Incentives to Improve Education

Incentives to Improve Education

A New Perspective

Robert W. McMeekin

Centro de Investigación y Desarrollo de la Educación
Santiago, Chile

Edward Elgar
Cheltenham, UK • Northampton, MA, USA

Published by
Edward Elgar Publishing Limited
Glensanda House
Montpellier Parade
Cheltenham
Glos GL50 1UA
UK

Edward Elgar Publishing, Inc.
136 West Street
Suite 202
Northampton
Massachusetts 01060
USA

A catalogue record for this book
is available from the British Library

Library of Congress Cataloguing in Publication Data
McMeekin, Robert W.
    Incentives to improve education : a new perspective / Robert McMeekin.
      p. cm.
    Includes bibliographical references and index.
     1. School improvement programs. 2. School management and organization. 3.
Institutional economics. 4. Educational change. I. Title.

    LB2822.8 .M39 2003
    371.2–dc21

                                      2002034710

ISBN 1 84376 068 1

Typeset by Manton Typesetters, Louth, Lincolnshire, UK.
Printed and bound in Great Britain by MPG Books Ltd, Bodmin, Cornwall.

Contents

Tables

Figures

Preface

BACKGROUND

In the late 1990s Guillermo Perry, then World Bank Chief Economist for Latin America, addressed a group of educators assembled at the World Bank Institute and remarked upon the great need to know more about 'the political economy of education'. He went on to explain that this meant learning how the 'power of market forces' could be brought to bear in the education sector in order to promote greater efficiency and better performance in the same way competition improves private sector organizations. Other social sectors such as health, said Perry, have made successful efforts to introduce market forces into areas previously considered the realm of the public sector. Why have there not been more such efforts in education?

With a doctorate in 'Political Economy and Government' and most of my professional life spent working to improve education in developing and developed countries, I took Perry's call for more knowledge about the political economy of education as a special challenge. The argument was familiar, as were both the examples from health and the difficulty of introducing market forces in education to which he referred. That marked the beginning of what has been a multi-year effort to understand the role of market forces in education, to examine whether other interventions and approaches to providing incentives to improve education have been successful or not, and why.

My early attempts to gather information revealed that the overwhelming majority of publications relating to the 'political economy of education' and introducing market-like forces into education concerned either (a) providing monetary rewards to improve teachers' performance, or (b) introducing competition through vouchers or other approaches to providing 'school choice'. This gave rise to the categorization of approaches to providing incentives used in this book. 'Rewards' include merit pay to individual teachers and merit awards to whole schools rather than to individual teachers, as well as changes in the traditional system of teacher compensation under which all teachers with the same experience and levels of education receive equal pay.

'Competition' includes all the forms of educational choice that have been the subject of intense study and debate throughout the 1990s and on into the present century. Milton Friedman's idea of providing vouchers so parents can send their children to schools of their choice is the main theme in this category of approaches to providing incentives. Vouchers enable parents to send their children to private schools – whether existing schools (church-sponsored or others) or newly started private initiatives – thus providing competition. Charter schools, which are financed with public funds but operated by individuals or groups with a vision of education that differs from traditional public schools, constitute another important subcategory. There are still other approaches to offering parents alternatives or choices among different forms of education that compete with the traditional schools and, in theory, bring about improvements in performance in both new and traditional schools. These include within-district choice, magnet schools, pilot schools and similar ways of offering choices between alternatives.

Often linked with these two categories of incentives is a third approach to improving educational performance: introducing external standards and making schools accountable for their performance. Standards based upon standardized tests provide the information parents need in order to exercise choice. By identifying which schools do the best job of educating children, standards inform authorities about how well schools are meeting their objectives, and may provide the basis for either rewards (whether positive rewards to teachers and schools or flows of enrollment to the schools with better results) or sanctions that can include closing a school that is performing poorly. While standards are not in themselves a market-like mechanism, they are linked to both rewards and competition by providing the information that enables markets to function. I call this category of incentives 'threats'. To the best of my knowledge, this three-way categorization of incentive systems has not been used before.

NEW INSTITUTIONAL ECONOMICS AND INCENTIVES TO IMPROVE EDUCATION

A parallel interest in New Institutional Economics (NIE), especially the work of Douglass C. North and Oliver Williamson, intersected with my interest in incentives in the education sector. The best-known work on NIE has focused on the theory of the firm, the role of transaction costs in influencing how economic activity is organized, and the importance of 'institutions' – what North calls 'the rules of the game'– in determining economic performance. Virtually all of this work has looked at firms, institutions and performance at a macro level; at national economies or at least large subdivisions thereof. But institutions exist at a more micro level as well.

Institutions as North defines them include formal rules, informal rules and enforcement mechanisms. The term 'institutions' has several meanings in English. In the most common usage it means 'things' like universities, hospitals, banks and other entities that NIE calls 'organizations'. But the term is also used to refer to the broad complexes of rules and norms that govern the behavior of individuals, organizations and firms. These include legal, political and regulatory systems, the policing mechanisms for enforcing laws, financial and insurance systems, a free press, the market system and all the rules and formal and informal enforcement mechanisms that operate within it.

The well-known phrase 'the institution of marriage' is a good example of this broad use of the term institution. Marriage is in some ways a legal contract with important financial implications, yet it also has powerful roots in religion and culture, and prevailing social norms and mores (about fidelity, for example) play a huge role in shaping and sustaining the institution. Society supports and enforces the rules surrounding matrimony, whether in courts, by providing 'marital deductions' in income tax, through the Church or through the strong influences of family, friends and society as a whole.

Do institutions exist at the extreme micro level, within schools? At a panel discussion at which Douglass North, Oliver Williamson and others were considering the distinction between organizations and institutions, I once asked whether institutions can exist within organizations. 'Absolutely', replied Williamson without hesitation. Yet there has been relatively little study at this extreme micro level. NIE examines economic factors at a more micro level than the mainstream theory of the firm, looking at factors that determine whether economic activity is organized through atomistic markets or into firms, but little work has been done on the institutions that operate within organizations. (Exceptions, such as Jensen and Meckling's work on organizational strategy, are found in the management literature.)

If institutions can exist within organizations (including schools) – that is, if formal and informal rules and enforcement mechanisms have an influence on performance at this extreme micro level – this implies that the body of knowledge we have about how institutions work can be applied to understand education better. Institutions influence performance by providing the confidence, stability and sense of security that enable economic actors to go ahead and engage in buying and selling, to enter into contracts and to take the risk that other parties will uphold their end of the bargain. Does the institutional environment within a school have the same sort of influence on the behavior of teachers, students and other actors that institutions have at a national level? Do within-school institutions reduce uncertainty and encourage actors to make commitments? If so, how does this affect how well schools produce learning? And what are the effects of interventions designed to provide incentives to good performance on institutions within schools?

These are the questions on which this book focuses. The first chapter develops a set of concepts that, taken together, constitute a model of how institutions function inside school organizations. A small empirical study described in Chapter 2 examines whether it is feasible to measure institutions within schools and whether there is an association between a school's institutional environment and its performance. Chapters 3 through 5 consider each of the categories of incentives identified above and how they relate to institutions within schools. A final chapter draws together conclusions and implications.

Acknowledgements

I am grateful to the Spencer Foundation for support that made possible the final development of the model as well as the empirical study presented in Chapter two.

A number of people have provided comments and suggestions on draft sections as well as encouragement during the preparation of this book. Of special importance among these are Patrick McEwan, Iris Rotberg, Bernardo Kugler, Becky Skinner, Elinor Ostrom, Sherwin Rosen, Vivian Heyl and Julian Rodriguez.

My colleagues at the Centro de Investigación y Desarrollo de la Educación (CIDE) – Marcela Latorre and Francisca Celedón – played an invaluable role in designing and implementing the empirical study. I am also indebted to Patricia Matte, President of the Sociedad de Instrucción Primaria and her senior staff who provided information and gave us access to the private voucher-paid schools in our study, and to the municipal authorities who granted access to the public voucher-supported schools. To the directors and staff of all the schools we visited, my colleagues and I extend our sincere thanks. My wife Lyn has provided moral support throughout the lengthy gestation of this book as well as careful review of drafts of the text.

My intellectual debt to Douglass C. North, Oliver E. Williamson, Henry M. Levin and many other economists and writers on education will be obvious to readers and is gladly acknowledged. None of those mentioned above should be blamed for any errors this work may contain, for which only I am responsible.

1.   The theoretical framework

1.1   INTRODUCTION

Few policy issues have generated greater interest and controversy than improving the efficiency and effectiveness of education systems. The debate over how to do this is intense and highly polemical. A central part of that debate concerns the provision of different systems of incentives that will bring the kind of competitive pressures found in the private sector to bear in education. Extensive research plus experimental programs of various sorts have sought to cast light on how to provide incentives. The outcome has been disappointing.

Surprisingly little clear information has emerged about what kind of incentives work, although advocates of one approach or another continue to argue for their preferred solution, and education authorities continue to make very large and important decisions about applying incentives. In the United States the 'No Child Left Behind' legislation of 2001 (signed into law in January 2002) mandates that, within a very few years, all US states shall implement accountability systems based on achievement tests and take other steps to provide incentives. The issue of incentives is very much alive.

This book offers a different perspective on the issue of how to provide incentives. Unlike large comparative studies that attempt to prove that one approach is better than another, it examines the effects that incentives have on the behavior of key participants at an extreme micro level, inside schools. Rather than view schools as 'black boxes' and attempt to measure their 'outputs' under different conditions, this study dares to ask what goes on inside the school. It explores how different incentive schemes influence the key actors in what I will call the school's community – the students, teachers, parents, school directors (to avoid confusion, I have used the term 'school director' to describe the senior official in a school) and school board – and the interactions between them.

In so doing, it bypasses a number of major roadblocks to understanding how to improve school performance. It develops an innovative theoretical framework, drawing on a body of economic thought rarely applied in education studies, that helps us understand why and how different approaches to providing incentives work. It presents the results of a small exploratory study that suggest that it is feasible to apply this theory in the real world and that the theory seems to work. Using this kit of tools, the book then looks at each of three categories of incentive systems – 'rewards', 'competition' and 'threats' – to understand their impact on the key actors, their behavior, and the 'transactions' between them.

What makes a good school?   Even though there is little persuasive, research-based evidence on the effects of different incentive systems, there is widespread consensus about many of the factors that characterize a 'good school'. These factors include:

- clear goals;
- high expectations regarding student achievement;
- leadership that is fair, consistent and supportive of teachers;
- an orderly environment;
- parents who are involved with the school and their children's education;
- evaluation of student performance, with feedback to all parties involved, especially the students themselves;
- a strong sense of 'community' within the school;
- a considerable degree of autonomy and freedom to develop a team of like-minded professionals and reward those who demonstrate professional excellence (sometimes called 'site-based management').

Even though these factors are recognized as important, we do not have a good explanatory model of how they interact, and how they encourage and enable all members of the school's community to perform their respective tasks to the best of their ability. The aim of this book and of the theory underlying it is to provide such a model and apply it to questions about educational incentives.

The environment for learning.   Note that the factors listed above do not include 'pedagogical' inputs such as able and well-trained teachers, sound curriculum and instructional methods, excellent materials, adequate infrastructure, and so on. Without question these have a powerful influence on how effectively teachers can do their jobs and how interested and motivated students will be. For this study, however, such inputs are not the main subject of interest. In an empirical study we would try to control for these inputs, as well as for student background factors, so as to focus on the effects of the institutional environment within which the education process takes place.

   A school's environment or organizational climate makes it possible for teachers to do their work, students to study well, and all members of the school community to function at their best. Without a good institutional environment, the pedagogical inputs cannot be fully effective (which is why it has been difficult to analyze the effects of the more traditional inputs when studies have ignored institutions). The environment is made up of a number of factors – a kind of 'syndrome' of a good school – that include many of those listed above. The following section explores how those factors interact to promote successful teaching and learning.

1.2 PRESENTING THE THEORETICAL MODEL

Institutions inside schools. This chapter, drawing on New Institutional Economics (NIE), introduces a conceptual model that helps explain what constitutes a 'good' environment and how it permits, encourages and facilitates successful teaching, studying and parenting that lead to good academic performance. Later in the book the institutional model will be used to analyze the ways in which different incentive systems influence school performance.

As explained in the Preface, the term 'institutions' is used here in its broad sense, meaning the collection of rules, norms and prevailing attitudes that shape people's behavior. Institutions can and do exist at an extreme micro level, inside organizations. They exist inside schools and have an impact on how well teachers can do their job and students do theirs.

Douglass C. North (1990) defines institutions as 'the rules of the game', and goes on to say that they include the formal rules, informal rules and enforcement mechanisms that shape the way societies operate. In his words, institutions 'structure incentives in human exchange'; 'institutions reduce uncertainty by providing a structure to everyday life'; '[T]hey are a guide to human interaction' (North, 1990, p. 3). In the larger society, institutions include political, legal and financial systems, courts and police forces, but also informal factors such as prevailing attitudes toward corruption. They govern behaviors with respect to marriage, social interaction, buying and selling, and the wide array of activities in which members of a society engage.

By reducing uncertainty, institutions make it possible for productive activities to take place, including economic investments, trade or the establishment of any sort of human activity ranging from organizing a club of football fans to starting a family. Without a set of institutions that reduces uncertainty, people are unwilling to risk entering into agreements because there is no assurance that other parties will keep their side of the bargain. If the risks or costs of making an effort are too high to make it worthwhile, then many useful things do not happen.

Most research on institutions has examined their role at the macro or national level. Viewed at this level, institutions have a powerful effect on whether countries develop or stagnate (North, 1990; Chong and Calderón, 2000). Unless there are institutions that reduce uncertainty and give people the confidence to enter into contracts or invest, much economic activity will not take place, jobs will not be created and an economy will tend to stagnate at or near the subsistence level. At the micro level, within organizations, institutions have the same effect of reducing uncertainty, making it worthwhile for people to enter into commitments and providing some assurance that the other party will uphold his or her end of the bargain.

Writing in the *Handbook of Research on Educational Administration*, Brian Rowan and Cecil Miskel (1999, pp. 378–9) state that:

> The new institutionalism presents a powerful set of explanations for the structure and functioning of educational organizations in modern societies. [Our review] did not find much organizational analysis of schooling using principal-agent theory and transaction cost economics. This is unfortunate because economists and political scientists are at the forefront of a movement to develop a 'positive theory of institutions,' one that can describe an array of governance arrangements that potentially can improve the efficiency and productivity of educational transactions … Immediate work is needed to see how the common governance mechanisms studied in transaction cost economics and principal-agent theory can be applied to the analysis of teachers' work and to improving the effort and engagement that students put into learning.

This book represents a step toward the sort of analysis these authors suggest.

Looking inside the 'black box'.   Metaphors are important because they shape the way we view the world. The metaphors economists generally use depict the education process as a 'black box'. Within the black box, so the usual argument goes, production processes take place about which we know very little. Much research has sought to specify production functions from outside the black box by measuring inputs and outputs. Analyses have (with a few exceptions) tended to assume that processes internal to the school are efficient, that transaction costs are insignificant, and that actors maximize their self-interest. They have assumed, as neoclassical theory directs, that schools are operating at their 'production possibility frontier'; that is to say, that all actors are making the best efforts they can and schools are operating as efficiently as possible. Some writers have argued that this is not true (for example, Levin, 1976; Hanushek, 1986) but because it is so difficult to specify what constitutes good teaching and how the 'production process' works, analysts have continued to use the black box metaphor and to assume that production processes are optimally efficient.

Research in the production function tradition has typically used a fairly limited set of variables to measure inputs and outputs. Well-known variables include school size, class size or student/teacher ratios, amounts of time devoted to schooling and similar variables that describe what goes into the education process. Other variables cover the availability of textbooks and materials, technology and other material inputs. Still others examine the characteristics of teachers (and in some cases school directors) in terms of their training, experience, turnover rates, and so on. (In a highly sophisticated analysis based on a rich data set, Hanushek, Kain and Rivkin (1998) found that teacher quality is the most significant of a number of variables.) Studies include control variables, especially factors having to do with the socioeconomic status of families and/or communities, parents' education and other factors external to the school itself.

With few exceptions, studies based on input data have not examined processes within schools. Even when they have included variables measuring parental involvement, for example, these have been based on whether parents have contact with the school, without attending to the nature and content of the contact. Output variables have focused on test scores or, in the developing world, where these are not available or reliable, on proxy indicators such as repetition and dropout rates. Fuller and Clarke (1994) examine the gap between research anchored in the production function tradition and studies that emphasize the effects of cultural factors operating within and around classrooms on the effectiveness of schooling. Their article points to the need to examine how cultural factors interact with material inputs to influence school performance but does not suggest a model with which to do this.

This study proposes a different metaphor: *that schools are governance structures within which various kinds of transactions take place.* As explained further below, this metaphor focuses attention on processes within the school, on the behavior of the most main actors in the school's community – especially students, teachers, parents and school directors – and on factors in a school's organizational climate that influence the behavior of the actors. Specifically it looks at how well the intra-organizational environment supports making and upholding various kinds of agreements and commitments – transactions between key actors – concerning how well each of them contributes to the tasks that produce learning. These transactions are, in effect, informal contracts, as will be discussed below.

What constitutes a good institutional environment?

Returning to North's definition of institutions as 'formal rules, informal rules and enforcement mechanisms', what are the characteristics of a good institutional environment in school settings?

Rules and enforcement mechanisms. Formal rules include the laws and regulations that govern a school's activities, such as the contract between the school district and the teachers' union, the legal requirement that children between certain ages must attend school, prohibitions on discrimination, requirements that handicapped persons have access, state provisions about curriculum, provisions regarding length of school day and year, possibly specification of approved textbooks and so on. In some school districts (and many private schools), there are written contracts between parents and schools governing parents' responsibilities regarding their children's education. There are requirements such as signing a release before a child can participate in a field trip. This extensive fabric of rules provides the framework within which the schooling process functions, and although some may consider the rules onerous, they also provide structure and confidence that things will proceed in a predictable, orderly fashion.[1]

The mechanisms for enforcing formal rules are also usually formal. They include the network of legal provisions that establish and guarantee that the rules will be observed, the court system that assures the laws will be obeyed, grievance procedures, truant officers and the like. There are courts to uphold the formal legal rules and procedures for union contract renewal and enforcement. Police may be called in extreme cases of rule violations. Many schools also have sets of regulations governing the behavior of all members of the school community, from support staff to teachers, students, parents and school director, and it is the school staff who are responsible for enforcing rules such as on-time arrival, formal dress codes and other behaviors inside the school. If enforcement works, it can be relied upon to assure that the rules are observed. This reduces uncertainty and provides a degree of confidence. If rules break down and there is poor enforcement, things do not work as intended, there is a feeling of insecurity and doubt about what one should do. In extreme cases, teachers and students may be anxious about their physical safety.

Informal rules also govern behavior, but are based on norms and customs rather than on written laws and regulations. They are, nonetheless, powerful determinants of the climate inside the school. They have to do with order, courtesy, and responsibility. They also have to do with student behavior (in class and elsewhere, toward teachers and each other) and with teachers' attitudes, work behavior and commitment to the school. Where informal rules are weak – where classes tend to be chaotic or there is little respect for fellow members of the community – then the environment for learning is damaged. Even an able and dedicated teacher cannot teach well. In part, the informal rules inside a school are influenced by the culture of the surrounding community, but some schools in extremely difficult surroundings manage to have sound systems of informal rules.

Enforcement of informal rules is essentially by informal means. Prevailing attitudes of community members or the approval or disapproval of the director, teachers or peers are among the most frequent and powerful influences on whether people adhere to informally established norms and standards of behavior. There is an extensive literature on the role of leadership in schools, and leadership certainly plays a critical role in establishing and maintaining the informal aspects of a school's climate. But leaders cannot function alone. The whole community is involved in upholding the informal norms of each school.

There are two other characteristics this study considers to be part of a school's institutional make-up: (1) clarity of objectives, and (2) whether there is a climate of cooperativeness and trust, sometimes called social capital.

Objectives. A key concept when examining institutions within organizations has to do with the objectives the members of the organization (in this case the school) seek to accomplish and how clearly these are articulated, understood and shared among members of the school community.[2] Schools are asked to do many things. Their role in imparting knowledge and cognitive skills is obvious, but they are also expected to help shape students' values, inculcate good habits that prepare them for the world of work, build good citizenship, help form their attitudes toward society and its members, and offer an array of desirable, education-related services that range from stimulating cultural and artistic interests, to practicing good hygiene and nutrition, to developing athletic skills and abilities. It is not possible for any individual or organization to do many things at once and all at high levels of effort. There have to be priorities and tradeoffs between different objectives. Establishing these is one of the most critical tasks of a governance mechanism.

The greater the consensus about objectives in an organization, the easier it is for all members to understand what is expected of them and to focus their efforts on what is truly significant. It is possible to pursue up to two or three high-level objectives at a time but no more than that, and there must be a sense of priorities and tradeoffs. If organizational objectives are not clear, if there are too many of them, if members of the community do not understand the objectives or believe in them and share them, several things go wrong. There is a lack of focus of effort. People work at crossed purposes. Incentives do not operate to encourage good performance. There is not a good basis for evaluating either the organization's accomplishments or those of its members.

Social capital or trust. There is increasing understanding of the role of trust in determining how well societies and economies, as well as organizations of all sorts, function. When a society or an organization has within it a high degree of trust and prevailing attitudes of cooperation, it is easier for its members to make arrangements of a quasi-contractual nature – commitments to carry out what has been agreed – than if the prevailing culture is one of betrayal and opportunism. Ever since James Coleman (1988) introduced the concept of social capital, educators have recognized that schools well endowed with this elusive quality tend to function more smoothly and effectively. In the present context, high levels of social capital create a context in which community members tend to make their best efforts – whether in teaching, studying or other tasks – toward achieving agreed-upon goals. Social capital provides the sense of security necessary for people to make commitments. Sociologist Francis Fukuyama (1995), one of the best-known theorists studying the phenomenon of trust in societies, finds that high levels of trust make it possible to organize in flexible ways, with greater delegation of authority, rather than rely upon bureaucratic rules and controls (p. 31). In the field of political science, Putnam (1993) is noted for his analyses of the importance of social capital for overcoming the dilemmas of collective action and making it possible for people to reap the benefits of working together to accomplish mutually beneficial ends. In schools where there is little trust, cooperation or assurance that other parties will uphold their side of 'bargains' or commitments, students and teachers cannot give their best in making learning happen.

Formal rules, informal rules, the mechanisms – both formal and informal – for enforcing these, clear objectives, and an atmosphere of trust and cooperation: together these constitute an institutional climate that makes good performance possible. They provide the security and the confidence for people to work together to accomplish a school's objectives. *The fundamental hypothesis underlying the model presented here is that the better a school's institutional environment, the better the school performs.*

With regard to the role of incentives, one of the most important questions is: what is the effect of an incentive on institutions inside schools? Specifically, how does it affect the environment in which key actors teach, study and carry out their role as parents? How does an incentive influence transactions between members of a school's community?

Terms and concepts

A number of terms and concepts, many from economics and NIE, will be useful for understanding the operation of institutions in schools.

Co-production.   An idea that lies at the core of this book is that learning takes place in the minds of students, as a result of the energy and effort they devote to their learning activities. Teachers play a central role in directing and encouraging students' efforts to learn, and the energy and effort that these exert in turn is also crucial for learning. Teachers and students are thus involved in a process of 'co-production', in which both the producers – teachers and schools – and the students who are the beneficiaries of schooling must work together to make learning happen (Davis and Ostrom, 1991; Ostrom, 1996). Other fields in which co-production occurs and where beneficiaries must participate in the 'production process' include health care and police crime-prevention work. Davis and Ostrom (1991) state that '[v]iewing the production of education as a process involving both the school and the students with their families as essential partners in a production process enables one to address questions somewhat differently than the more traditional view of looking at a school as the solitary producer' (pp. 324–5). This study incorporates co-production as a central element in the conceptual framework.

Transactions within school communities. There are many kinds of interactions between members of a school's community. Many of these are casual, social and unrelated to teachers' work or students' study, but many other interactions are transactions of one sort or another. They are, in effect, contracts. Some are formal, written contracts – for example, teachers have formal employment contracts that govern their pay, hours of work and related matters – but there are other kinds of formal and semi-formal contracts. In some school systems, parents are required to undertake formal commitments regarding their children's education, whether in terms of paying school fees or adhering to school regulations. Students are subject to various codes of behavior, ranging from attendance (required by law), to dress codes, to arrival on time. These are less formal than written contracts enforceable by law but still constitute semi-formal contracts. A very large category of transactions consists of purely informal agreements and arrangements between actors – including peer relationships between teachers or students, and hierarchical arrangements, such as teachers giving homework assignments. Some of these are extremely subtle – such as a tacit agreement between a student and a teacher about behavior in class, or understandings between peers about various aspects of behavior – but they are, nonetheless, contract-like transactions.

Property rights of students, teachers and others. The idea that schools are governance structures in which contract-like transactions take place may seem strange to some readers and merits a more complete explanation. The actors in a school community – most importantly teachers and students, but also school directors and parents – engage in multiple transactions or informal contracts involving property rights. North (1990) defines property rights as 'the rights individuals appropriate over their own labor and the goods and services they possess' (p. 33). The relevant property rights that teachers and students control are the energy and effort they devote to their respective teaching and learning tasks. Property rights in labor exist because it is costly (or simply not feasible) to monitor the activity and output of workers, who in education are the teachers and students. Since managers and supervisors do not have complete information about these co-producers, there is a fairly wide margin within which the teachers and students can vary the level of effort they expend. In other words, those who 'own' the labor can exercise considerable discretion over how they use it.[3] Transactions between actors take the form of micro-level contracts under which the participants negotiate and agree about how they will exercise that discretion and use their labor to perform the tasks assigned to them.

Neither educators nor education economists have given much attention to the existence, nature or functioning of property rights in schools; that is to say, the rights that teachers and students have over their 'labor' and how hard they work at their respective tasks.[4] There is tremendous variability between teachers in the energy and enthusiasm with which they approach planning and preparing their lessons, trying to communicate effectively with students, presenting each lesson in stimulating ways and evaluating whether students are learning satisfactorily. Time (both during school hours and spent out of class preparing lessons, grading papers, and so on) is a valuable and potentially measurable resource in teaching, but does not fully incorporate the dimension of how diligently the teacher uses the available time. Similarly, there is great variation between students in the attention they give to their studies both in and out of school hours, the time they spend on their lessons, and how hard and effectively they work to master the materials covered. The way teachers and students control and expend their 'labor' determines the degree to which the students learn both the formal and the 'hidden' content of the curriculum. In the aggregate, this determines the performance of the school.

Contracting and enforcement in schools.   As we have seen, the transactions or contracts with which this chapter is concerned deal with the way key actors use their property rights in the co-production of learning. Like most contracts in the real world, these are incomplete because it would be too costly (and perhaps simply impossible) to monitor and enforce every detail of a truly complete contract that covers all possible contingencies. In school settings, where members of the community interact with each other repeatedly and over extended periods of time (often for more than one school year), these are 'relational' contracts. That is to say, they take place between parties that have a long-standing relationship, in which the behavior of the parties in the future matters, and in which factors such as reputation, reliability, and playing by the rules have value. Relational contracts are influenced by different factors than those governing standard or 'classical' contracts; for example, by whether there is a feeling of trust between the parties. The subject of contracting, as it applies to schools, is complex. Readers who wish to explore the idea of contracting in schools in somewhat greater depth should refer to Appendix A.

In the business world, contracts are enforced by a variety of means, including the legal and regulatory rules that govern a particular category of business. But as anyone who has had dealings with the law knows, it is often extremely complicated and costly to rely on litigation to resolve differences. In many cases parties resolve differences and disputes privately on the basis of mutual understanding of what is fair, or what can be agreed upon without going to court or breaking the long-term relationship. This 'private ordering' plays a more central role in informal, relational arrangements and 'deals' than in formal agreements supported by written contracts, but it has a role in virtually all forms of contracting, and especially in the case of contracting in schools.

Enforcement mechanisms in school settings can be formal – a teacher can be fired, the Truant Officer may force the child (or the parents) to obey compulsory attendance laws – but in the overwhelming majority of cases, the enforcement is informal. A student who misbehaves faces an ascending order of sanctions. He or she may be reprimanded, kept after school, or sent to the school office or director. Parents may be informed of an infraction, or called to a conference with the teacher or the school director and, ultimately, a student may be expelled. But there are other, much less drastic but nonetheless significant, measures that tend to enforce contract-like agreements. These include approval or disapproval (of teachers by the director, or of students or teachers by their peers) that have great power as informal enforcement mechanisms.

Principals and agents.   Contracts are made between what economists call 'principals', meaning persons in positions of authority who want something done, and 'agents' who are those who perform the desired activities. (This use of the term 'principal' may seem jarring in a paper about education. To avoid confusion, this discussion uses 'school director' to describe the senior official in a school, as mentioned earlier.) There are several basic assumptions about relations between principals and agents:

1.   There is conflict of interest. Even though a teacher may love teaching and want the job, he or she probably does not want to do it exactly the way the supervisor wishes it done, or with the same intensity of effort. And although students may understand in an abstract way the importance of doing well on a test, they may not want to devote the time and concentration necessary to prepare for it.

2. The parties will have different information about the nature of the task to be performed and different opinions about what constitutes good quality performance. This asymmetry of information has frequently been noted with regard to teaching. There is no way a school director can monitor the performance of every teacher or even have the same view as the teacher about what needs to be done in a specific class.
3. Transactions between principals and agents have costs. These include the costs of making the agreement or contract, negotiating before and during the performance of a task, monitoring how well the agent implements the task and evaluating how well the original agreement has been performed. In transactions between teachers and students, tests can sometimes be valuable sources of information, but there are costs involved in designing, supervising and grading tests. Because transactions are costly and contracts are necessarily incomplete, informal rules and enforcement mechanisms take on added importance.

Drawing the concepts together.   In briefest terms, the framework is as follows:

1. From agency theory: when there is clarity about the school's objectives, then principal–agent relationships can be clear rather than diffuse. This reduces the difficulty and costs of making and enforcing agreements (contracting).
2. Clear, shared objectives improve the effectiveness of schools because all participants in the 'co-production' of student learning – especially teachers, students and parents, but also school directors and local boards – understand what is expected of them and are working toward the same ends.
3. Schools are governance mechanisms in which contracting takes place. It is possible to look at processes inside schools, the intra-organizational transactions and the institutions that govern them, and understand how these processes and institutions shape the ways actors use their property rights and how this influences the effectiveness of the co-production process.
4. A good institutional environment encourages actors to make and uphold agreements that have to do with making their best efforts to accomplish the school's objectives, thus promoting good performance.
5. These agreements or transactions are, in a sense, informal 'contracts' of a relational nature. That means they take place between actors who will continue to deal with each other over an extended period of time. Behavior under relational contracts is influenced by factors of reputation, loyalty, trust and sentiment, as well as concern for the future of the relationship

and the benefits and costs associated with protecting or betraying it. All contracts in schools are relational.

6. The contracts deal with the 'property rights' of the central actors involved in teaching and studying. These rights have to do with how hard and well the actors use their labor – their energy, attention and effort – in teaching as well as they can and studying hard and effectively. Parents also use their property rights by exerting effort to support the school, urging good study behavior, and encouraging their children to do well.

7. The property rights exist because of the transaction costs of establishing and monitoring contracts, both formal and informal. Because it is essentially impossible to monitor all aspects of a teacher's work (or a student's time and effort spent studying), the actors have discretion over how hard they work. Informal contracts and enforcement mechanisms fill the gap left by incomplete contracts.

8. Rules, including both formal rules and the mechanisms for their enforcement and informal rules and the subtle means actors have of enforcing these, structure the behavior of actors by reducing uncertainty and making it worthwhile to enter into agreements.

9. A climate of cooperation and trust also reduces uncertainty and encourages actors to make and uphold agreements and to use their property rights to accomplish the organization's objectives.

If a school's institutional climate is favorable, the school director can establish agreements with teachers to use their energy and effort to the best of their ability to accomplish agreed-upon goals; informal peer pressure among teachers will tend to enforce such behavior and the individual teacher will find it worthwhile to adhere to the agreement. Similarly a teacher can 'transact' with students about what they need to study and know. Examinations are the most obvious form of monitoring and enforcing these informal contracts, but approval and disapproval of teachers, peer pressure from other students, and parents' insistence that students study hard and perform well all operate to support the explicit and implicit agreements made. On the other hand if institutions do not function well within the school – if nobody really cares, or if there is no reliable benefit or 'payoff' to teachers or students for good performance and no sanction for bad – then the agreements or informal contracts will not be made or, if made, are unlikely to be honored. As a result performance will suffer.

1.3   A MODEL OF TRANSACTIONS WITHIN SCHOOL COMMUNITIES

A schematic model

Figure 1.1 presents a simple schematic model of the transactions between key actors in schools. Its purpose is to simplify later discussion of transactions within schools. The model considers the community of actors involved in an individual school, which operates in a school system or under some other administrative authority (called the school board here). In the model, each school or establishment has a community consisting of: (S) the students, (T) their teachers, (P) their parents or guardians, (D) the school director, and (B) the school board, and all are embedded in the society at large, which we call (E) the external environment. The school may be public, in which case it is governed by the local education authority (municipal or other), or private and under the oversight of its own school board. Winkler and Alvarez (1998,

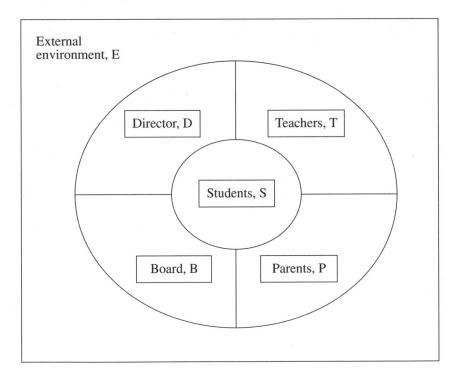

Figure 1.1   Conceptual model of transactions between members of the school community

p. 91) present a somewhat similar model that includes actors external to the school's immediate community. External actors include state or national-level education authorities, teachers' unions, communications media, employers and the job market, and such factors as whether there is drug use and trafficking in the external community.

The actors in the six categories in the model interact in various ways, including interactions within groups (especially between students or between teachers), plus all possible interactions between groups. Transactions can be unidirectional (a school director giving directions to a teacher or imposing discipline on a student) or a give-and-take exchange between actors (such as students and teachers talking about an assignment).

The transactions with greatest impact on school performance are those related most closely to the teaching and learning process: that is, T–S, P–S and, to some extent, T–P interactions. The three-way intersection of transactions between teachers, students and parents – the T–S–P nexus – is at the absolute heart of the co-production of learning. Interactions within groups – especially T–T and S–S interactions – are also of central interest because they may form part of the informal mechanisms for enforcing contracts. Other two-way relationships between actors will also enter the argument as relevant.

Assumptions about transactions within schools

There are some assumptions about the nature of these transactions (and the human beings that engage in them) that ought to be made explicit. The first is that human actors behave in a realistic, if not always pleasant, fashion. Members of a school's community have the characteristics of what Oliver Williamson (1989) calls 'contracting man'. That is to say that, no matter how nice or highly motivated they may be, in the final analysis they seek their own self-interest. They do so, however, within the constraint of 'bounded rationality'. They are not omniscient, nor can they calculate the long-run effects of every action. This is a very different and more realistic assumption than the usual concept of *homo economicus*, the all-knowing and self-interest-seeking calculating machines usually assumed in neoclassical economics. Moreover, real-world actors are capable of behaving 'with guile'. Williamson describes the last point as 'calculated efforts to mislead, disguise, obfuscate and confuse', also called opportunism, moral hazard and agency (1989, pp. 138–9).

The second assumption is that people shirk. Every human actor is tempted to shirk. Even the most highly motivated teachers, who are sincerely dedicated to their work, may not always exert their very best efforts. They may be tired; they may be exasperated by some administrative aspect of their work or some frustrating experience in dealing with a student; they may be distracted by some personal problem, or it may simply be close to the end of the term and they – like the students – are eager for vacation to begin. Under these circumstances even the best of teachers may not exert maximum effort in preparing the next day's task, in making constructive marginal comments on written work, or in ensuring that all students in the class have understood the content of today's lesson. If anything less than one's absolute best efforts all the time constitutes shirking, then we all shirk. A little honest introspection will reveal, I suspect, that readers of this chapter have been known to shirk.

Contracts are designed to minimize, if not eliminate, shirking. They seek to make clear what the agent will do for the principal and how the principal will reward performance of the task, subject to various kinds of conditions designed to protect one or the other party to the contract. Making, supervising and enforcing contracts, even implicit ones that relate to property rights for which established markets do not exist, involves transaction costs. Among these are the costs of information about agent performance.

This universal tendency to make life as easy and pleasant for ourselves as possible gives rise to the third assumption, which is that it is necessary to oversee workers and, in the context of education, to require a degree of accountability. There is a need for some degree of pressure to assure that agents perform well. One form of pressure consists of regulations and monitoring of compliance, which is the source of much criticism of oppressive bureaucratic controls that tend to stifle schools' autonomy and opportunities to innovate. The alternative approaches to generating pressure that will lead to diligent use of property rights and improved performance are the three categories of incentives discussed in later chapters of this book: rewards, competition and threats.

Several factors complicate the task of introducing incentives into education settings. First is the complexity of principal–agent relationships discussed above. Second is the difficulty and high transaction costs of monitoring the performance of teachers (if indeed it is even feasible to perform direct monitoring). The third has to do with the way the incentives influence institutions within schools. Does a reward system foster a positive institutional climate that encourages transactions between members of the community? Does competition really have a significant effect on the relationships between key actors, such as teachers and students? Does a system of standards and accountability lead teachers and students to use their property rights more diligently to raise academic performance, and does it promote the sort of performance we really value? These are the questions we will ask about incentive systems.

More on the relationship between principals and agents.   The definition of principals and agents in school settings is extremely complex, as other authors have observed (Winkler and Alvarez, 1998). To illustrate, let us look at the principal–agent relationships in which teachers are involved. Although school directors supervise the work of teachers and the teachers are in this sense their agents, they usually do not do the hiring. In many cases this is done by the local school board, but in some states and countries all teachers are the employees of a still higher-level board or agency that negotiates a common contract with the teachers' union covering all teachers in that jurisdiction. But since it is the parents who pay directly or indirectly for the education, including the salaries of teachers and school directors, in a sense parents are also principals. And the students are the true beneficiaries of the education, so they too are in the position of principals. To whom, then, is the teacher responsible?

Some relationships are two-directional. Teachers unions are formed to serve their teacher members, but Winkler and Alvarez (1998) speak of teachers as agents of the unions, as can be the case when the union depends on the teachers' votes or willingness to strike in order to exert its power. So the teacher is the agent of: the school director, the school board or other authority that hires him or her, the parents, and the students themselves. The teachers' union is also both an agent of the teacher and a principal that delegates responsibilities to the teacher. The more simple and direct principal–agent relationships are, the more easily and efficiently monitoring can take place and the more 'power' incentives have (Williamson, 1985; Holstrom and Milgrom, 1991, pp. 225–8). Looking only at the principal–agent relationships in which the teacher is involved illustrates the complexity of such relationships.

Various writers have incorporated the concept of principal–agent relationships in studies of education. Jane Hannaway (1992) suggests redesigning teachers' jobs to permit specialization in teaching either basic skills or higher-order skills, thereby clarifying responsibility for achieving the objectives desired and mitigating the principal–agent problem. Winkler and Alvarez (1998, pp. 95–6) describe the complexity of principal–agent relationships, the inability of parents or school directors to fulfill their roles as principals, and problems of establishing clear goals and incentives in Latin American education. William Savedoff (1998) describes the particular nature of agency relationships in social services in Latin America, especially problems of multiple principals. Geoffrey Rapp (2000) introduces agency theory in his examination of the effects of school choice and competition on teacher behavior. He finds that choice (especially intra-district choice, whereby parents can move their children freely between public schools in the same district) appears to ameliorate the 'agency problem' caused by the difficulty and cost of monitoring teachers' work effort.

Institutions and transactions within schools
The foregoing sections have sketched a model of what institutions inside
school organizations are and how they influence academic performance. Let
us look in greater detail at the transactions that take place within school
communities – especially those between teachers, students and parents – and
how they shape the performance of the actors and, ultimately, of the school.

Transactions between teachers and students.   The most important transactions are those most directly related to learning performance, in which the
teacher is the principal and the student is the agent who performs the 'services' of studying and learning. T–S contracts involve implicit agreements that
the student will study a given assignment, prepare for a test that will cover
specific materials, or produce a particular product (a term paper, for example). Anyone who has ever heard the questions that arise when a teacher
announces an examination – What pages will it cover? Will it be multiple
choice? How much of the material covered so far this term will be on it? How
much will it count for in the final grade? – will recognize these as a form of
contract clarification and, in some cases, negotiation.

Some such contracting is between the teacher and the class (single principal, multiple agents), but there are also implicit contracts – 'deals' – between
teachers and individual students, in which the teacher may use encouragement, persuasion or threat as well as clear explanation of what the student as
agent needs to do, as part of the contracting process. Note that having a
favorable institutional climate determines how well (or even whether) T–S
contracts will be made and upheld.

What is the quid pro quo in such contracts? The immediate item of exchange is grades, but there are other forms of rewards that apply, especially
the teacher's approval. In some instances students may be aware of the
importance of learning a subject (and making this clear is part of the teacher's
responsibility and contracting leverage).

In the transactions between students and teachers, the students have a
mechanism – a form of voice – for enforcing good teaching behavior. The
transactions take place between students as principals and teachers as agents.
They will deal with each other repeatedly over time and their attitudes and
behavior toward each other are part of the informal mechanisms for enforcing
the rules. Students want teachers to teach well – be interesting, well organized, skilled and fair – and if teachers don't live up to their part of the
contract, students will sanction them with disapproval, difficult behavior,
complaints, and so on. Most teachers will acknowledge that students' reactions to their teaching provide one of the strongest incentives they have. The
institutional climate has a very powerful influence on the strength of this
incentive.

There are various means of monitoring and enforcing contracts. Obviously testing is a monitoring device (and this aspect of transacting could be subject to quantification). Homework submitted is another monitoring device. Teachers also judge how well students are performing their learning tasks on the basis of performance in class including answers to verbal questions or participation in discussions, and may subtly warn a student who has been poorly prepared for the class. Grades are one way teachers compensate students for learning, and are also a means of sanctioning poor performance. Other means include disapproval (possibly criticism, either individually – 'see me after class' – or in the presence of others), report cards, meetings with parents, punishments such as staying after school or, in extreme circumstances, disciplinary actions involving higher authorities within the school. Very subtle influences in the form of the attitudes and expectations of other teachers and the administration, based on the student's 'reputation', may also enter the picture. When the academic climate of the school is favorable to learning, then the attitudes of peers may encourage good student behavior and high effort. If the climate is unfavorable, peer pressure may have the opposite effect.

Note that there are significant differences between school communities in terms of the rules that apply to teaching and learning and the mechanisms for enforcing the rules governing these transactions. In a 'good' school in which all parties value learning, transacting can take place readily because the parties agree on the desired outcomes and all the rewards and sanctions mentioned above are fully operational. At the other extreme, in a 'blackboard jungle' school, the students don't care about grades or teacher approval, parents have little interest in their children's schooling and peer pressures from other students may be counterproductive and reward negative or disruptive behavior with laughter or imitation. In these cases teachers have little bargaining power *vis-à-vis* students and the contracting process is much less effective and conducive to good performance. Rewards are not highly valued and only the most extreme sanctions – failure, suspension or expulsion – have any effect (and even that may be limited.)

From the days of Huckleberry Finn, students have been renowned for their propensity to shirk. Even in the learning environments established in the best of schools, students may not always make the best efforts they can in their studies. In less fortunate organizational climates, shirking and cheating are considered 'cool', the costs of transacting and enforcing agreements are high, the 'payoff' or chance of success is low, and performance of individuals and the school as a whole tends to suffer. Teachers also may shirk, and the tendency to do so is probably higher when making an effort and doing good work don't seem likely to make a difference. Unfortunately, these problems tend to be self-reinforcing. The less the institutions within a school commu-

nity favor the contracting process that influences the labor of students and
teachers, the more difficult it is to achieve good performance.

Transactions between parents and students.   In the crucial informal transactions or 'deals' that apply to how diligently a student undertakes the tasks
of learning, it is the child who is the agent of the parent. The substance of
P–S contracts is the child's 'labor'. There are formal rules governing attendance that originate outside the family and have the force of law (and
are binding upon parents as well as children). But simply being present at
school as required does not constitute studying and learning. So P–S contracts mainly have to do with (1) the child's behavior and effort in school,
and (2) the performance of homework. How is a child compensated for
performing well or sanctioned for not doing so? The parent-as-principal
transacts with the student-as-agent to exert effort in studying. The child
goes to school and tries to learn, in part out of filial duty but also because of
the terms of the transaction. Parents may also use more specific rewards for
exceptionally good performance ('You can sleep over at Sarah's' or 'You
can borrow the car') or for notable improvement in formerly inadequate
performance ('You're not grounded any more'). Parental approval is, of
course, a central part of the child's reward. (Note that where family structure is weak or broken, the force of parent's approval or disapproval is
weak and the P–S contract is debilitated.)

   Parents face measurement and information costs in connection with these
transactions. Children particularly, as well as teachers, know far more than
parents about how much effort they expend on learning. The parent/princi-
pal's main sources of information about work in school are report cards and
parent–teacher communications and conferences (usually reserved for problem situations). But a crucial source of information is conversation with
children and the answers to questions like, 'How was your day at school?',
'Have you learned your sevens table?' or 'How are you doing with the
algebra?'

   Regarding homework, parents are in a somewhat better position to observe
performance (although even concerned and attentive parents will find that the
information is necessarily incomplete). Total time spent on homework is a
useful indicator but does not reveal concentration or the degree of active
involvement in the task of studying. Working with children, helping when
appropriate or simply listening to their problems are among the best sources
of information. In the absence of such direct involvement, parents can ask to
see completed homework papers. Note that parents' close attention to the
child's studies plus communication with the teacher contribute to effective
supervision of the learning contract. This is the kind of 'parent involvement'
that influences performance.

Enforcement of transactions between parent and child are well known: disapproval, limited privileges and similar sanctions. (Whipping in the woodshed is now rarely applied.) As in the case of enforcement mechanisms open to teachers, there are many subtle ways in which parents can reward good behavior or punish poor performance. Much depends on parents' motivation and willingness to make an effort, on the tools they have at hand to encourage students to study well (instruments of parental control), and on the parenting skills they can bring to bear.

Children's motivation to uphold their part of the bargain depends in part on the degree of effort parents spend monitoring their children's effort and encouraging good performance. Peer pressures also play a role. Here the role of S–S interactions can be either an aid in enforcing good study behavior or counterproductive. There are also influences from the external environment (E–S): attitudes toward education in the society, inputs from the media, role models in the community, employment opportunities and credible information about the influence of education on life success.

Transactions between teachers and parents. We have said that the main transactions having to do with how well students learn take place at the T–S–P intersection in the model, where the interests of students, teachers and parents come together. The third kind of contract that occurs at this critical intersection is between teachers and parents. In comparison with the contracts between teachers and students and between parents and students, the contracts between teachers and parents are less frequent. If parents make it clear to their children that they expect and want them to do well in school and if they insist on and encourage hard work at school or on homework, this helps ensure that the child will make diligent efforts to perform well. Teachers can reinforce the parents' role, especially when there is good communication with parents. Reinforcement may deal not only with homework but also with such factors as the amount of sleep a child needs, nutrition, hours of television watching, and so on. Such reinforcement behavior has costs, however, and teachers' motivation depends in part on their perception of whether their efforts will do any good; that is, on their perception of whether parents are sincerely concerned. The idea of 'parent involvement' in schooling has been discussed at length in the education literature and there is a body of research devoted to the subject (see, for example, Epstein, 2001; Booth and Dunn, 1996). Tucker and Codding (1998, pp. 155–6) provide interesting examples of ways of implementing and monitoring agreements about parental involvement.

The point is that when teachers and parents have an agreement – a deal – to make sure a student makes a sincere effort to learn, this contributes to hard work on the part of the student. In effect, teacher–parent contracts are supplementary to T–S and P–S contracts. They deal with parents' behavior and effort in monitoring and enforcing desired behavior on the part of the student. In essence they play a role in directing parents' attention and effort toward supporting fundamental learning activities carried out by the student.

Transactions between peers.   There are two kinds of peer interactions that have an impact on teaching and learning: those between teachers (T–T) and those between students (S–S). The first category has to do with informal relationships between teachers to 'back each other up' in dealing with individual students or groups of students (for example, a history teacher agreeing with a language teacher to insist on good writing in history class). This cooperation extends to agreements to share or trade off duties such as supervising study halls or other tasks. Also included in T–T relationships are actions that provide either incentives or disincentives to professionalism and good teaching performance. The attitudes of fellow teachers tend to reinforce a school's norms regarding the quality of teaching and the effort expended by teachers. Obviously teachers also have tacit agreements regarding behavior and enforce informal school norms through their attitudes and actions toward their fellow teachers.

Peer pressure is one of the most powerful influences on student behavior. In high-performing schools, students tend to approve of hard work and high performance on the part of other students and to sanction poor performance or behavior contrary to the norm with disapproval and scorn. In similar fashion, if prevailing student opinion is that it is 'cool' to shirk on studies or disrupt classes, this makes it difficult for teachers to do a good job.

School directors' transactions.   School directors are in a position to influence school objectives and establish the environment in which contracting takes place. This leadership and orienting role is potentially extremely powerful. The director's role is less closely linked to student performance than the roles of teachers and parents; it can at best provide a context in which the transactions between teachers and students take place. Although it is frequently stated that school directors have little control or influence *vis-à-vis* teachers since they have little power over hiring and promotion decisions, informal D–T transactions complement the formal contracts between school board and teacher. Directors communicate, with greater or lesser success, the teaching performance they expect and have various instruments at their disposal for encouraging good performance or discouraging shirking. In their article on 'strategic ambiguity', Berkenheim and Whinston (1998) use examples of subtle rewards and benefits university professors receive from their deans, but the same kind of rewards and punishments can apply between school directors and teachers at the primary and secondary levels.

School directors also engage in transactions with students that sometimes constitute contracts at the micro level but often simply support the contracts between teachers and students. Examples of the latter are approval and recognition of students who are doing well or showing improvement. Contracting is more likely to take place when directors interact with students in a disciplinary situation, as in 'you're on probation until you get those grades up', or 'another incident like this and we will need to have a conference with your parents'. Directors do interact with parents (and not only in connection with discipline), but less frequently than with teachers and students.

Directors also establish and communicate the objectives of the school – the outcomes that various principals seek and agents are contracted to accomplish – and set a tone within the school that influences whether the sort of micro-contracting discussed in this chapter can take place. They set the formal rules and at best are firm, fair and consistent in enforcing them. Some directors do this with great skill, but it is an exercise that has its costs in terms of the director's energy and effort. The leadership role school directors perform is the subject of a growing literature (Leithwood, Tomlinson and Genge,1999; Heck and Hallinger, 1999). These studies emphasize the role of school directors in setting goals and establishing an environment favorable to making and adhering to informal contracts of the sort discussed above.

The school board's influence. Many observers criticize the role of school boards, viewing them as politicians and 'bureaucrats' who intervene in school affairs, impose requirements of various sorts and are largely interested in maximizing their own power and control. Boards have an influence on the institutional climate within schools. The board usually has control over hiring the teachers in public schools. They may impose external standards that are intended to provide an incentive for schools to improve their performance. In some jurisdictions, boards have the authority to grant charters to schools that seek to qualify as charter schools. They interact with various actors in the external community, including the relevant financial authorities that establish education budgets, teachers' unions at times of contract renegotiation, and other external entities. Boards may act to establish accountability in education in various ways, including not only external standards but also incentive systems such as merit pay for teachers or merit awards for successful schools. They usually operate through formal contracts and their influence on transactions between key actors within individual schools is indirect. In some instances they may serve as external authorities that uphold or enforce formal or semi-formal contracts or settle certain classes of disputes. In developing countries the local education authorities often have considerable political power through their authority to hire teachers. In some cases there are serious problems of corruption and this works to the detriment of teachers and schools.

The role of the external community.   The community within which a school exists influences students, teachers and parents, although this usually has more to do with generalized incentives – employment opportunities for graduates, respect for the teaching profession – than specific contracts. (Notable exceptions are cases in which an individual or firm in the community offers an explicit 'deal' to pay university tuition for students who do well in secondary school and qualify for admission.) In a sense the community is a principal and the actors within its schools are its agents. This is very clear with regard to community political decisions on taxes to support public schools. The community includes media that influence attitudes toward local education, teachers' unions and higher-level (state, regional or national) authorities, the requirements and standards of which influence what happens inside schools. The degree to which the community/principal makes clear its priorities with regard to education and the value it places on student learning has an influence on the attitudes and behavior of parents, directors, teachers and students.

1.4 INSTITUTIONS AND INCENTIVES TO IMPROVE EDUCATION

What is the relationship between institutions and incentive systems such as rewards or competition? In some ways, as we shall see in later chapters, incentives may tend to clarify goals (as in the case of well-conceived standards), or to strengthen teamwork and feelings of cooperation to achieve goals (as with merit awards to whole schools). In other ways the impact of an incentive system may differ from what its sponsors intended because its design did not consider its influence on institutions. Institutional factors may weaken the power of the incentive, or the incentive may undercut within-school institutions that promote good performance.

This chapter has set forth the conceptual framework within which to examine the relationship between institutions in schools and school performance. This theoretical framework, including concepts of schools as governance mechanisms, co-production, and contracting between key members of a school's community, provides the basis on which to examine the effectiveness of different approaches to providing incentives. A basic assumption is that the impact of an incentive to improve education depends on how it influences the interactions between participants in the fundamental co-production process of producing learning.

The next chapter seeks to bring the theory into contact with reality. It presents the results of a study of a small sample of public and private primary schools in Chile. It establishes that it is feasible to gather data on the institutional climate within an individual school (and that there is considerable variation between schools in terms of their intra-organizational institutions), and that having a 'good' institutional climate appears to be associated with strong academic performance. Chapters 3 through 5 look at how incentives based on rewards, competition or threats influence institutions in schools and the motivation and behavior of actors within them. The final chapter draws conclusions about institutions in schools and approaches to providing incentives.

NOTES

1. Note that the rules that promote successful transactions originate within the school community, optimally with participation by community members, and are accepted as valid and legitimate. Some rules, especially those imposed from outside the school, have little or no effect on the intra-organizational institutional environment and may even be counterproductive. In *Politics, Markets and America's Schools*, Chubb and Moe (1990, pp. 151–2) criticize bureaucratically imposed administrative constraints and requirements that schools comply with directives that impair schools' autonomy. These are not to be confused with rules originating within the school community.

2. Objectives are of greater importance within organizations than in larger entities or polities, where many individuals' objective functions operate through the political process. Organizations themselves do not have objectives; only the combination of the objectives of their members. Jensen (1998) says that the conflicting objectives of individuals are brought into a complex equilibrium through the multiple contractual relations within a firm (p. 57) but also that, within a firm, 'specification of the performance measurement and evaluation system *is* specification of the objective function, but it is not generally viewed that way' (p. 121). For convenience, however, I will use the phrase 'organizational objectives' to describe the 'complex equilibrium' of individuals' objectives in schools.

3. Barzel (1977) finds historical evidence that even slaves were able to appropriate some degree of control over their work, which constituted a form of property rights. This occurred because of the transaction costs of monitoring slaves' labor closely. Thus some slaves were able to use these rights in separate productive activities and eventually earn enough to purchase their freedom (Barzel, 1977, pp. 96–8; North, 1990, pp. 32–3). If even slaves had property rights over their own labor, clearly teachers and students do as well.

4. Teachers also possess human capital in the form of the knowledge they have accumulated and can impart, as well as the professional skill they have acquired through training and experience. Students have a form of human capital based upon the schooling they have obtained in earlier grades, plus the family background with which they are endowed and which has a powerful impact on their performance. Teachers and students combine their human capital with their labor in performing teaching and learning tasks.

2.   Institutions within schools and school performance*

2.1   INTRODUCTION

Chapter 1 presented a theoretical framework that helps explain why some schools have better performance than others; better even than schools that are quite similar in many respects. Is it possible to put any empirical content into this theory? Are the concepts defined earlier real and measurable? The following pages present the findings of a small exploratory study designed to test whether the theory 'works' in the real world. The aims of this study were, first, to determine whether it is feasible to gather data on variables that measure intra-organizational institutions within schools; and second, to explore whether a good institutional environment within a school is associated with good academic performance.

The study is based on interviews conducted in a sample of ten public and private primary schools in Chile. It focuses on factors associated with school management, such as clarity of goals, formal and informal rules, and enforcement mechanisms within the school. Much research on school administration has examined factors such as formal organizational structure, the training or leadership styles of managers, teacher management issues and other observable characteristics of schools. This study generates new data on institutional factors in individual school establishments. Although there is widespread recognition that management has an important influence on school performance, economic research has not produced clear findings about how that influence works or what could be done in a policy sense to make it work better.

Chile is an interesting setting for this kind of educational research. It is, for example, one of the few countries in the world with a nationwide system of educational vouchers. With this system, which has been in operation for over

*   I am especially grateful to Marcela Latorre and Francisca Celedón, both of CIDE, who were my fellow researchers in the conduct of the study described in this chapter; to the Sociedad de Instrucción Primaria and the municipal operators of the schools we visited, who gave permission for the interviews; to the school directors and administrators who gave us their time and candid information, and to the Spencer Foundation for support that made the study possible.

twenty years, plus a system of achievement testing and a program to provide merit awards to schools on the basis of performance, Chile has one of each category of incentives considered in this book. Before describing the study further, it will be desirable to sketch some of the key characteristics of Chile's education system that have a direct bearing on the study and its implications.

2.2 RELEVANT CHARACTERISTICS OF CHILE'S EDUCATION SYSTEM

Education in Chile is currently undergoing a major reform. Chile's model of education has been the subject of extensive research (Parry, 1997; Gauri, 1998; McEwan and Carnoy, 2000; Delannoy, 2000). The following brief comments will provide context information as well as explain some of the features and terminology used in describing the empirical study of institutions.

Voucher system. The military government decentralized control of schools to the municipal level, beginning in 1980, and permitted establishment of private schools that receive public voucher payments. These payments, called subventions, are based on the average student attendance (not enrollment) as measured each month. The per-student stipends are equal for both municipal and private subsidized schools. The amount of the vouchers is intended to cover the full cost per student. (Elite, fee-charging private schools are not eligible to receive voucher payments.) In other words, except for the elite schools, all primary and secondary education in Chile is publicly financed, even though some schools are privately operated. In 2000, at the primary and secondary levels, there were 1.75 million children enrolled in municipal schools and 1.16 million students in private subsidized schools that received voucher payments.

Testing system. Another feature of Chile's education system is its System for Measuring the Quality of Education (Sistema de Medición de la Calidad de la Educación; SIMCE). Introduced in 1988, the SIMCE provides standardized tests of Spanish and mathematics skills and has recently added other subject areas. SIMCE tests are administered at the fourth-, eighth- and tenth-grade levels, with repetitions every three years. The data used in our research were for the fourth-grade tests administered in 1996 and 1999. SIMCE provides information on the achievement of virtually 100 percent of students. The tests are standardized, which permits meaningful comparisons between the average scores of a school or group of schools between successive applications. Testing is almost universal, but reporting is on the basis of average scores for each school, not individual student scores.

System of merit awards to schools.   Chile has established a system of monetary prizes to school establishments (not to individual teachers) called the System for Evaluation of Performance of Subsidized Schools (Sistema Nacional de Evaluación de Desempeño de Establecimientos Educacionales Subvencionados; SNED). Key characteristics of the SNED system are: (1) competition is between relatively comparable establishments in 'homogeneous groups' (*grupos homogéneos*) or strata; (2) awards go to schools (regardless of whether they are public or private) that account for 25 percent of the enrollment in that stratum; (3) the awards are based on an index of six factors, including both absolute scores and changes in achievement since the last SIMCE tests, which together account for 65 percent of the total value of the index; (4) the remaining 35 percent of the index reflects factors such as parental involvement, equity-related variables, teacher and student organizations, and so on; and (5) the awards are fully competitive in the sense that schools can win repeatedly. For more detailed information on SNED, see also Mizala and Romaguera (2000), McMeekin (2000) and Ministerio de Educación, República de Chile (2000).

Education reform program.   Chile has undertaken successive waves of education reform. One of these was the 1980 decentralization/privatization of education and establishment of the voucher system mentioned above. The most recent wave of reform has come about since the return of democracy in 1990 and focuses on improving the content, quality and equity of education. This current reform effort has four main aspects or 'pillars': (1) extending the length of the school day, including the infrastructure investment necessary to make full-day schooling possible (double shifts are eliminated, which creates an immediate demand for classroom places); (2) programs to improve teaching and learning; (3) curricular reform; and (4) strengthening the teaching profession. Along with an extensive program of in-service teacher training, the SNED system mentioned above is part of the fourth 'pillar' of the reform. Delannoy (2000) provides an in-depth analysis of these reforms.

World Bank education projects.   Beginning in 1990, the World Bank has prepared and financed major education projects. The first, known by the acronym MECE (Mejoramiento de la Equidad y Calidad de la Educación), financed improvements at the primary level, while the second (informally called MECE Media) addressed secondary education. (Other projects have focused on higher and continuing education.) The World Bank projects have stimulated and financed educational innovations (through small capital grants awarded competitively to individual schools) and have supported key aspects of the reform. The projects have been part of a multi-pronged process that has raised the issues of educational equity and quality to the top of the country's policy agenda.

As noted, from the point of view of incentives to improve education, Chile offers examples of rewards, competition and threats. The SNED reward system avoids the pitfalls of merit pay to individual teachers. The voucher system is one of the few nationwide school choice systems in the world and has been in operation since 1980. The SIMCE tests are of the 'low stakes' variety and designed to generate information to guide parental choice and to promote educational improvement through better information. Because there is such an array of incentives, however, it is essentially impossible to separate the impact of any one of them from that of the others, or from other important aspects of the education reform program.

A note on terminology.   A number of terms, some peculiar to Chile and others generally employed throughout Latin America, are used in describing the study. These are listed in alphabetical order below, although the most important are the mission statement and internal regulations.

- *Basic education*: this term, which has different meanings in different countries of Latin America, refers to the first eight years of schooling in Chile; the equivalent of primary school plus two years of lower secondary or junior high school.
- *Board of Educational Assistance and Scholarships*: this is the Junta de Asistencia Escolar y Becas, or JUNAEB, which calculates an 'Index of Vulnerability' indicating the degree of poverty in communities.
- *Excellence awards*: the Premios de Excelencia Educativa awarded under the SNED system.
- *Homogeneous group*: the strata of schools that are comparable and compete against each other under the SNED system of merit awards.
- *Internal regulations*: every school has a *Reglamento Interno* that sets forth the main rules governing matters such as admission and teachers' work arrangements as well as the rights, responsibilities and duties of each category of members of the school's community, from director, to teachers, parents, students and support staff. These constitute one of the clearest indicators of formal rules. In some schools, parents are required to sign a statement (in effect a contract) that they understand and agree to abide by the *Reglamento*. This is an indication that the formal rules in a school are strong.
- *Mission statement*: this is an imperfect translation of the concepts of *proyecto educativo* or *ideario institucional*. A more adequate transla-

tion would be 'statement of the school's mission, vision of itself and educational philosophy', but the short version is used here for simplicity. As part of the education reform, every school develops its own *proyecto educativo*, with varying levels of clarity and coherence and degrees of participation. The statements provide insight into clarity of objectives institutions within the school.

- *Remedial classes*: some schools provide '*clases de reforzamiento*' or 'reinforcement' for students who encounter difficulties, in part to help retain students in school.
- *School operators*: this translation of '*sostenedores*' refers to either the private operators or the municipal authority (education department or corporation) responsible for financing and managing the school(s).
- *Subvention*: the Chilean form of capitation subsidies or educational vouchers that are provided to all students attending publicly subsidized schools, whether municipal or privately operated (elite private schools are excluded).

2.3   STUDY HYPOTHESES

The argument of the previous chapter (and of this book in general) is that successful schools have intra-organizational institutions that provide a favorable climate for learning. Institutions inside schools include processes for articulating the school's objectives, well-developed systems of formal and informal rules, mechanisms (both formal and informal) for enforcing the rules, and an atmosphere of trust and cooperation. The concepts of formal rules and formal enforcement plus the informal rules and informal forces that lead people to follow them come directly from North (1990). Clarity of objectives is highly important inside school organizations but is an addition to the usual factors included among institutions. It is included here because of its importance in clarifying principal–agent relationships and contributing to successful transacting between members of the community. Social capital – the climate of trust and cooperation – is something that North and others recognize as an important element that supports other dimensions of the institutional environment. It is easier to define and to measure this inside organizations than in the society at large, and the study team included this among the variables to be measured.

Together, these factors create a climate in which actors make and uphold relational contracts that complement the incomplete formal ones. Schools with the characteristics described here tend to be efficient in the way they produce learning and to demonstrate high performance.

Institutions take time to develop within a school and must emerge from shared experience over time. These characteristics cannot be legislated or imposed. Leadership – at the level of school operators and of directors of individual schools – plays a crucial role in the development of institutions. As noted in connection with the theory, the basic hypothesis of the study is this: *The more a school's institutional climate favors making and upholding relational contracts, under which teachers and students commit themselves to making their best efforts to achieve learning objectives, the higher the performance of the school.*

2.4   DESIGN OF THE STUDY

Information on institutional factors in our sample of ten schools came mainly from visits to the schools, interviews with each school director and with focus groups of teachers, observations of conditions within the school, and questions addressed to persons who knew the school intimately. Some information is objective and based upon documents, especially the schools' mission statements and internal regulations (written disciplinary rules). Other information is subjective and was gathered using qualitative methods, especially through interviews. The study looks at a small, purposively selected sample of municipal and private schools chosen with the aim of demonstrating the feasibility of measuring institutional variables and testing whether they are associated with school performance as measured by standardized tests and promotion rates.

The sample was designed to make it possible to compare schools that are very similar in many respects but that differ in terms of their internal institutions and processes. Because the sample has been chosen to maximize similarity, it includes high-performing schools from both the public and private sectors. In spite of the similarities, however, some schools have higher performance than others, and the study seeks to understand the reasons for these differences. The Annex at the end of this chapter provides a more technical description of the information-gathering methodology and measurement of institutional factors within the sample schools, including information on the interview questions and the responses of school directors and teachers.

Sample selection

The five private subsidized schools in the sample were chosen from among the fifteen primary schools operated by the Sociedad de Instrucción Primaria (SIP) in metropolitan Santiago. The SIP was established in 1856, before there was a public education system in Chile, with the explicit aim of providing good-quality education for children of families with scarce resources. This highly regarded network of private schools – better known as the Matte schools – has a long history of excellence and commitment to providing education for children of poor families. The SIP schools are of special interest for the study because they are specifically oriented toward educating children from poor families. They avoid selecting students on the basis of ability and make every effort to retain students in school and not to exclude or expel students who do not perform well. The SIP has a particular vision of primary education that is expressed in the mission statement for the society as a whole. Its schools are noted for their emphasis on developing values as well as for their academic success. The schools operate within the general framework of publicly financed education and receive the same subventions as other subsidized schools, both public and private. They also operate under a system of 'shared financing' (*financiamiento compartido*), which allows schools to collect limited fees from parents.

The first step in choosing schools for study was to select the sub-sample of five private schools. The SIP schools were originally located in communities with low income levels (although, with the passage of time, income levels have risen in some of these.) These factors make them more comparable to public schools. The SIP kindly agreed to allow our interview teams access to their schools and to facilitate the process of gathering information.

The five private schools chosen were all part of a single 'homogeneous group' as defined by the Ministry of Education for its National System for Evaluating School Performance (SNED) and designed to make the competition for merit awards fair. Choosing schools from the same homogeneous group was a first step in selecting similar schools. The sub-sample of municipal schools was then chosen from within the same homogeneous group of schools on the basis of criteria designed to 'pair' municipal schools with those of the SIP serving the same community. Schools were then further matched in terms of several criteria of similarity:

- Average education level of parents of students in the school, measured in years of schooling the parents completed.
- Schools that are very similar in terms of the vulnerability index compiled by the Board of School Assistance and Scholarships (JUNAEB), which is based on a set of variables that include mother's education level, height-to-weight relationships, and the medical, dental and nutritional needs of children in the school.
- Average income of the families of children in the school, in pesos per month, according to a questionnaire administered by the Ministry of Education.
- Family expenditure on education, based on the same questionnaire.

Variables indicating the institutional climate within schools
Review of documents and, most importantly, structured interviews with school
directors and focus groups of teachers provided information on key variables
that characterize the institutional climate within the schools and are related to
the specific hypotheses of the study. The variables are:

1. the clarity of the school's mission or objectives and the degree to which
    these objectives are understood and shared by members of the school's
    community;
2. the nature of formal rules within the school and the mechanisms for their
    enforcement.
3. the nature of *in*formal rules within the school and informal mechanisms
    for enforcing both formal and informal rules; and
4. the level of trust and cooperation – or the 'social capital' – that exists
    within the school.

These four variables were combined to create an 'institutional index', in which
each variable has a weight of 25 percent, with a total value of 100 percent. As
in any weighting scheme, this is an arbitrary distribution of weights, but there
was no overriding reason to assign different ones. The first variable, relating to
the school's objectives, was subdivided into two parts. The first of these is
based on the school's written mission statement. This part counts for 10 percent
and was evaluated on the basis of whether the objectives were clear, specific,
and limited in number. The second part of the 'objectives' variable counts for
15 percent of the total and is based on information from interviews about how
well the objectives are communicated to all members of the community, how
well they are understood and shared, and how much they influence behavior.
Again, the division of this variable was arbitrary, but gave less weight to what
was written and more to our observations about how well the written objectives
were understood and put into action. Variable number 2 on formal rules is
based on documentary information from the school's internal regulation and
interview information on how well the regulations are observed and enforced.
The variables for informal rules and their enforcement and for social capital are
based entirely on interview information and observation.

Teams of three interviewers visited each school and rated the variables
independently. The degree of consensus among interviewers was quite high.
No changes or adjustments were made in the interviewers' original ratings.

Indicators of school performance

The study examines the association between the schools' scores on the institutional index and three indicators of performance:

- Scores on Chile's national standardized test (SIMCE). We used test scores from two applications of SIMCE at the fourth-grade level, in 1996 and 1999. Separate scores on Spanish language and mathematics tests were averaged and these averages for each school for 1996 and 1999 are used as two of the dependent variables.
- Data on the schools' pass rate or promotion rate.

These data were made available to us by the Studies Unit of the Planning and Budgeting Division of the Ministry of Education.

2.5   ANALYZING THE RESULTS

Association between the institutional index and indicators of school performance

The relationships between our measure of institutions within the schools and the indicators of school performance appear to be strong, as Table 2.1 shows. The dependent variables are school average scores for Spanish and mathematics on two iterations of the SIMCE tests, plus the schools' promotion rate.

Table 2.1   Associations between institutional climate and outcomes

Dependent variable	Association (R^2)	Average for all schools	Range	Standard deviation	Standard error of estimate
SIMCE '96	0.69*	81.0	15.0	5.0	4.0
SIMCE '99	0.56	274.0	38.0	10.0	12.0
Promotion rate	0.72*	98.6	2.2	0.7	0.5

Note: * Significant at 0.05 level

Readers will note that the correlation between the institutional index and the 1996 SIMCE is higher than in the case of the 1999 SIMCE. The difference may be attributable to a major change in the testing methodology used between the 1996 and 1999 applications of the SIMCE. First the Ministry of Education extended the coverage of the tests to include 'comprehension of the natural, social and cultural environment', in addition to traditional tests of language and mathematics. Also, in 1996 and earlier years the SIMCE results corresponded to the percentage of correct answers, without considering the level of difficulty of the questions answered correctly. The 1999 SIMCE assigned higher points for correct answers to the more difficult questions.

The scores obtained by each student and the averages by subject and school were thus not truly comparable to those used in earlier years.

The second possible explanation for the difference is that the 1999 tests sought to measure accomplishment of the recently-established Fundamental Objectives and Minimum Content (FOMC), which is part of Chile's ongoing education reform. Items with different levels of difficulty were used to measure accomplishment, which made it possible to use item analysis to determine the depth of students' knowledge in the FOMC areas. There is room to question, however, whether curricula based on the FOMC were fully implemented before the 1999 tests, and thus whether the tests and the curriculum were appropriately aligned. (See the discussion of alignment of curricula and tests in Chapter 5.)

The correlation between the institutional index and the schools' promotion rates was also quite high (0.72), but the range of this dependent variable is very limited.

Analysis of the contribution of components of the index

Could it be that one of the four components of the index has such a strong impact on performance that it tends to explain the association of the whole index with the indicators of performance? We conducted additional analyses to determine whether there was a single component that had a much higher correlation with the outcome variables than the others. Table 2.2 shows the results of this analysis.

In general all the components of the index appear to be fairly strongly associated with the outcome variables and no single component consistently

Table 2.2   Associations between the institutional index and dependent variables indicating school performance

Institutional index and components	Associations with dependent variables: (R^2)		
	SIMCE 1996	SIMCE 1999	Promotion rate
Index total	0.68	0.56	0.72
Goals[a]	0.74	0.49	0.83
Formal rules	0.58	0.58	0.58
Informal rules	0.59	0.45	0.64
Social capital	0.59	0.51	0.59

Note: [a] The goals component includes both sub-components: the school's written goals and the degree to which they are understood and internalized by members of the community.

dominates the group. The goals component of the index appears to have a stronger association with the 1996 SIMCE scores and the promotion rate than the other three components – higher than the index as a whole – but even taking this into account, there does not appear to be one component that drives the association between the index and the dependent variables.

Bearing in mind that the sample of schools is very small and that one must exercise great caution when interpreting the results, the associations between schools' institutional climate and outcomes or performance appear to be strong. The institutional index seems to be a fair and balanced indicator of a syndrome of good institutional climate, in which no single component dominates all the others.

The influence of background factors

The small sample precludes the possibility of using multivariate analysis to control for background factors. We attempted to provide a degree of control for such factors by choosing schools from the same homogeneous group or stratum of schools according to data compiled for the SNED study. We also chose pairs of public and private schools in the same communities, and all the communities selected had low to medium average incomes. Questions may still remain, however, about whether the results of the analysis above truly reflect the role of institutions within schools or are instead the results of background factors. We have approached this possibility by looking one at a time at the associations between the background factors for which data are available and the 1996 and 1999 SIMCE outcome variables. The background variables we examine are: household income of the students' families, the amount the family spends on education, the number of years of schooling the parents have had, and the vulnerability index compiled by JUNAEB. We also considered the size of the school (total enrollment) and the student/teacher ratio. Table 2.3 shows the results of this effort to determine whether background variables are the source of the differences in school performance.

Research on factors associated with school performance usually finds that family or household income is the background factor that has the greatest explanatory power. Not surprisingly, we found that this factor is indeed strongly associated with schools' average scores on the SIMCE tests, especially in the case of the 1999 SIMCE. Since the one-way correlation between this variable and performance is of reasonably similar magnitude to the associations between the institutional index and performance, one can cautiously conclude that the institutional factors that are the subject of the study have roughly as much influence on student outcomes as household income.

Household expenditure on education and parental education levels have fairly low associations with performance (except for a fairly strong relation-

Table 2.3   Correlations between background variables and SIMCE scores

Background variable	Correlation with (R^2):	
	SIMCE 1996	SIMCE 1999
Household income	0.46	0.75
Household expenditure on education	0.05	0.22
Parents' education	0.10	0.54
Vulnerability index (JUNAEB)	–0.33	–0.59
School size	0.41	0.33
Student/Teacher Ratio[a]	0.80	0.40

Note: [a] The greater the number of students per teacher, the greater the positive correlation with SIMCE scores.

Source: Calculated from data provided by the Ministry of Education, Republic of Chile.

ship between parents' education and the 1999 SIMCE). The JUNAEB vulnerability index, an indicator of poverty, is negatively associated with performance, as theory would predict, and this negative correlation is strong in the case of the 1999 SIMCE. Some research has found that smaller schools tend to have better performance (Cotton, 1996; Johnson, 2002), and there is a moderate association between school size and the 1996 SIMCE and a stronger one in 1999. The student/teacher ratio, long the subject of research and controversy, shows a strong positive association, which is the opposite of what theory would predict. Schools with more students per teacher have higher performance on both SIMCE tests.

Like most educational research, the data in Table 2.3 show that background factors clearly have an influence on student and school performance. The associations are not overwhelmingly strong, however, taking into account what is widely known from years of educational research. In general it seems fair to say that the explanatory power of the institutional index is relatively strong in comparison with the background factors examined here.

Differences between public and private schools

There has been great interest in whether private schools perform better than their municipal counterparts in Chile. This study was not designed to address this question specifically, but some of the similarities and differences between public and private sectors are of interest in the light of the analyses above. The Matte schools do indeed have higher performance than the mu-

Table 2.4   Differences between subsidized private and municipal schools

| | All Schools | | Private Schools | Public Schools |
Variable	Average	Standard Deviation	Private Schools	Public Schools
SIMCE 1996	81	5	85	77
SIMCE 1999	274	10	281	267
Promotion rate	98.6	0.7	98.9	98.3
Institutional index	872	79	932	813
Enrollment (1999)	1006	270	1111	901
Student/teacher ratio	29	8	35	24
Household income	347,196	19,865	353,529	340,864
Household expenditure on education	33,503	3,477	34,207	32,789
Parents' years of schooling	11.3	1.6	11.3	11.2
Vulnerability index	12.7	6.2	10.6	14.8

Source: Calculated from data provided by the Ministry of Education, Republic of Chile.

nicipal schools in our sample, even though the sample was drawn from the same homogeneous group of schools. There are, however, many reasons why this is the case. Table 2.4 presents data on school performance, the institutional index, and background.

There is clearly a difference between private and public schools, with the private schools showing systematically higher performance on both SIMCE tests and the promotion rate as well as higher scores on the institutional index. Note, however, that the averages for private and public schools are within one standard deviation of the average for all schools. The detailed data show that the ranges for each category of schools overlap in the case of each variable. In other words, there are some municipal schools that rank higher than some private schools in the case of each outcome variable as well as the institutional index.

One issue that is relevant to the difference between private and municipal schools concerns selection of students. The study found that there is inevitably a degree of selection that operates in the case of every school that has more applicants than openings for new entrants. This is true of good schools in both the public and private sectors, even though selection on the basis of ability is formally prohibited in municipal schools and is contrary to the explicit policy of the Sociedad de Instrucción Primaria. There are two kinds of selection that can only be avoided if applicants are selected by lot: self-selection on the part of parents who value their children's education highly (over which the schools have no control), and the need to allocate places when there are more candidates than places. In the latter case, the SIP's policy is to give priority to brothers or sisters of children who are already in the school – a policy that is also practiced by the popular municipal schools and that is hard to criticize – or to children of former students of the school.

Selection that favors siblings or children of former students clearly reinforces the first kind of selection. What is the significance of self-selection on the part of parents who care about their children's education? In view of the role of parents as set forth in the conceptual framework, this is likely to have an influence on the successful co-production of student learning. In the case of admitting children of former students, the effect is even stronger, since both parents and students have prior knowledge of the reputation or 'mystique' of the school, and students must feel a special need (motivation) to adhere to the school's rules, participate in its culture and endeavor to be successful. On one hand, the existence of selection tends to weaken (or make more self-fulfilling) the finding that schools with better institutional climates are more successful. Later studies will have to attempt to sort out this factor. On the other hand, short of experimental programs in which places are allocated to students on a random basis, there does not seem to be a reasonable way of eliminating selection factors of the sort encountered here.

Another issue relating to differences between private and public schools concerns retention of students. One charge that has been made against schools that achieve high levels of academic performance, especially against some subsidized private schools, is that they take actions to exclude students with low performance or those that present behavior problems that make it difficult for teachers to teach and other students to learn. Such actions can include various means of encouraging students with actual or expected low performance to attend other schools where they will 'fit in' better. In the case of children with behavior problems that lead to disruptions in classrooms, actions could include not allowing the child to enroll in subsequent years (canceling the child's enrollment) or, in extreme cases, suspension or expulsion of the difficult child. In both the municipal schools in this study and the subsidized private schools of the SIP, it is an explicit policy to encourage students to complete their studies and to make every effort to keep them in school. The mechanisms the SIP uses to accomplish this include special remedial classes outside regular class hours (*clases de reforzamiento*), interventions (with child and parents) on the part of the school orientation specialist or the school's psycho-pedagogical unit, and, in some cases, peer tutoring through the use of 'monitors' (students who are good performers and who volunteer to coach). On the whole the schools in this sample showed high levels of student retention (as opposed to dropouts or 'push-outs'.) Recall that schools with the highest scores on the institutional index were those with high promotion rates.

With regard to background variables, enrollment in the private schools is higher than in the municipal schools, meaning that small and intimate size is not the reason for the differences in performance. The student/teacher ratio is, surprisingly, higher in the private than in the municipal schools. This is consistent with the unexpected positive correlation between the S/T ratio and performance. The private schools have more students per teacher and yet show higher performance.

Parental income in the private schools is higher than in the municipal schools but the differences are less than half a standard deviation from the average for all schools. The same applies to differences in family spending on education. Parents' education levels are somewhat higher for private schools but, as noted, the range for this variable is very small and the differences are hardly significant. As would be expected, the JUNAEB index of vulnerability (an indicator of poverty) is greater in the case of the municipal schools than in the private sector.

One of the differences between private and municipal schools is that the private sector allows what is called *financiamiento compartido*, an arrangement (to which a majority of parents in the school must agree) whereby parents make additional contributions up to half the amount of the voucher payment (with provision for reducing the public subvention as the private contribution increases). This system is complex and has been the subject of considerable controversy in Chile (Corvalán and Gaymer, 2002). If nothing else, it is an indicator of families' commitment to their children's education (and some argue that it contributes to that commitment). Four of the five private schools have *financiamiento compartido* arrangements, while none of the municipal schools do. The schools that have *financiamiento compartido* have higher performance on the SIMCE tests and higher scores on the institutional index, as Table 2.5 shows.

A factor that became clear during our research on the Matte schools is that being a member of the SIP network conveyed benefits that, our respondents reported, had a beneficial effect on their work and on student learning. This in turn resonated with other research CIDE has carried out (Swope and Latorre, 2000) on another network of schools – the Fe y Alegría schools operating in nine Latin American countries – that also performed better than similar schools that were not in networks. (And, because the Fe y Alegría are Catholic schools, there were also similarities with the findings of research on Catholic schools by Bryk, Lee and Holland (1993).) We concluded that membership in a network had a positive impact on institutions within schools. Appendix B treats this subject in greater detail.

Table 2.5   Differences between schools with and without shared financing
*(*financiamiento compartido*)*

Variable	All schools	Averages of schools	
		Schools with shared financing	Schools without shared financing
Institutional index	872	928	835
SIMCE 1996	81	84	78
SIMCE 1999	274	283	268

There is some feeling that single-sex schools tend to have better perform-ance than mixed schools. Both the public and municipal sub-samples of schools had three single-sex schools and two mixed schools, thus this does not explain the differences between the two sectors. With regard to the differences between single-sex and mixed schools in terms of performance, our data showed only slight differences between the two categories, and in fact the mixed schools showed higher performance on the 1996 SIMCE tests and higher institutional index scores. Table 2.6 presents these data.

Table 2.6   Differences between single-sex and mixed schools

Variable	Single-sex schools	Mixed schools
Institutional index	869	877
SIMCE 1996	80	82
SIMCE 1999	276	270

2.6   CONCLUSIONS FROM THE STUDY

Our exploratory study indicates that it is feasible to measure institutional factors in schools. The institutional index is composed of four components, and in the case of two of these (goals and formal rules) there were documents that provided part of the basis for evaluating each school. Other components involved subjective judgements on the part of the teams of evaluators but there was a high degree of consistency between the individually established ratings the three members of each team gave. The four index components are all weighted equally (which is arbitrary) but there do not appear to be marked differences between them in terms of their correlation with the outcome variables (see Table 2.2 above).

The findings also suggest that there is a positive association between a school's institutional climate, as measured by the index, and performance. The small size of the sample requires that these associations be interpreted with great caution and circumspection. All the associations are in the direction that theory would predict, however, and in my opinion a fair-minded reader will conclude that the findings suggest that institutions are indeed associated with performance.

We also examined the association between certain important background variables and performance and find that, while there are indeed the associations that both theory and a great body of educational research lead us to anticipate, these do not appear to be so strong as to overwhelm the effects of the factors measured by the institutional index. The study is small but its findings are suggestive. It would be desirable to replicate it on a larger scale and for different education levels.

ANNEX 2A   TECHNICAL ASPECTS OF THE STUDY

The study was a first attempt to gather data on institutional factors within schools. The institutional index that measures institutions within schools is based on fundamental features of an institutional environment: degree of clarity of objectives, strength of formal and informal rules and the mechanisms by which both kinds of rules are enforced, and the social capital of the school, interpreted to mean a climate of trust and cooperation. Future studies can elaborate on this index but, for the purposes of this exercise, it encompasses the most salient characteristics of a good institutional climate.

The interview and focus group methodology used a series of questions developed for this study. Examples of questions used for each component of the index appear below. Experienced interviewers on CIDE's staff were trained in how to apply these questions. As principal investigator, I attended all interview sessions but did not take an active part in asking the questions, in order to avoid possible signals of desired response. My role was to introduce our team to the school staff, observe the interviews and take notes. There was no communication between the three interviewers at each school before we gave our ratings on the institutional index and no changes were made in the original ratings. Inter-rater reliability was high.

Data on the dependent variables measuring educational outcomes – scores from three rounds of SIMCE tests at two levels (fourth and eighth grades), scores on the educational excellence (SNED) index, and promotion rates for the schools – came from the Ministry of Education and are public information.

Most of the information on background variables came from questionnaires administered to the families of children in the sample schools in connection with the Ministry of Education's SNED system of school evaluation.

Interviews were conducted with school directors and focus groups of six teachers chosen to be representative of the teaching force in terms of levels at which they teach, subjects taught and length of service at the school (as well as gender when there were any male teachers.) It would have been desirable to include interviews with parents but difficulties of sampling parents and arranging for interviews or focus groups, as well as tight resource constraints, made this impossible. No interviews were held with students in these primary schools because of the difficulty of interviewing such young children. It would clearly be desirable to gather information from these important members of the schools' communities and later replications of the study can do so; student interviews would be especially useful if applied at the secondary level.

Interview methodology and questions

The interviews with school directors and focus groups of teachers were based on questions designed to elicit information on the major institutional variables. Interviewers did not read from a questionnaire but tended to use prepared questions and to follow the structure in a conversational way. Key questions were designed for each major variable (with probes, for use when necessary). Some of the questions used appear below, together with examples of the kinds of answers received and recorded in the field notes of the study.

With regard to school objectives.

- How were the objectives established? Who was involved in decisions about the objectives?
- How do students, teachers and others learn about the objectives?
- What influence do the objectives have on the daily activities of teachers and students?

Most but not all schools in the sample indicated that there had been fairly high participation in preparing the mission statements. Substantial differences appeared in the dissemination of the statement to members of the school community (and measures to encourage adherence to the mission and objectives). Schools that scored high on the institutional index held special introductory meetings with groups of parents in which they explained and discussed the mission statement (as well as the internal regulations.) Teachers in schools with high institutionality made statements such as: 'we virtually carry the statement in our pockets', or 'we know it by heart', or 'we remind the children if they are not living up to the objectives'. The reverse was true in schools where objectives were not clear. A teacher in a public school said, 'I was in a school where the [mission statement] document wasn't available. You had to make an effort to find it.' With regard to the influence of the objectives, both teachers and school directors emphasized the aspects of the mission statement and the internal regulations having to do with values. Examples included respect (for self and others), orderliness, personal appearance (observing dress or uniform codes), and solidarity with classmates and with those less fortunate. Multiple comments from teachers indicated that 'without order you cannot teach'.

With regard to principal–agent relationships.

- What kind of relationship is there between this school and its operating authority (either the SIP or the municipal education department)?
- How does the national Ministry of Education influence what goes on in this school?
- How does the sustainer [operating authority] influence what goes on in this school?

The private schools indicated a close and positive relationship with their operating authority (SIP). Municipal schools indicated a variety of relationships ranging from support (with regard to some inspectors), to indifference ('they leave us alone'), to conflict. In one case the school did not have an approved mission statement because of 'philosophical differences' between the municipal authority and the school over the content of the statement. Attitudes toward oversight varied from positive ('they [supervisors] are helpful and constructive') in all the private and some of the municipal schools to no better than neutral.

With regard to formal rules.

- How do you monitor and control student behavior?
- In addition to giving grades to encourage studying hard, what other rules or requirements are there, and how are they enforced?
- What happens when a student's performance is very poor?
- What rules apply to teacher behavior; for example regarding attendance (and advising in advance if there will be an absence), punctuality, participation in extra duties or extra-curricular activities, preparation of study plans, behavior toward students, parents and others?

There was variation within a fairly narrow range within both the private and municipal groups of schools. All schools had written internal regulations, although in the case of one municipal school the only copy was kept in a folder and photocopies were made when necessary (as when requested by this study) and some of its pages were handwritten in pencil. Schools in which all parents received copies of the regulations and had to sign statements saying they understood and accepted the rules were rated highly on this variable. On the whole most schools possessed fairly strong formal rules. There were significant differences in enforcement, however. One school director spoke of going outside the main school entrance to ensure that students continued to adhere to the dress code, even when outside the school doors. There were statements such as: 'If there's no discipline, you can't teach.' Responses in schools with low levels of institutionality indicated that the rules were not always observed (for example, parents who 'forgot' to pay for repairing a window their child broke) or were difficult to enforce. 'There are things in the regulations that just aren't backed up; nobody makes people follow the rules', we were told in one school.

Regarding teacher performance, the private schools in the Matte schools network have a system of teacher evaluation whereby the school director writes an evaluation statement for each teacher and discusses it with him or her. The evaluation then goes to the headquarters of the SIP where it is reviewed and, in the case of teachers with exceptionally good evaluations, there is a system of monetary rewards.

With regard to informal rules.

- How do students feel about classmates who don't respect the rules or whose academic performance is very poor? How do they express these feelings? How do they communicate to such a student their approval or disapproval? Would you give some examples?
- What do teachers think of colleagues whose professional performance is very good? How do they express their feelings about this? Can you give examples?
- What do teachers think of colleagues whose professional performance is *less than* good? How do they express these feelings? Can you give examples?
- How does the atmosphere (culture) in this school compare with that in other schools where you have taught?

Schools with high institutionality indicated that students and teachers understood and respected the informal norms or codes that apply within the school. The survey team was also able to observe whether children demonstrated orderly behavior and adhered to the dress code. Directors and teachers in schools that were rated highly emphasized the importance of 'conversation' as a means of communicating approval, disapproval and guidance or orientation, both to students and among teachers. In spite of some degree of variation, there were generally expressions of solidarity among teachers. This was true in one school with a low institutional rating (although in this school, the opinion of the school director seemed to have nothing to do with the views of the teachers).

The interview team heard comments such as: 'teachers get annoyed when a colleague doesn't make an effort. They get frustrated when they see somebody who doesn't produce; who just jokes around.' When students misbehave: 'sometimes the other students support the teacher. They make comments out loud like "that's stupid" when another student acts up.' Another commented, 'In seventh and eighth grade, the students can be cruel to each other. They know when another student is wrong.'

With regard to formal and informal enforcement mechanisms.

- How do teachers encourage students to study hard and learn the materials?
- What happens in this school to encourage teachers and students to do their best?
- Would you describe any informal agreements or 'deals' that you [teachers] make with students about their studies, such as 'learning contracts' or informal commitments? What about informal encouragement of good studying, such as approval or disapproval, or assigning tasks that are seen as rewards or punishments?
- In addition to teachers' formal contracts, what other standards apply to teachers concerning their professional performance, their behavior toward students, or other aspects of their performance? Please give examples.
- What activities or events are there that serve to recognize or reward teachers or students for good performance: awards ceremonies, etc. Are there activities or occasions that promote teamwork and cooperative effort?
- How do you publicize the names of students who are on the honor roll?

Teachers in particular said they used approval and disapproval as means of encouraging and rewarding good behavior or punishing bad, but observed that this was more effective at the lower primary level (grades 1–4) than for the upper grades. Schools with high institutionality had more elaborate arrangements for providing recognition and praise: honor rolls, prize ceremonies and awards for a variety of good behaviors (in addition to academic success) such as 'best companion' or 'has achieved greatest improvement this month'. In a number of schools, teachers indicated that symbolic rewards – recognition within the class, giving honorary duties or assignments, and 'pat on the back' gestures – are very important. For older children there were also certificates and gifts such as books. With regard to 'contracting' *per se*, there was little mention of things such as learning contracts, although some teachers gave examples of ways of encouraging good study behavior that approximated to contracting. The most clear contract-like activity indicated was specific arrangements with students designed to encourage them to change or overcome misbehavior in the future.

Questions to directors and comments on informal rules and enforcement mechanisms.

- In addition to the supervisory meetings you hold with teachers, and reviews of performance, what do you as director do to communicate to the teachers whether they are performing well or badly?
- How does a teacher know what is expected of him or her in terms of behavior and effort?
- Do parents sometimes complain about teachers they feel are not doing a good job? What do they complain about? To whom do they complain, and what happens when they do?
- What do students think and do when another student is misbehaving?
- In addition to grades and various forms of reward and punishment, what tools do you have at your disposal when a student is being difficult and disturbing the teacher and the rest of the class?

Directors in schools with notably good institutional climates emphasized the role of 'conversation' with teachers. One outstanding director, when asked about methods of communicating desired behavior and levels of effort to teachers, replied 'By my example!'

It was more difficult to obtain information on informal enforcement mechanisms, in part because it was difficult to explain the question without signaling the answer desired. Nonetheless, it was possible to gather some information, as in this example: 'The teachers promote discipline by their presence, by what they say, their attitudes and examples.' As in the case of rewards for good behavior, teachers gave importance to symbolic measures – forms of disapproval – as effective tools for shaping behavior.

With regard to levels of social capital, solidarity and trust.

- How do the students feel about studying and learning?
- How do the students show their 'school spirit' or feelings toward the school?
- How can you tell if a teacher has a feeling of commitment to the school and the students?
- When a new teacher comes to the school, how is s/he introduced around, to new colleagues, students, the rules and general norms and culture of the school?

The level of solidarity among teachers was observed to be relatively high in most cases, although there were differences. In some schools with favorable institutional climates the teachers had all worked together for long periods. In a school with little rotation of teachers: 'they only leave when they retire. Once they get into this school, they don't want to leave. Sometimes we have differences – different styles of doing things – but nobody wants to leave. Here we're treated like people, because the director doesn't impose her will on us; we do things by consensus.' In more than one school, teachers spoke of their relationships (with students as well as fellow teachers) as 'like a family'. 'There is a lot of mutual support among teachers; good communication between us; at lunch, in the halls, at meetings and training courses.'

Respondents in such schools indicated that students feel a strong bond with their classmates and their teachers, that students spend time at the school after school hours (in formal extracurricular activities or just playing). 'There's a mystique about this school.' Former students frequently return to the school and indicate that they miss it and their teachers. 'They come back to see us, even when they get older. Every week one or two students come back to visit.' Teachers in schools with less favorable institutional environments did not say that there was little solidarity but did not have positive examples or express interest in the subject.

Rating system

The study rated each school in terms of the components of the institutional index. The rating sheet presented in Figure 2A.1 shows the weights assigned to the components. The weights add to 100. Schools were scored on each variable on a ten-point scale, with '10' being 'the best that could reasonably be expected'. The sum of the weighted scores of the variables yields the school's institutional index score. The theoretical maximum is 1000. Index scores ranged from 685 to 955. Interviewers familiar with many schools in

School Name _____ Director _____

Address _____

Interview Team _____

FACTOR EVALUATED	WEIGHT	FACTOR SCORE (Scale of 10)	WEIGHTED SCORE (Weight X Score.)
Clarity of objectives (from Proyecto educativo or vision statement)	10		
Objectives understood by members of school community (school staff, students and parents)	15		
Formal rules are clear, internally consistent and enforced.	25		
Informal rules are clear and consistent with formal rules, influence behavior, and are enforced through informal means.	25		
Spirit of cooperation and trust (social capital)	25		
Total weight:	100		Weighted Score:

Figure 2A.1   Rating sheet: institutional index

Chile said that if the study had included schools more diverse in terms of quality, this range would have been much greater.

For readers interested in the basic data the study produced, Table 2A.1 presents the data the study gathered and that were used in the analyses above.

Table 2A.1   Database: empirical study

	Sample schools									
	1	2	3	4	5	6	7	8	9	10
Independent variables										
Institutional index	861	955	947	947	949	821	685	928	870	760
Sum of goals*	207	241	242	245	228	205	178	228	220	168
Formal rules	229	246	239	248	233	208	150	219	217	200
Informal rules	196	229	231	229	245	204	191	242	204	204
Social capital	229	239	235	225	243	204	166	239	229	188
Dependent variables										
SIMCE 1996	82.72	84.66	83.77	85.19	86.91	78.94	79.01	79.74	75.48	71.56
SIMCE 1999	280	285	273	277	288	292	255	273	254	259
Promotion rate	97.78	99.63	99.19	98.93	99.07	98.78	98.10	98.42	98.57	97.44
School variables										
Enrollment, 1999	929	816	1256	1312	1243	1146	578	824	1333	624
Number of teachers	30	24	34	34	35	51	29	31	43	34
Student/teacher ratio	31	34	37	39	36	22	20	27	31	18
Boys/girls/mixed	Girls	Boys	Mixed	Mixed	Girls	Boys	Mixed	Mixed	Girls	Boys
Shared financing	Yes	Yes	No	Yes	Yes	No	No	No	No	No
Background variables										
Household income	331,097	365,321	339,017	346,293	385,915	360,636	315,330	351,754	334,991	341,607
HH expenditure on education	33,425	34,193	28,683	37,947	36,789	35,022	30,888	27,350	34,818	35,913
Parents' years in school	11.3	11.8	10.4	11.1	11.9	11.5	10.2	11.6	11.3	11.4
Vulnerability index	15.5	0	18.1	5.6	14	8.4	20.1	14.8	17.2	13.6

Note: * Combines both subcomponents of goals indicator: clarity of written goals and degree to which they are disseminated and internalized.

Source: Data for the independent variables, school and household variables provided by the Ministry of Education, Republic of Chile.

3. Rewards for good performance

3.1 INTRODUCTION

There are three broad approaches to providing monetary incentives to teachers for good performance: (1) merit pay (usually a one-time bonus) to individual teachers for their unique contribution to school performance in a given year, whether based on the school director's evaluation of that contribution or some more objective measure of performance such as test results; (2) awards to whole school establishments in the form of a bonus divided between all members of the team of people involved in producing the academic performance; and (3) development of a compensation system based on a multi-dimensional evaluation of teacher performance and a scale of compensation that rewards knowledge, skills and actions directly associated with professional performance rather than purely on seniority and academic degrees.

Research on merit pay to individuals as a way to provide market-like incentives concludes that there are many reasons why this intervention has rarely been successful. This includes both the work of Murnane and Cohen (1986) and Malen, Murphy and Hart (1987) as well as more recent studies such as Odden and Kelley (1997). Malen, Murphy and Hart (1987, pp. 96–108) provide an extensive critique of individual merit pay. They conclude:

> In sum, the merit pay strategy operates as a relatively weak vehicle for reallocating salary and a potentially counterproductive means for conferring status. The current experience echoes previous experiments. Although merit pay policies have been enacted, removed, revived and retried for decades, few endure ... The strategy does not appear to be a viable approach to the redistribution of economic rewards in school settings. (p. 99)

In spite of such clear consensus in the research literature, the idea of rewarding individuals for performance, as in a piece-rate system, seems to have great intuitive appeal and still finds advocates. Local and national jurisdictions continue to attempt to implement approaches based on merit pay to individuals.

There is less knowledge about merit awards to whole schools. The number of examples of merit awards to whole establishments is limited (far less than the number of experiments with merit pay to individuals). There is little evidence about whether providing market-like incentives to whole teams of teachers and other school staff successfully avoids many or all of the problems of merit pay, although a number of writers argue that it is a useful tool for motivating teachers. Odden and Kelley (1997, pp. 111–38) devote a full chapter to 'School bonuses for improved student performance', concluding: 'We believe that a performance award at a small level, particularly when combined with real site-based decision making and restructuring … will also strengthen the focus on improving student achievement results' (p. 138). Odden and Clune (1998) cite several sources supporting their argument that 'performance awards are most appropriately provided to groups or all individuals within an organization because the work is best conducted in collegial, team-based settings' (p. 171). These authors cite programs in Kentucky, Maryland and North Carolina as well as the Dallas, Texas, and Charlotte-Mecklenburg, North Carolina school districts as examples of a functioning system of school-based awards. One interesting example of awards to whole schools is found in Chile, and section 3.3 of this chapter includes a case study of this example merit awards to whole schools, which appears to be working successfully.

The third category of reward systems – changes in evaluation and compensation systems – is really a management intervention rather than an attempt to bring market-like forces into the education arena. There is something of a movement developing around the idea of basing teacher compensation on 'what teachers know and do' (Odden and Kelly, 1997) rather than on seniority and degrees obtained, as in most standard 'single salary' contracts governing teachers' pay and promotion. Section 3.4 of this chapter considers this approach to rewarding performance.

The institutional model developed in Chapter 1 helps explain some of the differences between these three approaches to providing monetary incentives in terms of their success in improving performance. The discussions of the three approaches later in this chapter do not attempt exhaustive reviews of the extensive literatures on each but rather focus on the ways these interventions influence institutions within schools.

Sherwin Rosen (1987) traces the idea of paying university teachers on the basis of 'teaching quality assessed by students' as far back as Adam Smith, and cites other sources that mention student fees at the University of Bologna in the Middle Ages. Payment for training in specific skills is probably as old as the development of skills themselves, but paying differential amounts based on quality - especially to individual teachers - has not emerged as the dominant model.

Economists recognize a principle of 'survival of the fittest' according to which successful innovations survive and prosper while others do not. The well-known approach of paying elementary and secondary teachers a 'standard salary' rather than differentiating between them seems to have great survival ability since it is so consistently used, worldwide and over a long period of time. There are various possible explanations for this, including the transaction costs of alternative approaches, equity concerns (both in hiring teachers and in providing services), and political factors. Understanding this fully would truly be a study in the political economy of education, but relying on markets – as is common in so many other aspects of life – has not evolved as the dominant model in education. Why have efforts to introduce market-like organization of activity into the education sector met with such poor results? It must have to do with the nature of 'production' of the 'output' of education: teaching and learning.

Earlier chapters have looked inside school organizations and found that institutional factors – formal and informal rules, enforcement mechanisms, principal–agent relationships, trust and related matters – have an impact on the productivity of education activities. The next sections of this chapter consider three approaches that use rewards as means of inducing better performance, and the influence they have on institutions in schools.

3.2   MERIT PAY FOR INDIVIDUAL TEACHERS

Research on experience with merit pay.   The idea of paying teachers a monetary reward for doing a good job of teaching seems reasonable on the surface. It has been tried since early in the twentieth century in the US and there have also been attempts to introduce merit pay for individual teachers in some developing countries. Education reform programs in a number of countries include activities designed to reward good teaching through bonuses, much as a good salesman receives commissions or bonuses for successful sales performance. The history of such programs indicates that merit pay schemes raise many problems and have not, on the whole, been successful. As with most of the approaches to providing incentives to improve education considered in this book, merit pay is a controversial subject, with strong advocates and opponents. The advocates argue:

- Merit pay to good teachers will encourage them to continue giving their best.
- It will also encourage other teachers to make greater efforts in order to win awards in the future.
- A system of merit pay will tend to attract bright and ambitious people into teaching and discourage teachers who do not win merit awards and cause them to leave teaching, providing openings for able new comers.

- Without some system of accountability, human nature will lead teachers and whole schools to shirk and give less than their best efforts.
- Parents and taxpayers will approve of and tend to support a system that rewards good teaching through merit pay.

Opponents, on the other hand, hold that:

- Using achievement tests for determining which teachers are performing best raises many concerns about whether tests really measure desired outcomes.
- Observing and evaluating what individual teachers do inside their classrooms is difficult if not impossible.
- Since good teaching requires adapting the instruction to the needs of the specific learner(s), there is no objective standard by which to determine whether a teacher is doing as well as possible.
- It is impossible to sort out which teachers are responsible for good results in what is essentially a joint activity.
- Money rewards will encourage teachers to be competitive rather than maintain cooperative relationships with their colleagues, to the detriment of good internal functioning of the school.
- Teachers may engage in strategic behavior, such as focusing their attention on students who are most likely to improve their test scores rather than on the best students (who are already doing well), or those who are lagging and need a great deal of the teacher's time and help. Or they may simply 'teach to the test', as has been observed in some experiments.
- School directors must inevitably disappoint the majority of teachers who do not receive awards, thus undercutting the director's role as instructional leader and damaging morale and good internal relations.
- It is difficult to design a system that continues to encourage good performance over time because of the great difficulty of measuring improvement (value added) and continuing to reward top performers while stimulating others to improve.

Hanushek et al. (1994) are generally in favor of providing monetary incentives for good performance, but recognize that there are difficulties, especially in changing from current systems to others based on strong incentives (pp. 95–7). 'In practice', they say, 'designing a workable system of merit pay has proved elusive' (p. 95). 'Unfortunately, the history has been one of varying state commitment, with funding being driven more by politics and budgetary pressures than by evaluations of success or failure' (p. 97). Despite the recognized problems, these authors remain hopeful about the possibility of successful merit pay systems in the future.

Murnane and Cohen (1986) review the history of individual merit pay in the United States, looking at 115 school districts that had merit pay systems in 1978 and examining in detail the experiences of six of the 47 school systems in which merit pay was used for at least five years. In general they find that the majority of merit pay systems did not survive for more than a few years, and in those cases in which they have survived, they evolve into something other than true systems of pay for performance, such as extra pay for extra work or mechanisms for improving the salaries of all teachers in the system.

From the point of view of institutions within schools, these authors draw on the economic literature of contracts, concepts of opportunistic behavior, and the negative effects of injecting competition into a school's environment on both cooperation between teachers and the leadership role of the school director. While they do not mention the phrase 'transaction costs' in their 1986 article, they clearly recognize the difficulty (and, implicitly, the cost) of obtaining adequate information on teacher performance in the classroom as a significant barrier to implementing merit pay.

Murnane and Cohen (1986) distinguish between what they call 'new-style merit pay', in which merit bonuses are based on improvements in student learning as measured by achievement tests, and 'old-style merit pay' that is based on the school directors evaluation of teachers' performance (including such factors as teamwork). The former, they say, is similar to a piece-rate compensation system, like paying workers so much per bushel of apples picked. It is subject to two kinds of problems. The first has to do with the compensation schemes or 'payment algorithms' on which such systems must be based and the tendency of any such scheme to give rise to opportunistic behavior on the part of teachers. The second set of problems has to do with what they call 'the nature of teachers' work' (and here is where information problems arise).

With regard to payment algorithms, any payment scheme needs to specify what improvements in test scores will be rewarded. It must necessarily include some outcomes – for example reading scores – while excluding others. In effect this places a zero value on gains in the excluded areas. Narrow specification of outcomes that will lead to rewards leads teachers to focus on these out-comes, or on the students with whom they can produce the most gains in return for their time. Murnane and Cohen (1986, p. 5) cite evidence that teachers working under new-style merit pay do appear to adjust their efforts so as to maximize improvements in outcomes that will bring them rewards. They refer to a 1975 study, sponsored by the US Office of Economic Opportunity, in which private firms were compensated on the basis of reading-test score gains. The study observed opportunistic allocation of teachers' time between different groups of students so as to maximize test score gains.

Turning to the nature of teachers' work, the authors find that new-style merit pay is rarely used, even in private schools where there is a high degree of consensus on goals and management is free of outside regulations. They argue that teaching does not satisfy the conditions under which piece-rate compensation is efficient: that it is possible to measure clearly the quantity and quality of work performed by each worker, and to do so at a reasonable cost. Moreover, such schemes do not recognize that teaching is a collaborative and cooperative activity in which all the teachers in a school are engaged.

The second or 'old-style' form of merit pay is based on performance evaluations by the school directors, who are in a position to observe teachers reasonably closely in their work. Murnane and Cohen (1986, pp. 7–10) cite Alchian and Demzets (1972) and Williamson (1975) on the subject of compensation based on supervisors' assessment of individual workers' performance. Merit pay is efficient when it is possible for supervisors (school directors) to answer two questions that teachers who do not receive merit bonuses raise: (1) Why does worker X get merit pay and I don't? and (2) What can I do to get a merit bonus next time?

The nature of teachers' work makes it difficult if not impossible to answer these questions in a satisfactory manner. Two teachers may both be highly effective, yet use totally different techniques, so it is not possible to identify or measure specific teaching actions that are associated with success. Given this imprecision, and the fact that teaching largely takes place behind closed doors, school directors have difficulty gathering the information necessary to answer the two crucial questions. Under these conditions, teachers may engage in opportunistic behavior to win approval from directors. The problem with old-style merit pay, the authors state, lies in 'the lack of a blueprint for effective teaching' that prevents supervisors from providing convincing answers to teachers' two primary questions about merit pay.

Other important points are: (1) that merit pay tends to interfere with school directors' efforts to promote good teacher performance through pedagogical leadership, encouragement and steps to improve teacher morale; and (2) that it tends to introduce an adversarial atmosphere and create incentives for teachers to conceal problems. 'Merit pay turns my job from being a coach into being a referee', said one school director (Murnane and Cohen, 1986, p. 9).

Bruno Frey and his associates at the University of Zurich have studied the phenomenon of 'motivation crowding', whereby monetary incentives – extrinsic rewards – tend to undermine or crowd out intrinsic motivation. Frey and Jergen (2000) survey empirical studies that indicate that the phenomenon is observable in both field and experimental studies in the areas of voluntary work, on-time behavior of parents of day-care children, on-time flight performance of airlines, readiness of communities to accept toxic waste deposits, and civic virtue in fulfilling tax obligations, among others. Frey and Jergen (2000) mention some teachers accepting lower pay 'who want to work in government schools because they believe in the virtue of public education' (p. 22).

For all these reasons, specialists in teacher compensation, such as Odden and Kelley (1997, pp. 32–4), are skeptical about the benefits of merit pay to individuals. They cite research both before and after Murnane and Cohen's work that comes to much the same conclusion. Poor implementation of merit pay systems and uncertain funding due to budget problems can be added to the list of problems. 'Pay strategies that differ from the single salary schedule must overcome the fatal flaws of past merit pay programs. And unless funded over the long haul, even well-conceived new pay approaches will not provide the incentives for a skeptical teaching force to adopt new behaviors' (Odden and Kelley, 1997, p. 33).

How does merit pay affect institutions inside schools?

The incidence of merit pay. The main impact of merit pay is intended to be on teachers. It provides a payment incentive for better performance. It may, however, generate tensions between peers (T–T transactions). As noted above, it complicates the D–T transactions between teachers and school directors. Since the essence of merit pay is that some teachers receive bonuses while a majority does not, the gains in motivation of one group tend to be offset by dissatisfaction of the others. Teachers who do not receive awards feel aggrieved, especially if they do not accept that the awards are fair and based on valid and important outcomes.

Under the best of circumstances, students may sense the effect of merit pay in terms of greater effort on the part of teachers. Or they may become aware of anxiety on the part of teachers regarding the students' success on standardized tests. With regard to parents and the community at large, there are some indications that merit pay schemes meet with favor in the community and tend to legitimize educational expenditure in the eyes of those who pay taxes.

Strength of the impact. How much better will teachers teach as a result of merit pay? If all teachers begin to work as hard and well as they can in the hope of gaining a merit award, this would tend to produce significant improvements. For several reasons, however, the total impact is likely to be limited, especially over time. First the magnitude of merit bonuses is constrained by the budget. Usually the amount of the bonus a successful teacher receives is fairly small. Murnane and Cohen found that, even in those school systems in which merit pay schemes survived for at least five years, a number of teachers did not compete for merit awards because the pay increments were not worth the extra work necessary to meet the criteria for the awards. Second, merit bonuses should not be large in any event, since substantial rewards would tempt teachers to behave opportunistically. Finally, any teacher's ability and effort are limited. While it may be the case that many teachers are performing well below their best, the amount of improvement in professional performance that can be stimulated by a merit bonus is constrained. And while there may be improvements in the initial years of such a system, disenchantment is likely to set in over time as teachers find reasons to distrust or dislike the merit pay program.

Effect on clarity of objectives. On one hand, basing a portion of teachers' pay on performance – whether measured objectively through tests or subjectively on the basis of supervisors' evaluations – provides a powerful means of focusing attention on the objectives that the school system or the supervisor want to maximize. In order to bring forth the desired behavior, a merit pay scheme must indicate what behavior it proposes to reward. But if the desired end or 'payment algorithm' is too narrow and specific, this focuses attention on a few narrow (usually easily measured) outcomes such as reading and mathematics scores. It can lead teachers to give more time to students who are likely to show the greatest improvement, or simply to teach to the test. Or it can produce 'grandstanding' behavior whereby teachers give greater attention to how well they appear to be working than to truly optimizing their performance. While clear statement of objectives generally has the effect of improving principal–agent relations (by specifying exactly what performance the principal desires), the introduction of extrinsic rewards tends to produce undesired distortions in agents' behavior.

Effect on formal rules. Merit pay necessarily requires a body of rules and regulations that spell out what will be rewarded, how performance will be measured, who will receive the rewards and related matters. These formal statements of the 'rules of the game' of merit pay are similar to a contract with teachers: if you do x, we will reward you in the form of y. As discussed in Chapter 1, it is essentially impossible to write a complete contract covering all contingencies, which means that there will be 'gaps' that are likely to lead to misunderstandings or feelings of unfairness on the part of teachers. If teachers come to feel that these new 'rules' are unfair or improperly specified, they will not respect them, which may foster cynicism and disrespect for all the formal rules.

Merit pay incorporates its own formal enforcement mechanism: those who meet the criteria will receive a bonus; those who don't will not. The literature on merit pay indicates that some teachers feel they are already making their best efforts to meet objective or subjective criteria, and even that they have made significant progress or contribution, yet if they are below the 'cutoff line', they receive no bonus. This would have a negative effect on motivation and effort. Or teachers may feel it is unfair that a peer who made no greater contribution received a bonus. Such outcomes undercut acceptance of or confidence in the fairness and justice of the whole fabric of enforcement mechanisms, which damages the institutional environment.

The body of formal rules that establish the basis for a merit pay system may loom large in comparison with other statements of formal rules, sending the signal that merit pay is as important or nearly as important as some less specific expressions of desired outcomes, such as statements of the school's mission and vision. The rules associated with merit pay are an addition; an overlay on the basic set of formal rules. It is difficult to specify and communicate them clearly without reducing the relative importance of other aspects of formal rules.

Effect on informal rules. Informal rules are: '(1) extensions, elaborations and modifications of formal rules, (2) socially sanctioned norms of behavior, and (3) internally enforced standards of conduct' (North, 1990, p. 40). The mechanisms for enforcing them are also informal and are generally based on individuals' internal perception of desirable behavior (including the perception of the probability of 'getting caught' and of resulting social disapproval). Malen, Murphy and Hart (1987) mention cases in which teachers who received merit pay were ridiculed and disrespected by their peers, who did not accept that the merit pay system was fair or that it evaluated meaningful performance. But even less overt sanctions, including very subtle indications of disapproval, can have considerable power. Internal sanctions – one's own beliefs and preferred behavior – can be among the most powerful sources of enforcement, giving rise to behavior in accordance with the informal rules, even when it is not in the individual's apparent self-interest. The work of Frey and associates on the way extrinsic rewards 'crowd out' intrinsic motivation supports the argument that the reaction to merit pay may be strongly influenced by informal rules (Frey and Jergen, 2000; Bohnet, Huck and Frey, 2000).

Social capital and trust. This is perhaps the area in which merit pay has its greatest impact, and it tends to be uniformly negative. First, teachers may perceive that measurement of performance is either improper or untrustworthy. 'Old-style merit pay', based on supervisors' observation and ratings, takes an especially high level of trust that the supervisor knows who is performing well and has the integrity to reward the truly meritorious teachers. And in the case of 'new style merit pay', based on more objective measurement, teachers' professional judgement as educators may be that the outcomes measured are not the most significant ones, or that they are not accurately measured.

The second area in which merit pay may conflict with trust is in relations between peers. Even if there is no perception of unfair behavior on the part of peers (that is, even if teachers do not feel others are 'grandstanding' or 'boot-licking'), transforming teachers into competitors for limited numbers of bonuses damages feelings of collegiality and trust. As for trust between teachers and supervisors, this clearly suffers when a merit pay system is instituted. There is no way a school director can avoid making some teachers unhappy. This in turn damages morale, the quality of principal–agent agreement, trust, voluntary effort and cooperation.

Conclusions about merit pay

Is merit pay to individuals a desirable way of using the power of market-like forces to improve teacher motivation and performance? The balance of research-based literature indicates it is not. Malen, Murphy and Hart sum up their assessment as follows:

> The merit pay strategy relies on a narrow band of incentives – a salary supplement and presumably status benefits. Although these rewards have a role to play, like people in other organizations teachers 'seek simultaneously many kinds of satisfactions, not just those with economic roots' ... Because the merit pay strategy is confined to a single set of rewards and to what teachers define as the least salient set of rewards, it is not compelling to most teachers. Because the reward offered is not particularly attractive and is consistently viewed as tentative, it is not very potent. (p. 108)

Yet the concept continues to have adherents and there are still policy makers who advocate rewarding individual teachers for good performance.

Looking at the effect of merit pay on institutions within schools enables us to go somewhat farther than earlier studies toward understanding why this approach to providing incentives does not work. The institutional perspective reveals the effects of rewarding a few teachers on the willingness of the whole teaching staff to give their best – use their property rights in labor – in helping to achieve the school's goals.

3.3   MERIT AWARDS TO WHOLE SCHOOLS

There is much less information on or experience with group-based or whole-school performance awards than on merit pay. Craig Richards and Tian Ming Sheu (1992) examined the South Carolina School Incentive and Reward

Program as a specific case of financial incentives to whole operating units. Helen Ladd (1999) studied the Dallas, Texas experiment with school-based awards. Other examples are found in Kentucky, and in the Charlotte-Mecklenburg, North Carolina school districts. The programs seem to be working, although it is difficult to determine clearly what their impact on performance has been.

The following discussion of this approach to providing incentives will consider:

1. Design issues: what are the key factors that must be considered in designing such a program?
2. Implementation issues: is the implementation process fair and equitable, effective, and likely to result in improvements in student outcomes?
3. Issues of intra-organzational institutions: what effect does the program have on the institutional climate within the school?

Design issues

What kind of reward? There is consensus among researchers that merit award programs should be one-time bonuses to the teachers in a school, that they should be based on 'value added' (that is, on improvements in performance rather than absolute levels), that the awards must be won in each time period, and that they should be divided among recipients on a basis that is fair and equitable.

Odden and Kelley (1997, pp. 112–38) devote an entire chapter to school-based performance awards, which they feel are a desirable complement to changes in the system of teacher compensation. They favor performance awards to all the teachers in a school, or to identifiable groups of teachers within the school, such as a 'house' or a faculty responsible for teaching a specific group of students whose performance can be evaluated.

The frequency with which rewards are made is an issue. The bonuses must be earned in each time period, but how long should the time period be? Can measurement systems capture changes in value added within a one-year time period? In the Chilean case study discussed below, the selection of schools to receive the awards takes place every two years, with payments distributed quarterly over the full two years.

Similarly there is a question of how to divide the bonuses: equally, as a percentage of each teacher's base salary, or on some other basis. The related issue of how to determine which teachers in a team made diligent efforts is dealt with in the section on opportunism and free riding.

Maryland has a school based award system under which the reward goes to the school (not the teachers). This is an interesting development, no doubt designed to avoid some of the problems associated with cash payments to teachers. It constitutes an explicit recognition that teachers are motivated by factors other than or in addition to monetary rewards. Odden and Kelley (1997) recognize that monetary bonuses are not the only, or necessarily the most meaningful, form of rewards:

> The symbolic significance of group performance awards ... might be more impor-
> tant than the fiscal incentives they would provide. An important education goal
> within each school is to create a collective focus on results and to encourage
> collaborative actions to improve results. A performance award is a formal, tangi-
> ble symbol from the system that this goal is important, but the behaviors that such
> an award motivates or rewards are probably more critical than the economic value
> of the bonus itself. (p. 113)

What indicator of performance?   This is one of the most vexed questions associated with reward-based systems of incentives. For independent schools or small networks of schools, it is possible to design what Murnane and Cohen (1986) would call an 'old-style' evaluation system. That is, a system in which the school director decides who receives the awards on the basis of observation and possibly some objective indicators of teacher performance. Ideally teachers should participate in developing such a system, and possibly participate in observing their peers' work in classrooms. To be successful this kind of personal evaluation of teachers must be perceived as accurate and fair.

For merit award systems in larger education authorities – districts, states/ regions or whole countries – a system to evaluate all teachers on the same basis has to be based at least in part on some form of standardized test. This raises all the complex questions about testing discussed further in Chapter 5. One question is whether the tests are criterion-referenced or norm-refer-enced. Odden and Kelley (1997, p. 124) 'strongly urge states and districts not to use norm-referenced standardized achievement tests; they do not connote that all students can achieve to high set standards'.

Many of the issues arising in connection with performance indicators are similar to those discussed in connection with individual merit pay, with the key difference that it is the performance of the whole school that is being evaluated rather than the work of individual teachers. That avoids some problems, especially identifying the individual contributions of members of a team, but there are other problems, including the quality of the tests them-selves, whether they evaluate all the qualities and skills students should acquire, and how high the stakes should be. Chapter 5 considers these ques-tions in detail.

How to avoid opportunism?   If individual teachers can engage in opportun-istic behavior in order to win awards, cannot whole schools do the same?

Devoting most teaching effort to groups of students who are most likely to show substantial improvement while giving short shrift to others is one form of opportunistic behavior. Focusing on those aspects of the curriculum most likely to be tested or, at worst, teaching to the test is another. In some British Commonwealth countries where the Cambridge Overseas Examinations determine which students will gain access to the next highest level of education, some teachers and headmasters urge poorly performing students whose scores would lower the school average and who have no chance of a good score to stay home on the day of the examination. Odden and Kelley (1997, pp. 121–3) use the term 'gaming' to describe such opportunistic behavior and mention such possibilities as schools making special efforts in one year (in order to show high value added) and slacking off in the subsequent year in order to be able to show a high gain in year three. This would tend to assure that the school received a merit award in every second competition. The design of an award system should minimize the possibilities of such opportunistic behavior.

A different category of opportunism is free riding. Free riders coast along, making minimal effort but benefiting from the reward shared among all teachers in winning schools. By avoiding the problem of identifying which individual teachers are performing well or poorly, merit award systems open themselves to problems of free riding. The Chilean example of merit awards described below addresses this problem by keeping the awards fairly low.

How do you both reward improvement while also aiding the neediest?   This question raises a policy puzzle. The idea of merit awards is that teachers in those schools that are doing best – have achieved the greatest gains or value added – should be rewarded. But there is another policy imperative, which is to improve the performance of schools at the bottom end of the distribution. Some local authorities use pay premiums to attract good teachers to work in schools where performance has been low. Others provide extra resources for schools to reform and improve. It is difficult to both reward excellence and finance efforts to improve schools in trouble. This means that schools at both ends of the spectrum receive awards.

Other challenges.   Schools that have a high proportion of special students – whether they have learning disabilities, are handicapped, are language minority or otherwise disadvantaged students – cannot compete for awards with schools that have fewer such students. Schools in communities where there is high mobility (especially where there is a constant inflow of language minority students) are likewise at a disadvantage. High student mobility means the school cannot fully control or influence the learning that will be tested. Some means of providing a 'level playing field' is needed. In Chile, good eight-year basic education schools lose their best students after the sixth grade, when they have a chance to obtain a scholarship or gain admission to an especially high-quality secondary school the entry level for which is grade six. No means has been found to account for this loss of competitiveness.

Implementation issues

Having an award system based on a sound design is certainly desirable, but there are also issues having to do with how that system is developed and put into practice. How transparent and comprehensible is the system? Is there provision for 'voice' or expression of disagreement or discontent with the system?

Consultation about the design. One essential attribute of a successful award system is 'legitimacy', and one approach to providing this is to give members of the community a voice in the design of the system. Participation is relatively easy to provide when scale is small, as in independent schools, but much more difficult when an award system covers a larger district, or a whole state or country. Consultation between system designers and teachers' representatives helps provide a sense of participation. Obviously the design of a system should be based on research and experience with successful systems, and not on the conclusions of a committee, but some form of consultation is essential, not only for its legitimizing effect but also for the insights that those affected – who know the local reality well – can bring to the design process.

Voice. In addition to consultation at the design stage, teachers (and parents and others) should have a chance to make their views known once the system is in operation. In part, voice can serve as an early warning device, signaling that there are unfavorable perceptions of the awards system. Most importantly, however, voice – including the mere opportunity to express one's views – provides an outlet for dissatisfaction, an indication to participants that the system's managers want it to be accurate and fair, and a contribution to legitimacy.

Evaluation and fine tuning the award system. It should be clear from the outset that the award system will be evaluated and, if necessary, modified to make it as fair, transparent and effective as possible. Especially in the initial years of application, evaluation of how the awards process is being implemented and how it is perceived by teachers, administrators and others helps to make necessary adjustments in the design as well as adapt it to any changes the system causes (such as the occurrence of opportunistic behavior).

Chile's system of merit awards to schools: a case study

Chile is experimenting with a 'National System to Evaluate School Performance' (Sistema Nacional de Evaluación del Desempeño de los Establecimientos Educacionales Subvencionados; SNED) that provides merit awards to all the teachers in winning schools. The SNED awards are based on an index in which student outcomes weigh heavily but other factors also enter the picture. The system was designed with care, taking into account the findings of research about reward systems. It is applied every two years and, after three rounds of evaluation and awards (1996–97, 1998–99, and 2000–01), it appears to be well accepted and functioning successfully. Information for this case study was drawn from Ministerio de Educación, República de Chile (2000), Mizala and Romaguera (2000), Delannoy (2000) and McMeekin (2000). Readers interested in greater detail should consult these sources.

The SNED evaluation system provides awards to school establishments at the basic (grades 1 through 8) and secondary (9 through 12) levels, with the funds used for bonuses to teachers. The awards are based on a school's performance as measured by an index comprised of six factors. The index includes the absolute levels of SIMCE scores and improvement in scores (value added) since the last SIMCE tests, as well as other factors associated with quality, parental participation and equity. Awards are made to the best-performing schools in each of a number of strata, which means that competition is between relatively comparable schools. SNED evaluations take place every two years and the awards are distributed over a two-year period. Any municipal or private-subsidized school is eligible to win an award, and may win in successive evaluations. That is to say, SNED awards are fully and permanently competitive.

Awards based on index scores. One of the interesting features of the SNED system is the use of quantitative indicators combined into an index as the basis for the awards. Data come from the SIMCE tests and a questionnaire completed by parents at the time those tests are administered, from a special survey carried out for the purpose of SNED, from reports prepared in connection with the subvention or subsidy payments to the school, and from the Ministry of Education statistics unit. The index of school excellence includes six factors in which student outcomes weigh heavily. The factors, including their percentage weights in the total index, are as follows:

1. Effectiveness: most recent scores on Spanish and mathematics tests of the SIMCE (37 per cent).

2. Improvement: change in these SIMCE scores since the last application, a longitudinal measure (28 per cent).
3. Initiative: indicators of activities designed to strengthen the school's plan for improvement, to improve teaching and curricular offerings, encourage student activities, and so on (6 per cent).
4. Improvement in working conditions: rating of the school by the regional inspectorate, whether the school has a full complement of teachers and brings in substitutes if teachers are absent (2 per cent)
5. Equality of opportunity: student retention and promotion rates; whether there are indications of discrimination (for example, expulsion of students during the school year or students who repeat, expulsion for pregnancy, refusal to readmit students who attended the previous year). Note that discrimination enters the index as a negative factor (22 per cent).
6. Participation and integration of teachers, parents and guardians: existence or creation of a teachers' council or of a parents' association with participation of parents and integration into school affairs; existence of a students' association; clear mission statement and internal regulations for the school; information and explanation to parents of SIMCE outcomes; parents' perceptions and approval of the school's work and especially of the language and mathematics teachers (5 per cent).

For schools serving handicapped and special education students and for two- and three-teacher schools in remote rural areas, there are additional criteria for evaluating each factor. The weights assigned to each factor were adjusted between the first and second rounds of SNED competition, giving slightly less weight to the SIMCE scores and increasing the weight of factor 5 (equality of opportunity), in accordance with the policy of evaluating and adjusting the SNED. Some of the key characteristics of this award system are discussed below.

Stratification and competition within homogeneous groups of schools. A central aspect of the SNED system is that it establishes competition between schools that are roughly comparable in terms of the student populations they serve, the socioeconomic levels of the communities in which they are located, and other external factors that affect student outcomes. For this the schools are organized into 'homogeneous groups' in a two-stage process. First, schools are divided into four main categories: urban basic and rural basic schools, and urban secondary and rural secondary schools (the last can include schools that have both basic and secondary levels). Schools that provide only special education constitute a fifth category, but are evaluated on the basis of the index. There are sub-groups of schools within each category that are evaluated on the basis of different criteria: rural primary schools with single teachers or multi-grade teaching, adult education schools, schools in penal institutions and free-standing pre-schools. The evaluation criteria for these subgroups are complex and differ depending on the type of school and level of education. For purposes of brevity and focus, this description will not deal with them at length.

Once grouped into categories, schools within each category are divided into the 'homogeneous groups' on the basis of statistical cluster analysis. This analysis considers variables that influence the schools' performance but are outside their control, such as average family expenditure on education, level of education of the parents, kind of community, physical accessibility of the school and an 'index of vulnerability' compiled by the entity responsible for distribution of scholarships and student aid (Junta Nacional de Auxilio Escolar y Becas; JUNAEB). The vulnerability index indicates the socioeconomic level of the families of children that attend each school. Schools are then grouped.

SNED establishes homogeneous groups within each of Chile's 13 Regions in each of the categories above (urban basic, rural basic, and urban and rural secondary). Breakdown by region means that there is even greater similarity between schools in each stratum or comparison group than if the grouping process were nationwide.

Allocating awards.   SNED ranks schools within each group according to their scores on the index and gives awards to schools in rank order, up to the point where the enrollment in the winning schools accounts for 25 percent of the enrollment in that group. Award funds can be used only for bonuses for teachers (including head teachers or school directors). Ninety percent of the funds are distributed on the basis of the number of hours a teacher worked in the school. (This is the most equitable basis for distributing awards, especially for secondary schools, where teachers may work less than a full day in a particular school. If primary school teachers in a school all work full time, the awards to each are equal.) Each school establishment decides how to allocate the remaining ten percent to the teachers who have made the most 'outstanding' contribution to professional performance. The special awards made from the unallocated ten percent are explicitly designed to overcome the 'free rider' problem of teachers who make little effort on behalf of the school's improvement program. This final ten percent is distributed in various ways: in the same manner as the basic 90 percent, through peer decisions by 'the education professionals in the establishment', or at the school director's discretion.

Approximately 31,000 teachers have received bonuses in each round of SNED awards. The average amount of the bonus per teacher per year has been approximately US$450 per year, with adjustments for cost of living. The relatively low amount of the awards has the effect of keeping the SNED process from becoming too much of a 'high-stakes' exercise. This in turn tends to avoid opportunistic behavior on the part of the teachers, such as focusing most of their attention on only those subjects that will be considered by the SNED. Evaluation of SNED after one round of competition did not indicate instances of opportunistic behavior, but the same evaluation found that most teachers (even in winning schools) did not know much about SNED. As the system becomes better known, there may be more of a tendency toward opportunism.

Municipal and private subsidized schools compete against each other. The distribution of awards between these two sub-sectors did not differ greatly. The portion of private subsidized schools receiving awards was slightly higher than in the case of the municipal schools. Few private subsidized schools eligible to receive vouchers have been established in remote rural or urban slum neighborhoods, so the municipal sector is more heavily represented in communities with low socioeconomic status. Table 3.1 below shows the percentage of schools in each sector and the percentage of awards going to that sector for the 1998–99 application of SNED.

Table 3.1   Awards to municipal and private subsidized schools, 1998–99

	Municipal subsidized schools		Private subsidized schools	
	% of schools	% of awards	% of schools	% of awards
1998–99 SNED	69.1	67.5	30.9	32.5
2000–01 SNED	67.4	67.9	32.6	32.1

Source: Mizala and Romaguera (2000, pp. 23, 38).

The information base for the SNED.   Chile offers an unusually rich body of data, especially the outcome data from the SIMCE tests, which is not equaled in most other Latin American countries. This has meant that the incremental cost of the information needed to establish the SNED system has been low.

The most important source of information on educational outcomes is the SIMCE tests. The tests of Spanish and mathematics administered at 4th, 8th and 10th grade levels are combined into school average scores that account for 65 percent of the total value of the index (including both the cross-section and longitudinal comparisons). Special surveys carried out for SNED provide data used for the indicators that form the basis for the 'initiative', 'equality of opportunity' and 'participation' factors. School data, which do not change greatly from year to year, come from regularly reported statistics, and are used for the 'working conditions' factor and the rates of student survival and promotion indicators for the 'equality of opportunity' factor. Other information on schools' activities and practices for the 'equality' factor come from the SNED survey. For the final factor, 'participation and integration of teachers, parents and guardians', information comes from a form completed by school directors in connection with the SIMCE tests and from a special questionnaire completed by the parents.

Evaluation of the SNED experience. The design and management of the SNED system has been well informed, sophisticated and careful. The Ministry of Education commissioned a body of evaluation studies of both the design of the SNED system and its implementation. The studies aimed to improve the SNED system by examining its design and methodology, the way it has been implemented, the information used, the attitudes of actors toward the process, behavioral-motivational factors, the time dimension, and costs.

The evaluation of the SNED design included a review of international literature on providing incentives for school improvement. It was found that the SNED system avoids the main problems associated with merit pay to individuals and incorporates features that international research finds desirable.

Interviews with school directors and with focus groups of teachers, as well as survey-based information gathering, provided the basis for the evaluation. In part, the study investigated the attitudes of respondents not only to SNED but also to the context in which it operates: Chile's system of vouchers, with public and private providers competing for students. Directors' and teachers' opinions of the SNED system constituted the main portion of the evaluation.

With regard to design and methodology, the evaluation found the following:

1. There was strong support for the establishment of homogeneous groups so that schools compete with others in similar circumstances. One recommendation was that the homogenous groups be established within each Region, not for the country as a whole.
2. There should be changes in the weighting of factors used in formulating the SNED Index. (Table 3.1 above shows the changes that were made.)
3. There should be improvements in the way the factors were measured, especially incorporation of more and better indicators.
4. All indicators should be normalized to improve the calculation of the index.
5. Information-gathering instruments should be refined so as to improve data gathering for the index.

Interviewees and focus group participants came from both municipal and private-subsidized schools, from representatives of the Regional Secretariats of Education (SEREMIs) and Provincial Departments of Education (DEPROVs), and from knowledgeable people in the central Ministry of Education. The findings and recommendations of this phase of the study were the following:

1. There is notable consensus that a system for evaluating school performance is a good idea, although there were suggestions for improvement.
2. Respondents approved linking the evaluation of performance with the payment of monetary awards.
3. Stratification into homogeneous groups so that schools are competing against equals is highly desirable.
4. Respondents recommended modifying the weighting of factors in the index (reducing the importance of absolute and value-added SIMCE scores) and the way some factors are measured.
5. Respondents urged that the evaluation system be transparent and that schools have access to the information used to determine which schools receive awards.
6. Regional and Provincial authorities recommended that they have greater participation in the process, especially in identifying the homogeneous groups in their regions.
7. Schools that won awards suggested that, in addition to the money awards themselves, that there should be greater publicity attached to winning the awards so that parents and the community at large should be aware that their school was a winner.

School directors' and teachers' opinions of SNED.   Information gathered through the evaluation made it possible to assess: (1) the perceptions school directors and teachers have of the SNED system; (2) whether SNED contributes to improved teaching performance; and (3) the degree to which SNED encourages competition between schools to improve educational quality (Mizala and Romaguera, 2000, pp. 25–32). The interview-based information provides insights not available from the survey.

The general attitude of school directors toward the SNED system is positive. This includes directors both of schools that won awards and of those that did not. The directors, whose point of view is somewhat aligned with 'management', see the SNED evaluation system as a way to recognize differences in the performance of schools. The design of the system is generally satisfactory, in their view, although they are somewhat concerned about the heavy emphasis accorded to SIMCE scores through the combined weight of the effectiveness and improvement factors in the SNED index. In this context some directors expressed the view that some of their competitors, especially private subsidized schools, practice selection of students (even though this is against regulations and the SNED system itself penalizes such behavior).

Directors are in favor of a system of monetary rewards for teachers. In their view, teachers' salaries are too low and awards under the SNED system represent a partial step toward rectifying this problem. It is interesting that, although SNED regulations reserve ten percent of a school's award to be allocated to 'outstanding' teachers at the director's discretion, a substantial majority of directors said that they distribute this ten percent on the same basis as the main portion of the award (Mizala and Romaguera, 2000, p. 26). This tends to support findings of earlier studies of merit pay to individual teachers that the difficulties of gathering information and justifying individual awards, plus the negative effect on teamwork and feelings of solidarity in the school, outweigh any positive effects of individual rewards. The directors indicated they would oppose a system of rewards to individual teachers.

School directors care about their school's prestige and its ability to attract students. Some directors of winning schools made efforts to publicize the awards but others did not. There was skepticism about whether the SNED awards would have an impact on parents' decisions about where to enroll their children. More meaningful, in the directors' opinion, was a school's long-term reputation in the community, especially its role in developing strong values in the students. Directors feel that families judge a school on the basis of its values, the commitment of teachers, what other families are choosing, and pragmatic factors such as distance from home to school, as well as on its achievement scores. The SNED awards cannot, in their opinion, alter more deeply rooted reality.

Directors' comments on teachers' reactions. When asked their opinions about what teachers thought of SNED, the directors gave a somewhat different picture. In their opinion, teachers have more reservations about a system based heavily on standardized achievement tests. They mentioned a 'teachers' culture' (*cultura docente*) in which teachers see themselves as motivated by values and commitment to their vocation. According to the school directors, teachers see themselves as doing the best they can, even under difficult circumstances. In this view the SNED awards are seen as acknowledgement of what teachers are doing in any event, rather than as recognition of excellence or special efforts. To a considerable extent directors' comments indicate that they understand and even share these views.

In the same vein, directors emphasize that teachers would object to evaluations of their work based solely on the SIMCE tests, which do not take into account factors such as student learning in areas other than Spanish and mathematics, nor the teachers' role in inculcating values and attitudes in the students. This criticism has been voiced by the teachers' union, although the union has not opposed the SNED system.

Some directors doubted that SNED would motivate teachers to greater effort. The evaluators quoted statements indicating that the contribution of SNED to teacher motivation is 'fragile' because of the strong teachers' culture. Some directors felt that what would make a difference in teacher performance would be a general salary increase of significant magnitude, greater public recognition of teachers' efforts, and substantive participation of the teachers' union in the design and implementation of education policies. In the directors' opinions, teachers tend to be convinced they are doing a good job on the basis of their own professional commitment and values, regardless of monetary awards.

Survey data on teachers' reactions. A survey administered to samples of teachers found that they tend to accept 'the Chilean model of education', including the voucher system and competition between coexisting municipal and private subsidized schools. There is not much difference between the attitudes of teachers in award-winning schools and others, but teachers in private subsidized schools showed significantly greater acceptance of the 'Chilean model' than those in the municipal schools.

There was fairly high acceptance of the concept of evaluating schools and awarding prizes on the basis of performance, especially on the part of teachers in private subsidized schools. Teachers in both municipal and private schools that won awards agreed with statements that such awards can bring about improvements in education. Teachers in losing schools were less in agreement with such statements.

Teachers' responses indicated a generally positive attitude toward the design of the SNED system, although a significant percentage found the design complex. There was some concern about the indicators used in the SNED index, including both the categories and their weightings. In general the concern focused on the relatively heavy weight given to achievement test scores. This concern was greatest on the part of teachers in private subsidized schools that did not win awards.

Teachers expressed concern that SNED is based heavily on the SIMCE achievement tests, bearing out the opinions of the directors. Some teachers would have preferred more use of qualitative indicators, although at the same time they approved of the relative transparency of the present design.

The survey found that teachers evaluate their own work quite highly, regardless of whether their school won an award or not. Seventy-four percent of teachers in schools that did not receive awards classified their own teaching performance as good or very good. This finding coincides with comments of directors that teachers are fairly complacent about the quality of their own work.

The survey was administered in 1997, shortly after the first round of SNED evaluation and awards. It found that teachers did not have very complete or accurate information about SNED, especially teachers in schools that had not won awards. This, together with similar findings about directors' knowledge of SNED, led the evaluators to recommend strongly that the Ministry of Education undertake an information campaign to increase understanding of SNED. Unless there is full and accurate information about the system, it cannot have the desired impact on the quality of teaching. As a result, the Ministry has taken effective steps to implement an information campaign.

Group-based awards and institutions within schools

Clearly awards to whole schools avoid many of the problems of individual merit pay, including problems of damage to the institutional environment inside the school. Group-based awards may even strengthen teamwork. Let us briefly examine the effects of awards to whole schools on institutional factors.

Incidence of impact. Teachers are the actors most directly affected by the awards, although there are influences on school directors, on transactions between directors and teachers, and in some cases on students and parents. An educational authority would tend to urge school directors under its juris-diction to strive to win awards. This effect would be stronger in contexts where there is real competition for students.

If the amount of the awards is not very great, as in the Chilean experience, teachers do not seem to be greatly affected by them regardless of whether they win or lose. The findings of the SNED evaluation, that teachers tend to be complacent about their own work, is significant (and has implications for all types of incentives). Larger awards would have greater impact, but would also tend to stimulate opportunistic behavior. A fairly delicate balance is called for.

Group-based awards would tend to strengthen relationships between school directors and teachers, placing everyone 'on the same team' in pursuing better performance (as measured by the award system). Awards would tend to motivate both directors and teachers to urge students to make greater efforts, thus students would feel the effects of the awards system indirectly.

The impact on parents would tend to be via the perception of the school as a 'winner' with good performance, as well as possible increased efforts on the part of teachers to encourage parents to urge their children to study well and try to succeed. In theory, some parents would be influenced to enroll their children in award-winning schools, which is why boards and directors would be motivated to press for good performance.

Effect on opportunism. As mentioned earlier, there is a tradeoff between having awards that are high enough to bring forth greater efforts on the part of teachers, on one hand, and stimulating opportunistic behavior on the other. Whole schools, probably led by the director, could behave opportunistically in order to maximize the school's performance on the indicators used by the award system. Within a particular school community, individual teachers are unlikely to change their behavior toward their peers. They might engage in free riding, making minimal effort and hoping to benefit from any award the school might receive, but probably would not behave much differently than in the absence of a reward.

Effect on clarity of objectives. Group-based awards would have the same effect as individual merit pay in terms of specifying what performance will be measured in deciding which schools win awards, with the same combination of desirable and undesirable effects. Insofar as the payment algorithm manages to incorporate a fairly full spectrum of outcomes that corresponds to the school's objectives or preference function, an awards system will tend to focus attention on achieving these outcomes. If the factors to be rewarded constitute a narrow set of outcomes – test scores on language and mathematics, for example – this will encourage concentrating on these outcomes to the exclusion of others, with undesirable effects on aspects such as creativity, problem-solving ability, participation in group activities or development of values such as honesty or cooperativeness.

Effect on formal and informal rules and social capital. Since the formal 'rules of the game' established for group-based awards apply to the whole school rather than individuals, their specification would not occupy a central position in the array of formal rules that govern behavior inside the school. They would be of relatively minor importance for teachers and hardly any importance for other actors in the community. With regard to informal rules, the externally determined awards to the whole school would have scant influence on the behavior of the key actors. The introduction of extrinsic monetary awards might have the effect of 'crowding out' behavior based on intrinsic motivation, as studied by Frey and Jergen (2000), but it is not clear whether this would happen. The effect of awards to all teachers in a school would have little effect on social capital. If there were an effect, it would tend to be positive, encouraging teachers and their school director to work together to win the award.

3.4 CHANGES IN TEACHERS' COMPENSATION SYSTEMS

The third category of incentive systems involving money payments is not based on direct performance bonuses in the same way that individual merit pay or group-based awards are. Compensation systems that base teachers' pay on attributes that include knowledge and demonstrated skill are really management interventions, not incentive schemes that attempt to elicit performance on the basis of rewards.

A compensation system that bases pay and promotion on assessment of knowledge and skill obviously depends on economic incentives to encourage desired performance, but not by introducing competition or 'market-like forces' in the same way as the previous two cases. Further evidence of the difference between the incentive systems discussed above and modified compensation systems is that some authors advocate a combination of teacher compensation based on knowledge and skill with a group-based performance reward system. The impact of such a system on transactions between members of school communities is also different from that of individual and group incentive pay, although issues of transaction costs and principal–agent relationships are still present.

Changes in compensation arrangements have attracted considerable attention in recent years and tend to be viewed favorably by some of the same authors and organizations that favor extrinsic reward systems. They have not, however, generated the same kind of controversy as other reward-based systems or incentives based on competition. While teachers' unions have tended to resist departures from the single salary schedule, with its transparency, predictability and guarantee of equity, there appears to be increasing willingness on the part of the unions to consider changes that result in more pay for higher performance.

The nature of compensation based on knowledge and skill

Relating teachers' pay to knowledge and skills – 'competencies' – rather than pure seniority and academic degrees involves basing some portion of total pay on factors such as their command of the subject area or areas in which they are teaching, the pedagogical methods and skills they use in teaching their subject, additional relevant abilities such as techniques for using technology to enrich instruction, and certain management-related abilities that the teacher can apply to the benefit of the school. The portion of total pay based on such competencies may be a modest addition to a basic salary, which is still largely a function of seniority and degrees, or it can approach all or a very large portion of the salary increases a teacher can obtain above the basic starting salary for a beginning teacher.

Competency-based pay differs from the traditional single salary scale that has dominated teacher compensation systems throughout much of the past century in that teachers with the same number of years of experience and academic degrees or number of 'units' of graduate study can earn different amounts, depending on evaluations of their relevant knowledge and skills. Unlike merit pay or merit awards, the pay additions are permanent rather than one-time bonuses that have to be won in each time period. The increases in pay – and all teachers are expected to obtain some increases as they gain experience and become more proficient – result from teachers making an effort to acquire and apply the desired competencies. A fundamental component of such a compensation scheme is an evaluation system that will certify that the teacher possesses certain competencies and is eligible for the salary increase.

What competencies are rewarded?

One of the leading proponents of basing teachers' salaries on knowledge and skills is Allan Odden. He and various co-authors have published widely and advised a number of education authorities and organizations on the subject. Odden and Kelly (1997) do not specify in detail the competencies that teachers should have because they feel this is something that each education authority should determine for itself, because the competencies needed vary between levels of education and in schools with different characteristics. They identify three general categories of competencies: classroom instruction techniques, other educational tasks, and school management and leadership (Odden and Kelley, 1997, pp. 76–80).

Classroom instruction. The bedrock of competencies needed to teach is knowledge of the subject matter taught. Beginning teachers must have at least a basic command of the subject, and are expected to continue to strengthen and deepen their subject matter knowledge fairly rapidly at the early stages of their careers. Some states have several stages leading to a provisional license to teach a subject and finally to a full license. In addition, there are other established systems for evaluating professional command of subject matter and other pedagogical skills. In the US there are several systems for evaluating teachers that give districts alternatives from which to choose. The National Board for Professional Teaching Standards (NBPTS) was developed as an outgrowth of studies and efforts by the Carnegie Forum on Education and the Economy to establish a basis for certifying that teachers meet professional standards (Tucker and Codding, 1998, pp. 40–3). The Council of Chief

State School Officers sponsors the Interstate New Teacher Assessment and Support Consortium (INTASC) while the Educational Testing Service has developed a third, parallel program to evaluate teachers' competencies, known as PRAXIS (Odden and Kelley, 1997, pp. 17–20). Associations of teachers of specific subjects have also joined the movement to develop professional standards in their own fields, the best known being the National Council of Teachers of Mathematics, whose standards for their profession have been widely adopted (Tucker and Codding, 1998, p. 42). Other professional associations that are moving in the same direction include the National Council of Teachers of English, the National Science Board and the American Association for the Advancement of Science.

Teachers may add qualifications to teach in a second subject area (or more), thereby gaining a salary increment. Having the ability and preparation to teach in more than one subject makes the teacher more useful to the school because it provides flexibility in case of a need for the second specialty when no other teacher is available to fill it. Skills related to the curriculum range from basic knowledge of the curriculum in one's subject area to abilities to enrich or revise the existing curriculum or develop new modules. More experienced teachers may learn how to mentor newer teachers or, eventually, they may qualify to become subject area leaders in their field. These are some of the readily recognizable competencies that qualify teachers to receive higher pay.

Other pedagogical competencies. Other skills that make a teacher more valuable to the school include skills in using group study methods and related techniques, and cross-cutting skills like writing instruction (which can be applied not only in language courses but also in history, social studies, sciences and other classes). Ability to develop assessment techniques, especially techniques for evaluating projects, portfolios, performances and similar outputs of student activities, is another relevant competency, as is ability to evaluate instructional materials or technologies, or to advise students on education plans or transition from school to work. These are a few examples of the kinds of competencies that are valuable to schools and contribute to a teacher's 'tool kit' of competencies, and that can be rewarded with pay increments.

Administrative and leadership competencies. While one desirable aspect of competency-based compensation is that it enables teachers to progress up a professional career track without the need to switch to the administrative track in order to continue advancing, there are various ways in which a teacher can assume administrative and leadership roles without making such a switch. They can learn skills of planning, project preparation, operating in or leading team-based activities and task forces, guiding the professional development of their peers, negotiating skills, interacting with parents or other actors in the external community. Under some circumstances it may be feasible and desirable for teachers to learn and apply the more traditional administrative skills such as budgeting or course and facilities scheduling. Again, these are merely examples of competencies that educational authorities may choose to reward.

How to evaluate competencies?

As in the case of the other two approaches involving rewards, evaluation is an essential element of the system. Instead of trying to evaluate 'performance' on the basis of outcomes – especially learning outcomes as measured by standardized tests – competency-based compensation requires evaluating whether teachers have acquired useful competencies that the education authority values, and whether they are applying them in their work. It differs from direct and subjective evaluation of performance on the job by supervisors, in that the criteria for determining whether the knowledge and skill are present are clearly specified and relatively objective.

The way the evaluation system is designed and implemented, as well as its transparency and 'legitimacy' in the eyes of the teachers, have a powerful influence on whether the system functions effectively. Optimally, teachers or their representatives should be involved in designing both the evaluation and compensation aspects of the system from the outset. This is not possible, however, when the system covers a state, province or other large polity. Scale matters. The nature of an evaluation system for an independent school or a small network differs greatly from that of a system covering many schools and hundreds if not thousands of teachers.

Who will carry out the evaluation? Will it be a teacher's peers (from within the school, or from elsewhere in the system), the school director or some objective system such as INTASC, PRAXIS or NBPTS? Certainly someone from within the teachers' own school should have a voice in the evaluation, but this introduces the possibility of bias or favoritism. Where the evaluation process covers a large education system, the tendency is for it to be based most heavily on an objective, external system.

Evaluation of knowledge and skills has costs; far more than establishing the teacher's years of service and the advanced degrees or graduate study units accumulated. Probably the greatest cost is the time required for evaluators (supervisors, peers or specialists) to observe the teacher in action. In cases where teachers prepare 'portfolios' to substantiate their professional skill, both preparing this material and evaluating it require time. And some systems leave open the possibility of disagreements, appeals and negotiation costs. But evaluation of knowledge and skills does make it possible to answer the two critical questions: 'Why did teacher X get a reward when I didn't?' and 'What can I do in order to get a reward myself?' Advocates of such systems argue that the substance of the evaluation – the abilities the teacher must have in order to be approved for advancement – are much more relevant to good teaching than mere seniority and degrees recognized by the single salary system. And offering teachers the chance to get ahead and earn more by acquiring the requisite knowledge and skills and putting them into practice provides the right incentives, differentiates appropriately between teachers who demonstrate interest and effort, and contributes to raising professional standards and, ultimately, to improving the quality of students' education.

Evaluation in an independent school.   On a personal note, I am a member of the board of a private international school in Santiago, Chile. The school engaged specialist John Littleford, who has advised hundreds of schools in establishing evaluation and compensation systems based on teachers' professional performance, to visit the school, provide advice on how to design and implement a system, and conduct a workshop for teachers. In the workshop, held at the end of his stay, Littleford asked the teachers to consider the advantages and disadvantages of a compensation system with evaluation based on observation of their performance by peers and the school director. The advantages the teachers saw were the following:

- *Feedback*   Teachers said they would welcome knowing more about how they are performing, even if this entailed constructive criticism and suggestions for how to improve in the future. Some said they felt they were working in a vacuum, without information about their own performance.
- *Praise*   Although the previous system – essentially a single salary ladder – sheltered them from criticism, it also kept them from hearing that they were doing well.
- *Higher salaries*   The system would mean that, if they were truly doing well, they could break out of the rigid pattern of advancement based on seniority and earn more.
- *Promotion*   Similarly the new system would enable them to move to higher paths on the matrix of promotion tracks.
- *'Mirroring'*   The new system would give them a realistic perception of how they were performing.
- *'Justice'*   Some thought it would be fairer for better teachers to be recognized and rewarded over those who did not perform as well.
- *Training*   One result of the system, the teachers understood, would be

the opportunity to receive additional training in how to master the skills and abilities the school wanted them to have.

- *'Sharing'*   Peer evaluation would involve all parties, the evaluators and the person evaluated, in the process of professional development, and all teachers would have a chance to play both roles.

The disadvantages the teachers could see were these:

- *The risk of getting fired*   If one were really not performing well, there would be sanctions; the most extreme being dismissal.
- *Insecurity, lack of predictability*   Again, there was the perception of greater risk; and the new system would not offer the assurance that one would progress up the scale at a predictable rate.
- *Embarrassment*   Unlike the previous system, which shielded teachers from negative appraisals of their work, there would be the possibility of receiving a poor evaluation, and of slower advancement if they did not meet performance standards.
- *Criticism*   Similarly, the teacher would possibly hear criticism of his or her work.
- *Possible bias or favoritism*   In a system in which subjective assessment of performance plays a key role, the teachers recognized the possibility of personal bias or favoritism entering the evaluation process.

On the whole, however, the teachers favored abandoning the previous, well-known compensation system (which had developed serious flaws over time) in favor of the new system based on evaluation by peers and supervisors. There was concern about the time and effort it would take, but willingness to give it a try. At the time of writing, committees made up of teachers and members of the administration and board have participated actively in designing the new system, which will be pilot tested late in 2002 and implemented (with any adjustments) in the following school year.

Impact on institutions within schools

How does a compensation system based on evaluation of teachers' performance and on their professional knowledge and skills influence the institutions – the objectives, formal and informal rules and enforcement mechanisms, and climate of trust – within the school?

Clarity of objectives.   Like other reward systems, a compensation system based on knowledge and skills tends to make clear the professional performance that the school values. Because the set of criteria for advancement can be extensive and is evaluated both objectively and subjectively over a period of time, the system offers a rich basis for assessing teacher performance. This avoids the tendency for systems based on test scores in a few subject areas to distort teacher behavior in undesirable ways or to stimulate opportunism. A well-designed system can specify a broad range of teaching abilities, including skills in working with students at all ability levels and in promoting both cognitive and non-cognitive development of the students.

Formal rules. The performance criteria become incorporated in the fabric of formal rules in the school. They increase the clarity of the formal rules. As noted, the criteria articulate the school's objectives in the area of professional standards. The compensation system is, in effect, part of the system of enforcement: meet the requirements and, according to the rules, you will be rewarded with higher pay and more rapid advancement. Objectives, criteria and enforcement are aligned. All this places a heavy burden on the evaluation criteria. That is not necessarily bad, however, especially if teachers are involved in designing and implementing the system and if there is an opportunity for voice, for evaluation of the system itself, and evolution of and improvement in the set of rules.

Informal rules. It is possible that basing teachers' compensation on a clearly articulated body of knowledge and skills will tend to increase the importance of the formal rule structure and reduce the role of informal rules and informal enforcement – the subtle play of approval and disapproval – in shaping the behavior of teachers. Human nature being what it is, however, it is unlikely that informal rules will disappear from the picture. For example, there might be a tendency for some teachers to 'grandstand' and adopt behaviors intended to influence the way they are perceived by supervisors and evaluators. Fellow teachers – peers – have powerful sensing apparatus to recognize such behavior and all the tools of informal enforcement at their disposal to sanction it. The same applies to free riding: if teachers tend to coast and not give their best (within the limits allowed by the evaluation system), their peers are likely to know about it and employ informal enforcement mechanisms to counter it. This was the case in the Matte schools described in Chapter 2.

Social capital. A system that is transparent and perceived as legitimate and fair contributes to feelings of security and trust. If teachers are involved in designing and implementing it, if they have a voice to criticize and improve it, and if they themselves serve as evaluators, this would tend to build trust. A system that is perceived as fair and just, rewarding those who deserve to be rewarded, contributes to social capital. Given such a system, the quality of personal and professional communication within the school community, especially among teachers, would tend to be open, trusting and professionally rewarding. Even if a teacher receives negative feedback from the system, the criticism should be accompanied by advice and support concerning how to overcome the problem. Edmondson (forthcoming) reports that hospital medical teams that have a high degree of trust are much more likely to display clear and open communication about problems and errors than ones with lower trust. This in turn prevents errors from having serious consequences.

Summary assessment of compensation based on knowledge and skill

If one can assume that a compensation system that rewards good professional skills and performance is well designed, that the essential evaluation system that accompanies it is sound in terms of the professional qualities it evaluates, and that the latter is transparent and accepted as legitimate by those evaluated, then such a system would have many advantages. It entails considerably more information and transaction costs than the single salary system, but it offers potential benefits to all actors in the educational community, including the teaching professionals who are evaluated and rewarded by the system. Its impact on intra-organizational institutions would tend to be positive. Establishing the system would present multiple challenges, but the result could be worth the cost and effort.

4. Competition

4.1 INTRODUCTION

Among the different approaches to providing incentives to improve education, the most salient and hotly debated is competition. Terminology is complicated in this category of incentives. The word 'choice' is an umbrella term, covering privatization measures – mainly vouchers – as well as other ways of offering parents options for educating their children, such as charter schools. Vouchers are a financing mechanism providing parents with the resources to send their children to private schools. They create competition if parents withdraw their children from public schools and the money from the public sector budget follows the child to the private sector. According to the theory espoused by Milton Friedman and other voucher advocates, this reduced financing for public sector schools would produce the healthy pressure of market-like competition.

Other approaches to privatization and parental choice do not involve vouchers. These blend public financing with private provision of services, sometimes through granting a charter and at other times by contracting with private sector providers. At one extreme this can mean true 'privatization', as when a school district contracts with an organization to simply take over and manage some or all the schools in a district (Hill, Pierce and Guthrie, 1997). Education management organizations (EMOs) such as the Edison Project are private, for-profit chains of schools that undertake contracts to manage schools and that seek to improve education by introducing management techniques from the private sector. There have been cases in which districts make contracts for instruction in a particular subject area such as English or mathematics (Mac Iver and Stringfield, 2000).

Charter schools, an approach to providing school choice that has developed in the United States since the early 1990s, constitute a variation on the voucher idea. Charter schools operate with public funding but outside the main public school system. Under this form of choice, groups of educators, parents or others with a vision of educational excellence establish schools that provide alternatives to traditional public schools. The operators obtain a 'charter' from the local or state authority that describes the educational model or approach to be applied in the school, imposes a few limits such as nondiscrimination and minimum health and access standards, specifies what level of performance the school proposes to provide and how this will be evaluated, provides for review of the charter at certain intervals and, in the event that the school is not living up to the standards provided in the charter, for terminating it. Within these fairly broad parameters, the school is relatively free of other bureaucratic control by the district and can (in many cases) hire the teachers it wants and manage the school in the manner its operators choose. Different US states have different legislation governing charter schools and some allow greater freedom than others.

A variety of related approaches offer different ways of providing parents with a degree of choice within public systems. These include measures such as open enrollment that allows parents to choose among schools within (or even outside) their local district, pilot schools, magnet schools and other variations. Not surprisingly such approaches to providing choice within the public school system are viewed with greater favor by those with a stake in the existing system than either privatization or charter schools.

All the forms of competition listed above fall under the heading of 'choice'. In theory they put pressure on traditional public schools, both by attracting students away and by providing information about the quality of the education offered by schools outside the traditional public system. They have different degrees of success, and sometimes the results of an intervention such as charter schools are mixed, with different outcomes under different circumstances. Their effects on institutions within school organizations are also different, since their impact on different actors in school communities varies.

This chapter will consider the incentives provided by different kinds of competition – voucher programs, charter schools and within-district choice – and the way they influence performance in the 'new' schools as well as the existing public schools with which they compete. While each section will briefly review the state of knowledge about each approach to providing competition, the main frame of reference will be the institutional model presented in Chapter 1. The discussion will focus on how the different approaches to providing competition influence institutions inside the school and the transactions between key actors within individual school communities. In particular, the discussion will examine the impact of vouchers, charter schools and other forms of choice on the relational contracts between teachers and students, the transactions involving the property rights of each group over their own energy and effort or 'labor', and other aspects of the co-production process of creating learning.

4.2   VOUCHER PAYMENTS TO PROVIDE SCHOOL CHOICE

The indecisive debate

No approach to providing incentives to improve education has stirred more controversy and polemical argument than that of creating competition through vouchers to enable students to attend private schools. The best-known proponent is Milton Friedman (1955, 1962, 1997). Friedman proposed using vouchers that would enable parents to choose where to enroll their children. This, he argued, would introduce market competition into the field of education, which would provide the same incentives toward efficiency, high performance and innovation that drive private sector firms in markets. Many other writers have adopted the same position, notably Chubb and Moe (1990).

Extensive research on various voucher pilot programs and experiments has produced great quantities of data – some providing interesting insights – but few clear conclusions. Moreover, much of the research on the subject has sought to strengthen the position of either advocates of vouchers or opponents. It is hard to find truly objective studies, and when one does, they rarely examine cases that truly represent what a full-fledged voucher program would look like if one existed. Examples of balanced views on the issue of school choice are found in Henig (1994), Levin (2000a) and McEwan (2000b).

There has been extensive and usually heated debate on vouchers, as for example in the exchange between Carnoy (1997) and West (1997). The research that has fueled this debate, has been disappointing for anyone who believes that information should guide policies. The research, largely in the production function tradition, has not produced clear answers to the basic questions: (1) whether providing vouchers will lead to healthy, market-like competition, and (2) whether this will lead to better school performance (in both the voucher-paid and public schools) as Milton Friedman and the advocates of vouchers argue.

The problem of definitions and dimensions

What do you mean by 'voucher'?
Part of the problem is that there are many different ways of providing public payments that enable parents to choose (subject to the availability of places) the school their child will attend.

1.   Milton Friedman imagined a system under which parents would receive the equivalent of a check for tuition payments that they could hand to schools. Of the various voucher systems that have been tried to date,

none has taken this idea literally. In most cases, schools receive a payment from some public source for each child enrolled under the program. In Chile this is a monthly capitation payment from the central Treasury (that does not pass through the Ministry of Education) on the basis of the number of children attending the school that month.

2. The size of the voucher payment can be an amount roughly equal to the cost per child in public schools, or it may be some lower amount (which parents can supplement with their own funds). In some cases there are compensatory payments that enable children of poor families to pay the additional sum. The question whether parents are allowed or required to make payments in addition to the voucher has obvious equity implications.

3. Vouchers may be awarded to all children in the publicly financed sector, including those who attend schools operated by public authorities and those owned and operated by private providers. Or they may be reserved for poor children, with the aim of enabling them to 'escape' from public schools in their neighborhoods to better-quality schools elsewhere. This raises various knotty questions about how to determine who is eligible to receive a voucher payment.

4. One of the big questions concerning voucher systems is their 'scale': whether vouchers are provided for all children in a school system (which may vary from a municipal system, as in some cities in the US, to a nationwide system as in Chile or New Zealand). A number of experiments in the US (for example, Florida, and Milwaukee, Wisconsin) have made vouchers available for students in poor-performing schools or who are otherwise selected on the basis of need. Some national systems provide vouchers for all students. McEwan (2000a) considers the issues involved in programs of different scale, concluding that there is not sufficient evidence to indicate whether large-scale voucher programs would be beneficial.

5. Within the private sector, providers may operate on a for-profit or not-for-profit basis. In Chile, both are allowed. Levin (2001) considers the issue of for-profit provision of education under contracts with profit-making schools or EMOs, finding a number of reasons to be skeptical that this approach to privatization will lead to significant improvement in student learning (Levin, 2001).

6. The voucher scheme may or may not provide additional funding for transporting the students from their neighborhood to the school of their choice.

7. The voucher scheme may or may not make special efforts to provide information and counseling to parents about the different schools to which they can send their children. Since the benefits of choice depend

on parents making informed judgements about what school would be better for their child, valid choice systems must assure that parents have adequate information.

8.   Within any voucher scheme, questions arise about who is to be admitted to schools that are oversubscribed. (And it is probable that any school that gains a reputation for excellence will soon have more applicants than places.) Some programs such as the Milwaukee, Wisconsin voucher program have resolved this question by awarding places in oversubscribed schools on a lottery basis (Hanushek et al., 1994, pp. 110–11).

So opinions about voucher-based systems for providing school choice may vary depending on the characteristics of the voucher system in question.

What are the criteria for evaluating voucher programs?

In addition to the different kinds and designs of voucher programs, there are different criteria with which to evaluate voucher systems. Levin (2000b) sets forth a comprehensive framework for evaluating voucher systems with the aim of clarifying the debate about voucher-based approaches to education finance. He proposes four criteria (Levin, 2000b, pp. 12–14).

- *Freedom of choice*   Providing parents (and students) the opportunity to choose the school the child will attend from among a reasonably wide set of options is a valuable addition to personal freedom. For some advocates of choice, this is an end in itself. This is especially true for families for whom factors of religion, values, and views about what kind of education they want for their child are of great importance.
- *Productive efficiency*   Most of the empirical research that has been conducted on voucher-based systems focuses on this aspect. Ever since Friedman's earliest pronouncements on the subject, advocates of vouchers have argued that 'competition improves the breed' (which it certainly does in some fields and circumstances). The advantages of allowing competition between public and private schools are, according to pro-voucher spokespersons: (1) private schools are more efficient and effective because they are free of bureaucratic control (and, in the view of Chubb and Moe 1990, they are not subject to 'democratic institutions' of political control), and (2) if public schools have to compete for students, they will be forced to improve their own efficiency and effectiveness.
- *Equity*   Friedman and those who follow him argue that poor and minority children are 'trapped' in low-quality public schools in their (usually poor and urban) neighborhoods. Vouchers would offer the

opportunity to escape from the monopoly of public schools and to attend private schools that are better. By allowing freedom of movement, vouchers would reduce the social stratification caused by *de facto* segregation of children living in ghettos. Others, however, fear that vouchers will increase stratification – for example, Fiske and Ladd (2000).

● *Social cohesion* Levin (2000b, p. 13) says that 'a major public purpose of schooling is to provide a common educational experience that will orient all students to grow to adulthood as full participants in the social, political and economic institutions of our society'. This objective of public education is often overlooked. Proponents say vouchers will not undercut this objective, but opponents argue that they will do exactly that.

Levin (2000b, pp. 18–21) points out that there are tensions and internal inconsistencies among these four criteria. Success in providing freedom of choice and productive efficiency might conflict with equity and social cohesion. Balancing all four objectives calls for careful tradeoffs between them, which can best be achieved through political means.

The tools available to adjust program designs include 'finance, regulation and support services' (Levin, 2000b, pp. 14–16.) Finance means making sure that the amount of the voucher is sufficient to truly allow children from low-income families to attend any school they choose. A significant related issue is whether schools are allowed to impose supplementary charges in addition to the voucher, which would make it harder for children of very poor families to attend. But a voucher program with this feature might also provide 'scholarships' to such poor children to cover the extra fees. Regulation applies to rules governing selection and admission, avoiding discrimination and requiring some degree of common curriculum for all schools. By support services Levin refers to providing transportation so that children can get to schools outside their immediate neighborhoods, and information to parents so that they can make informed choices. In spite of all that can be done through these three tools, '[t]here is no optimal system that provides maximal results among all four criteria' (Levin, 2000b, p. 20).

Other considerations. In addition to Levin's four criteria for evaluation, there are other questions one must consider when weighing the merits of a voucher-based approach to providing incentives. One of Friedman's fundamental arguments in favor of vouchers was that competition among schools would bring forth the same sort of innovativeness that results from competition between private sector firms. Private schools can indeed innovate without being subject to any demands for uniformity imposed by public authorities, but in a climate that increasingly favors some degree of freedom of choice, there are also opportunities for innovation that do not require vouchers or privatization. Charter schools and various forms of pilot schools and within-district choice in public systems offer ample flexibility within which schools can innovate. Education seems, however, to be highly resistant to innovation, regardless of the opportunities offered or the technologies available. Most of the innovations observed in successful schools of all sorts tend to be made by fine-tuning the traditional model of education rather than substantial innovations.

Another argument in favor of market-like competition between schools is that this will improve the quality of teaching. Advocates argue that people with higher educational qualifications will be motivated to enter the teaching profession because, in a system based on competition between schools, there are greater opportunities for advancement and higher pay for superior performance. Similarly, it is argued, competition will encourage good teachers to remain in the profession and enable schools to weed out those who do not perform well. Hoxby (2000) finds evidence indicating that when schools face competition, they tend to hire teachers with better educational preparation, especially in mathematics and science, and who show higher degrees of effort and independence.

Finally, voucher-based competition provides a means of applying pressure to improve educational performance. The theoretical argument is that teachers are like everybody else: they shirk when given the opportunity. Teachers also tend to view themselves as doing well and to blame most problems on students or their families. Many observers hold that this is why incentives, especially competition, are necessary. The questions are: how do you establish incentives – apply pressure – in ways that will (1) produce the kind of behavior you want, without leading to distortions such as teaching to the test; (2) avoid too narrow a focus on readily testable outcomes; (3) leave schools the freedom to innovate and pursue their own vision of education; and (4) not crowd out intrinsic motivation?

How do vouchers influence institutions in schools?

Does competition 'improve the breed' in schooling as it undoubtedly does in auto racing and other endeavors? There are reasons to believe that it should, but experience does not indicate that this is an automatic outcome or that the effects are great. Research that looks at schools from the outside, examining their inputs and characteristics without studying the effects of competition on internal processes, has not produced findings that provide much guidance for policies or program design. The following sections apply the concepts from the model in Chapter 1 to explore how market-like competition through vouchers influences the institutional environment within schools and the transactions between the main categories of actors in school communities.

The impact of voucher-based competition on the institutional environment

Is competition likely to influence the clarity of the objectives a school community seeks to accomplish? Do schools in a situation of competition have clearer formal and informal rules and effective enforcement? Does competition between schools promote trust and cooperation within them? Let us examine each question in turn.

Clarity of objectives and principal–agent relationships. If a school has a high degree of autonomy and the freedom to establish clear consensus about objectives, this helps clarify the relationships between principals and agents. If the objectives are disseminated to all members of the school community and supported by the formal and informal rules, this tends to make the transactions between all principals and agents more efficient, including those between directors and teachers (D–T), teachers and students (T–S), parents and students (P–S) and other relationships.

Does competition through vouchers lead schools to establish clear objectives and the rules and enforcement mechanisms that support achieving them? What are the effects of competition on different kinds of schools in this respect? There is no doubt that private schools have greater freedom to set their own objectives than public schools. Whether they do or not depends on many factors: whether the school operator itself is clear about the objectives it wants the school to pursue; the ability of the leadership and key members of the community to build consensus, articulate a sensible set of objectives and communicate them effectively to the community; the degree of homogeneity among the families whose children attend the school; and the nature of other aspects of the institutional environment within the school. In the case of for-profit schools, there are also tradeoffs between academic objectives and making profits. Public schools can also establish clear, sound objectives and gain the advantages that this offers, but this depends on how much freedom (or clear guidance) the local education authority provides, as well as factors within the school. There is no guarantee that a private school will be successful in establishing clear objectives, nor does being a public school preclude the possibility of doing so.

With regard to the effects of competition on objective-setting, one of the main questions concerns whether the objectives will tend to focus narrowly on those outcomes that influence the school's competitive position. There are two potential problems here. First, if schools believe that the way to compete is to raise test scores, pursuing this objective can turn the school into a 'cramming academy' and encourage behaviors such as teaching to the test. Second, if school operators believe that the way to compete is to emphasize non-academic features or to devote resources to marketing, this will reduce the importance of high internal standards for learning. Experience in Chile (Gauri, 1998, pp. 104–5) and New Zealand (Fiske and Ladd, 2000, pp. 178–209) indicates that schools in a competitive situation use a variety of strategies to attract students, not all of which give highest emphasis to academic excellence. Competition can divert attention from academic excellence in both public and private school sectors.

Effects of competition on formal rules. If a school is in a situation of competition, and if this results in pressure to attract more student 'clients', the effect on its system of formal rules is not likely to be great. Any effect resulting from competition will depend on what the school considers to be attractive to parents (not necessarily students) who are in the position of making a choice. If the school's leaders (and its operator, if it is a private school) conclude that the best way to attract students is to improve academic performance, they might strengthen rules concerning the behaviors of teachers and students that relate to teaching and studying. Rules pertaining to orderly behavior and other factors relating to the environment for teaching and learning might also be strengthened. At least as likely would be changes in the enforcement of existing rules. It is difficult, if not impossible, to make and enforce rules about the way teachers and students use their discretion over how hard they study and work, even in public schools, since this is virtually unobservable.

On the other hand, school officials might conclude that parents are as interested in a disciplined and orderly environment as in grades, and emphasize rules that would produce this outcome. In addition to establishing the rules, a school would also need to develop a reputation for thoroughgoing enforcement.

Effect of competition on informal rules and enforcement mechanisms. The influence of competition on a school's informal rules and their enforcement would be felt indirectly, as a result of the school director and teachers deciding to establish a culture with characteristics that would make the school a more successful competitor. Such efforts would be directed in part at teachers themselves (perhaps using the threat of competition as a motivator), in part toward parents, but mainly toward students. It would be very difficult to measure changes in informal rules and show they resulted from competition.

Effect of competition on cooperativeness and social capital. The New Zealand experience makes it clear that competition reduces cooperation between schools (Fiske and Ladd, 2000, pp. 244–5). What happens within schools is another matter. If competition led members of the school community (especially the director and teachers) to make special efforts to improve academic performance, this could lead to a strong feeling of solidarity and teamwork among the staff. (There are films about schools rising to challenges that illustrate the way this might happen.) Just as evaluation systems that reward the whole school community for academic success might foster cooperation and trust (as discussed in Chapter 3), the pressure imposed by competition might have similar results.

The effect of competition on transactions between key actors

Transactions between teachers and students.   When a student transfers to a 'new' voucher-paid school (let us call it a private school), this has little if any effect on the teachers and other actors in that school. Whatever institutional patterns have influenced transactions between teachers and students in the past are likely to continue. Only if the private school receives large numbers of new students (which might both strain capacity and tend to change the social environment within the school) would there be much impact, and most private schools would close off new admissions before this happened. The entering student might find that, after a period of adapting to the new ways of doing things, the relations with teachers were different and presumably better than in the previous school. One can imagine a transfer student making new and more serious efforts to respond to teachers' directions, rise to their expectations, and give greater attention and energy to studying. This could be a notably positive experience for the transfer student but the impact on the receiving school would be slight.

   The effect on the school the student leaves would be greater. If schools begin to lose students, this may lead to budget cuts and possible loss of teaching positions. Teachers will begin to worry about their jobs. Directors, sensitive to the loss of enrollment and its implications about their performance, may put pressure on teachers to try to improve their performance. This could lead to changes in the relations between teachers and students. The larger or more rapid the loss of enrollment, the stronger these effects would be. One can imagine circumstances in which teachers make special efforts, work to the best of their ability, encourage students to make greater efforts to learn, and help all students achieve greater success. The degree to which this happens depends on whether the school's institutional environment permits and encourages such behavior. In some circumstances the effect of losing students on teacher–student transactions might be positive. Yet if it is the best students who leave, or if the difficulties in the school environment are very great and teachers feel there is little chance of making improvements, the effect may be despair and lower motivation rather than improvement, or teachers might simply focus their efforts on raising test scores by teaching to the test.

From the point of view of students who remain enrolled in either the private school that gains students or the public one that loses them, the effect of the change is slight. An influx or exodus of students might cause changes in the social fabric of student life, but the effect on the co-production of learning – the joint work of teachers and students – is not likely to be great.

Transactions in which parents are involved. Parents who have made the effort (and sometimes the financial sacrifice) to transfer their child to a better school can be expected to care whether the child is doing well, to communicate with the new teachers and to support the rules and requirements of the new school. They are likely to check on homework and encourage the child to study hard. Whether it is parents such as these who select themselves into the group of families that take advantage of choice is virtually impossible to test. Evaluating this would require experimental programs that assign students to choice and non-choice pools on a random basis.

In cases where students have not transferred, the mere possibility of choice would be unlikely to lead to changes in transactions between parents and their children. This would be true in both the public and private schools.

Transactions in which the school director is involved. School directors would be subject to pressures from the board to improve their school's performance if many students leave. The directors, in turn, would exert pressures of various sorts on teachers. These might take the form of exhortation and encouragement, or warnings of possible sanctions including layoffs or, in extreme cases, school closure. Directors in public schools usually do not have the authority to use pay, promotion or dismissal as means of rewarding or punishing teachers, but there are informal means of exerting pressure. It is possible that teachers might exert pressure on the director to take actions (sanctions on disruptive students, for example) that would promote better performance. In a neutral situation, school directors have the opportunity to use positive encouragement to create a favorable academic environment and encourage teachers and students to perform well. Once a problem such as loss of students arises, however, directors have fewer tools available to them and may tend to use fear and coercion to encourage better performance.

Concluding thoughts on vouchers and competition

Looking at vouchers from the perspective of institutions within schools, it becomes somewhat clearer why experiences with this form of choice have not produced unambiguous evidence that market-like incentives lead to the desirable outcomes Friedman and others predict. While it is probably true that the greater autonomy enjoyed by voucher-paid private schools can make it easier for schools to create an institutional environment that encourages all members of the community to make their best efforts, there are several serious reservations. First, the existence of an opportunity does not guarantee that it will be taken. Not all private voucher-paid schools have become models of good institutional environments. Second, the reactions to competition may not lead to changes in behavior or in institutions that are desirable. Finally, it is not necessary to be a private school in order to develop such a good environment. Some public schools manage to do so quite well. Outstanding examples include the Comer Schools in New Haven, Connecticut (Comer, 1980), PS 261 in New York City (Darling-Hammond, Ancess and Falk, 1995) and the many Accelerated Schools established to serve students at risk (Finnan, St John, McCarthy and Slovacek, 1996), and there are many other excellent public schools that have not been the subject of special study. Such examples, plus the theoretical arguments above and the empirical study in Chapter 2, support the position that innovation and excellence are possible in the public sector. In other words, privatization is neither a necessary nor a sufficient condition for having an institutional environment conducive to high performance.

4.3   CHARTER SCHOOLS

An alternative to vouchers

Charter schools offer another way of introducing competition into the world of education. Finn, Manno and Vanourek (2000, pp.14–15) define a charter school as an 'independent public school of choice, freed from rules but accountable for results', and add that charters constitute 'a new species, a hybrid, with important similarities to traditional public schools, some of the prized attributes of private schools – and crucial differences from both'. Independence from bureaucratic control and freedom to follow their own educational vision are among the most outstanding characteristics of charter schools, although the degree of independence allowed varies from state to state. Since charter schools are part of public school systems, they provide freedom of choice for families without directly attacking the concept of public education. And since they are public, and operate under charters that make explicit commitments concerning the education they will offer, charters are accountable to public authorities. They represent a middle point in the spectrum of choice, between vouchers on one hand and within-district choice between public schools on the other.

Advantages that charter schools offer

Being a charter school has a number of advantages, although there are disadvantages as well. The following paragraphs discuss some of the key advantages.

Freedom to construct and follow a unique vision of educational excellence.
One of the criticisms of traditional public education is that the diversity of interests and objectives of different groups within school districts makes it hard or impossible to establish a clear set of objectives or a special vision of education (Chubb and Moe, 1990). Charter schools are often established with the specific aim of creating a school according to a vision of education shared by its founders. Advantages that charter schools enjoy include freedom from the need to (1) accommodate all the political interests that shape public education in a community, and (2) adapt the school's vision and objectives to continually shifting political winds and educational fashions. Clarity of vision, together with commitment to the vision on the part of the founders and staff and the parents who choose the school, means that all members of the school community are 'pulling in the same direction'. Clear goals reduce principal–agent problems and are an integral part of a good institutional environment.

Autonomy and flexibility.   The same freedom makes it possible for the school director to hire and develop a team of professionals who share the school's vision and are committed to working toward it. If the pedagogical vision calls for variations in standard class periods, or authentic teaching methods and approaches to evaluation, the charter school is largely free to make these variations. Similarly there is great freedom to establish a set of formal rules (and build social consensus around complementary informal rules) that govern the behavior of members of the community. Cooperation, trust and social capital are likely to be high when a school is free to shape its own rules and culture. The degree of flexibility a school enjoys depends on the legislation in a state concerning charter schools and on the attitude of the local board, but, in general, charter schools have more freedom than public schools.

Commitment on the part of all members of the community.   Almost by definition the founders and original staff of a charter school are highly committed to the school's goals. Parents who choose to send their children to a charter school likewise have a special degree of commitment. At best this leads to the kind of parental involvement that strengthens the informal incentives for children to do well. In such a setting, students are likely to be influenced (both at home and in the school itself) to make their own commitments to doing the best they can in the co-production of learning.

Small scale. Charter schools tend to be smaller than public schools. This may be the result of choices on the part of the school operator, or of limited demand for the specific kind of education the charter school offers. But it may also be because of geographic factors, or because there is no pressure from the local board to increase size in the interest of economic efficiency. Whatever the reason, charter schools tend to have smaller communities, in which teachers and students can form personal relationships that contribute to both the strength of informal rules and enforcement mechanisms and the development of trust and social capital among members of the community.

Problems that charter schools face
There is great diversity among charter schools, which makes it hard to generalize about them. Part of the diversity is because the very idea of charter schools is that their operators are free to innovate and follow their own particular vision of what education should be. Another reason for diversity, however, is that different US states have very different legislation regarding charter schools. Observers of the charter school phenomenon characterize state laws as either 'strong', meaning they tend to give charter schools a great deal of flexibility and discretion, or 'weak', which means that the laws include so many restrictions and constraints that charters hardly differ from traditional public schools.

Differences in state legislation. Charter schools flourish in states with strong charter school laws. Finn and his colleagues say that states with strong charter laws are 'hospitable to the creation of many vigorous schools' and find that the 24 states with strong charter laws had 97 percent of the charter schools in operation as of the end of 1999 (Finn, Manno and Vanourek, 2000, pp. 101–4). The two states with the strongest laws, Arizona and Michigan, had one third of all charter schools.

States with strong charter school legislation (a) provide substantial autonomy from local boards; (b) allow considerable freedom from state and local labor contracts; (c) provide for adequate funding of charters, optimally based on statewide average costs per student; (d) allow various authorities (not just local boards) to grant charters; (e) do not establish a 'cap' on the number of charter schools or students enrolled in them; and (f) have clear and sensible systems for holding charter schools accountable for results. Hamilton (1999) provides a detailed review of the state of charter school legislation in each of 50 US states plus the District of Columbia, including an assessment of the future prospects for charter schools in those 19 states that still had no charter school laws as of 1999. She uses twelve criteria for evaluating whether a particular law is 'expansive' and facilitates development of charters, including the number of schools allowed, the variety of authorities able to issue charters, diversity of entities eligible to apply for charters, whether schools can be converted from public to charter status, freedom from collective bargaining agreements, legal and fiscal autonomy, whether per-pupil funding automatically follows students who enroll in charter schools or must be negotiated with local Boards, and whether charter schools have access to start-up capital.

Opposition to charter schools, which has come from teachers' unions and school boards in some states, often takes the form of political maneuvering to weaken charter school legislation. Finn, Manno and Vanourek (2000) criticize as 'weak' legislation that restricts who can obtain a charter and how many charter schools can be formed in the state, and that limits the authority to grant charters, the funding available for charter schools, and the freedom from rules and regulations that are the key to charter schools' autonomy.

Administrative burden. Becoming a charter school entails all the managerial challenges and problems of starting a business. Gifted and committed leaders with exciting pedagogical visions are often not well equipped to deal with these, or happy to spend as much time and effort on administrative matters as is necessary. Finn, Manno and Vanourek (2000) recognize this and devote a chapter to what they call 'Trials by Fire' (pp. 100–26). In addition to the political and administrative problems associated with obtaining a charter and dealing with political opposition (even after a charter has been granted), they identify problems of finance, lack of business experience and acumen, and problems of establishing a system of governance. To these can be added administrative tasks of budgeting, accounting, public relations and advertising; securing physical infrastructure and adapting it for school use when necessary; permissions, licenses, insurance and other sorts of purely administrative paperwork; personnel management, and so on. Schools must struggle to pass through the start-up period when most of these burdens and demands on staff are greatest.

In an early article on the experience of charter schools in California, Eric Premack (1996) describes some of the problems as follows:

> Starting a new school from scratch is exceptionally difficult ... Assuming the charter is approved, most developers find the first years a major challenge. Myriad critical tasks and issues have to be successfully addressed all at once. From-scratch schools need to secure facilities, develop budgets, select staff members, assemble curriculum, establish a governance structure, recruit a board of directors, obtain insurance and professional services, devise student assessment plans and tend to numerous other tasks ... Developers and conversion charter schools describe their experience as similar to changing a flat tire on a car while driving at 65 miles per hour. (p. 63)

Such demands and challenges have not deterred hundreds of charter school developers and charter school operators from pursuing their visions and launching either from-scratch or conversion charter schools. More recently, there have been programs, including the No Child Left Behind initiative in the US, to provide at least some start-up capital for new charter schools. But the tasks of launching a charter school do constitute a serious burden on educators who are not experienced business managers.

Does competition from charter schools improve public school performance?

One of the big questions surrounding charter schools concerns their effects on existing public schools in the district or area. There are two dimensions to competition from charter schools. The most obvious is that, if state legislation is structured so that resources 'follow the child', every student who moves to a charter school takes financing away from public schools. The other way in which charter schools have an impact on the public sector is by demonstrating excellent performance in comparison with public schools. Does subjecting public schools to this kind of competition lead to improvement in their performance? Charter school advocates argue that it does. Finn, Manno and Vanourek (2000) provide examples of districts taking steps to provide greater choice within the public system (pp. 204–9) and list the ways charters encourage districts to free public schools from red tape, promote innovation, overcome problems of low-performing schools, offer a degree of choice within the public system, and generally become more alert to the need to be more responsive to parental preferences (pp. 211–17). These authors feel that the existence of charter schools and evidence of their success is changing the debate on educational reform at the state and national level by challenging long-time opponents of choice and change. On the basis of a study of four districts in Massachusetts, New Jersey and the District of Columbia, Teske, Schneider, Buckley and Clark (2000) conclude that public schools '*are* reacting to charter school competition when they have reason to feel threatened' (p. 24). The effect would be stronger, in their opinion, if public schools were not shielded from the full competitive effects of losing students to charters.

The effect of being a charter school on institutions in schools

As in other sections in this chapter, let us look at how this approach to providing competition influences institutions within school establishments.

Effects on clarity of objectives.   Even more than voucher-based competition, charter schools have clear objectives that, in the best of circumstances, all members of the community share. Their leaders have taken the risky and challenging step of establishing a charter school, and are committed by definition to its goals. Leadership assembles a team of teachers who share the educational philosophy and vision that led to creating the school. Parents electing to enroll their child in the school are aware of its goals and presumably committed to helping accomplish them. At least during a period following establishment of a charter school, its goals are strong and clear and virtually all members of the community are aware of them and have shown by their actions their willingness to participate in accomplishing them.

Effects on formal rules and their enforcement. One of the reasons for establishing a charter school is to escape from at least some of the externally imposed rules emanating from the local authority. Another is to be able to create a new set of rules governing activities and behaviors within the school. Along with the school's goals, its rules are likely to be salient, and both teachers and parents who 'join' the community may be required to enter into fairly formal contracts to uphold and support the rules.

Effects on informal rules and enforcement. In the informal sphere as well, being a charter school tends to create an environment in which members of the community believe in the goals, accept the rules, encourage fellow members to do the same and express their disapproval of those who fail to adhere to the formal and informal rules of the school. The great diversity of charter schools and their visions makes it difficult to generalize about the kinds of informal rules that develop, but the tendency of charter schools to develop strong community feeling argues for the existence of informal rules consistent with the school's vision.

Effects on social capital, cooperation and trust. This is an area where the positive effects of being a charter school are strong. Although charter schools constitute a form of competition, and tend to increase competition between schools and between the traditional and charter sub-sectors, the atmosphere within most charter schools is not competitive but cooperative. With the strong unifying effect of being special, the self-selection of staff and families, the clear articulation of an educational vision, strong consensus around a set of objectives, and greater accountability for results, charter schools tend to create strong internal communities in which cooperation between actors is the norm. These factors, plus freedom from most outside intervention, tend to promote trust and a feeling of being part of a team. There tends to be agreement and understanding between principals and agents (and among agents as peers).

Effects of being a charter school on transactions between key actors. There
are factors in the structure of the charter school situation that tend to promote
good institutional environments that favor successful transactions between members of school communities. In fortunate situations, in which the enabling
legislation permits true autonomy and flexibility, and in which an able team of
professionals with a clear set of objectives has a chance to do its best, the
atmosphere for transactions between all members of the community is highly
favorable. All parties have become members of the school community on
purpose, with fairly good and clear information about the vision and goals to be
pursued and with a willingness to work together to accomplish the goals. This
creates a situation in which there are fairly high levels of understanding and
agreement between principals and agents. The startup period may well be
difficult but, assuming the school succeeds in meeting the challenges of startup,
even having done this together strengthens the bonds within the community.
The role of formal rules is likely to be less strong than that of informal rules,
especially during the early years of a charter school's life. All parties tend to
want the school to be successful, and to define success in much the same way.
These factors tend to be stronger in new charters than in conversions of existing
schools, but even in the latter case members of the community have been aware
and participated in decisions to become a charter school.

Under favorable circumstances, charter status encourages the development
of a strong sense of community and an environment of confidence and trust.
This in turn promotes the making and honoring of transactions that lead to
good school performance. There can be something like a virtuous circle
operating. The positive incentives that accompany charter status contribute to
the success of this model of choice, perhaps more than the pressure of
accountability or the fear of failure and losing the charter.

4.4   CHOICE WITHIN THE PUBLIC SYSTEM

With interest in vouchers and choice becoming an increasingly salient issue
in policy debates, some school districts have acted to provide greater choice
for parents within their system. Districts have offered options and a degree of
choice for many years, including pilot schools, magnet schools and various
special schools that differ from the traditional model of public education in
terms of either their pedagogical approaches (for example, Montessori-like
kindergartens and lower grades) or their content (for example, vocational
orientation). These options have sometimes extended to enabling parents to
send their children to schools outside the district.

Such options are available for schools that are under public management
and are fully financed with public funds. They do not involve voucher-like

subsidy payments to non-public schools or the establishment of special charters. Admission is open to all students in the district, although issues of selection do arise in the case of special schools for which demand for places exceeds supply. The transportation infrastructure already existing in the district can be used by students to attend schools of their choice, and possibly extended to accommodate students who need to travel longer distances.

Approaches to providing choice within the public system seem to offer many of the advantages of choice based on vouchers and private provision while avoiding some of the concerns (including many of the concerns of local school authorities and teachers' unions). What are the differences? Perhaps most importantly, final authority over the alternative schools remains in the hands of the existing educational bureaucracy, and many advocates of vouchers and choice feel that it is the bureaucracy that is the root of many problems. A related issue is that alternative public schools may not have as much autonomy to set goals, choose their team of teachers or pursue innovative teaching methods as either a charter school or a private establishment.

Myatt and Nathan (1996) describe the experience of a recently approved charter school in the Boston school district that opted to be a pilot school within the public system rather than a charter school. Motivated by new charter school legislation in Massachusetts, the Boston Public Schools took steps to permit a category known as pilot schools. Fenway High School, with a long tradition of innovation and excellence, chose to return its charter and become one of the pilot schools. The authors cite the advantages of pilot status including for example financial security, the opportunity to select their own team of teachers, freedom to establish a curriculum and evaluation system based on student portfolios and exhibitions, for example, and on a fairly high degree of autonomy. Disadvantages included having to 'educate' and persuade a highly traditional district bureaucracy concerning what it means to manage a pilot school without choking off its necessary freedom, as well as conflicts with teachers' union rules that threatened to infringe on the integrity of the teaching team. After three years of operation, the authors could look back upon many successes, but still found it necessary to struggle constantly to maintain the autonomy they needed to pursue their own educational vision. Pilot status conferred benefits that being a charter school did not, but operating under the control of a traditional school district bureaucracy entailed difficulties and threats to the school's treasured autonomy.

If a district has been motivated by the threat of competition to offer more choice options, it should be sensitive to these differences and allow considerable freedom from control. This is not certain to occur and there is always the possibility that the alternative schools will come to be as heavily regulated as other schools in the district. These are fine points, however, and cannot be answered except on the basis of experience over time.

Effects on institutions within the school

Let us consider the effects of within-district choice on the institutional environment within the alternative schools, assuming that a district that offers such choice also permits the alternative schools to have a considerable degree of flexibility and autonomy.

Effects on clarity of objectives.   When a public authority opens an alternative school for the purpose of offering a degree of choice to families within its community, the objectives of the school tend to be relatively clear for several reasons. First, there is some special rationale for the school to exist, whether to provide high-quality education in some special field such as a magnet school specializing in mathematics or science, or to offer a pedagogical approach different from the prevailing mode in most traditional schools in the district, or for some other reason. Fulfilling this special purpose gives the school's objectives a special focus and coherence. Second, the students enrolled have come because their families chose to send them (often at some special effort) precisely because they wanted the kind of education offered. Thus there is both a higher degree of homogeneity among the families represented and built-in congruence between what the school offers and what the 'customers' want. This tends to reduce both diversity of opinion about what the school's objectives are and related principal–agent differences and problems. Third, the teachers in such a school tend to be there because they believe in the school's special purpose and objectives and/or are skilled in the school's area of specialization. Finally, since it is the local education authority (LEA) that has established the school with its special orientation and purpose, problems of differences between the LEA and the school over objectives are likely to be reduced. While a school offering within-district choice may not have as much autonomy as a charter school, it does avoid some of the administrative and financial concerns that charter schools have. It is also less exposed to competition and is not required to expend effort and resources on marketing as a purely private school competing for voucher-paid students would be.

   While there is no guarantee that such a within-district alternative school will take advantage of all the opportunities available to it, or that the 'honeymoon' with the LEA will last indefinitely, the school is likely to have a considerable degree of autonomy and flexibility to establish its own clear set of objectives and to build support for them throughout the school community.

Effects on formal and informal rules and enforcement mechanisms.   Being a special school may create some need to establish rules that differ from those of traditional public schools. Pilot schools may be based on pedagogical philosophies and practices that call for different relationships between students, teachers and parents. Students may work in teams producing joint projects rather than individual work. Nathan and Myatt (1998) describe the need to explain Fenway School's system of student portfolios and exhibitions to both parents and a school board that was determined to apply the same external standards as in traditional public schools. A pilot school may establish an honor system rather than a command-and-control model as a basis for monitoring behavior and enforcing rules. Or a school may observe a different dress code than the traditional schools in the district. It is essential for parents to understand and support these rules, which means that the school will either have to require a formal, contract-like parental commitment or make special efforts to communicate information about the rules to parents.

Effects on cooperation, trust and social capital.   Because of homogeneity of interests and aims among all parties within a pilot school or other special school, levels of trust and cooperation tend to be high. Teachers who have self-selected or been selected to work in an alternative school are likely to have feelings of cooperativeness and trust, and to have high expectations of students who have self-selected because of an interest in the school's special characteristics. Parents likewise approach the school with positive expectations and a propensity to trust and support its staff and programs.

Effects of within-district choice on transactions between key actors

Transactions between teachers and students.   In a situation where a school has a special reason for being, whether to offer education with a special focus or to respond to a specific demand, teachers and students all understand the purpose of the school and why they are there. At best, teachers in such circumstances have high expectations regarding students' performance, are stimulated by having students with special interests and motivation to work hard, and will work with enthusiasm to provide the best possible instruction.

If the school is a magnet school, students have an interest in its specialty virtually by definition. They are likely to have taken part in the family's decision about the school and will tend to be highly motivated and to participate willingly in their part of the co-production process. Students are likely to have high expectations of teachers and to interact with them in ways that stimulate high levels of professional performance.

Transactions in which parents are involved.   In the best of cases, one would expect parents who have chosen to enroll their child in an alternative school to be interested in the child's education and closely involved with the school.

Such parents will tend to support the school's objectives and practices, trust its teachers, have high expectations about their child's performance and encourage him or her to study hard.

Transactions in which school directors are involved.   The director of a special-focus school within a public system is in a position somewhat similar to that of a charter school director. Both have considerably more autonomy than a public school director, can select their teaching team, and can develop a quality of communication and trust that is rarely possible in a purely public school. The director is free from most pressures of competition and the need to market the school, and is somewhat sheltered from financial pressures because the school is within the public system. The director interacts with a community of students, teachers and parents who have 'bought into' the system and its objectives; thus transactions tend to take place in a positive context.

Relations with the district authority are closer than for either a voucher-paid private school or a charter school and may be relatively positive. On the other hand, Myatt and Nathan (1998) make it clear that interacting with a district bureaucracy requires effort and sometimes entails disadvantages that directors of private or charter schools do not face.

Final thoughts on within-district choice.   There are many reasons why schools that offer parents and students an alternative within the public system have advantages, and why the institutional environments within such schools would tend to be good. While intra-district choice offers desirable opportunities to establish a good institutional environment that is conducive to high performance on the part of students and teachers, school leaders must still make an effort to clarify their objectives and communicate them clearly to all members of the community. Offering a variety of public school alternatives provides both freedom of choice to parents and considerable autonomy to the school, although the autonomy is not as great or as secure as in the case of charters or private schools.

4.5   CONCLUSIONS ABOUT COMPETITION AS AN INCENTIVE

Providing parents a variety of schools to choose from and the freedom to select the school their child will attend has several benefits. It enhances individual liberty, and in the process tends to create a higher degree of interest in and commitment to the school of choice than is likely under a system dominated by geographic monopoly. The existence of alternatives and free flows of students between schools provides a degree of competition for traditional public schools, although even in the case of vouchers, this may not fulfill voucher advocates' hopes and expectations. Some degree of pressure is probably necessary to overcome the natural human tendency toward complacency and avoidance of hard work in sheltered environments. And, if schools in a district have latitude to innovate and improve their performance, this can both provide information and stimulus to other schools about ways of improving their own performance and a yardstick effect that challenges less successful schools.

There are, however, problems associated with any approach to choice. One is that it is virtually impossible, barring true random assignment of students (which is not free choice), to avoid some degree of selection. If good schools have more applicants than places, there must be some basis for deciding who enters; and even if this is limited to taking siblings of students already enrolled, that in itself is likely to produce a group of parents and students with a high level of commitment to the school. If selection is inevitable, then some degree of stratification is also an unavoidable outcome. In cases where considerable selection takes place, as in New Zealand, the stratification effect is strong (Fiske and Ladd, 2000). This leads to what I have called the 'endgame problem': there will always be some students 'left behind' and some schools where children with problems of various sorts tend to be concentrated. Dealing with this problem (without establishing conflicting kinds of incentives) is a continuing challenge. Solving the problem will necessarily call for special interventions tailored to the needs of the schools in trouble, and not 'blunt instrument' policies applied to all schools in the district.

Privatization and vouchers. Privatization provides an opportunity for schools to establish their own goals and means of achieving them. Being private gives schools the flexibility and autonomy to develop institutional climates that are favorable to high performance. But having the opportunity does not guarantee that a school will take it. Private schools do not automatically develop the characteristics of effective schools. This may explain why experiences with privatization and vouchers have not produced the powerful positive effects that their advocates assume will follow.

A separate problem of establishing a voucher system, especially on a large-scale basis, is how to effect the transition from a traditional system to one based on privatization, and how to implement the policy in ways that ensure both effectiveness and equity. In no case are policy makers starting from a *tabula rasa* situation; there are always existing schools that need to be either converted, as in New Zealand, or allowed to operate in parallel, as in Chile.

Charter schools.   This approach to providing choice and competition does not involve privatization. Charter schools are public, but have greater freedom than traditional public schools to shape their own instructional program and establish institutional climates with their own unique goals. Clear goals reduce principal–agent problems. Having clear and sound sets of formal rules and enforcement mechanisms, informal rules consistent with the goals and the formal rules, and communities in which cooperation and trust prevail all contribute to good performance. Of the several approaches to providing competition, charter schools appear to have the most positive impact on institutions inside schools.

The degree to which charter schools can function with autonomy and achieve the benefits of charter status depends heavily on the state charter school legislation under which they operate. In some states charters are so hemmed in and limited by the enabling legislation that many of the benefits are lost. Furthermore, the burden of managing a free-standing charter school may overwhelm sponsors whose greatest interest is in pedagogy. This is especially true where governing authorities provide very limited budgets to charter schools.

Choice within public school systems.   This approach is purely within the public sector, yet it offers parents a variety of options for the education of their children. If there is no need to structure a single model of education that suits all the preferences of a diverse community, this reduces to some degree the principal–agent problems that Chubb and Moe (1990) decry. It is also easier to get within-district choice options adopted and supported over time than either vouchers or strong charter school legislation because this approach to providing choice does not threaten the political interests or strong ideological positions that favor public education. Choice within public systems may provide many of the same positive influences on institutions within schools as charter schools. Under the best of circumstances the leadership and key staff of pilot schools or other public alternatives are self-selected on the basis of commitment to the school's educational model. Parents who elect to send their children to such schools also self-select and tend to favor the educational philosophy and vision that guides the school. In general there is a greater possibility to forge a strong sense of community and mission in a pilot or experimental school than in a traditional public one. But, as Nathan and Myatt (1998) make clear, the local district or other governing authority must truly grant genuine autonomy if these desirable outcomes are to be fully achieved.

5. Threats: external standards and accountability

The subject of standards and accountability could hardly be more relevant today. The recently enacted 'No Child Left Behind' legislation in the US brings the Federal government's power to bear by mandating that all US states will adopt some form of accountability for school performance based on a single test (see Madaus and O'Dwyer, 1999). States that fail to do so will lose a portion of their funding under the Elementary and Secondary Education Act. The reaction to this ranges from applause to deep concern, as recent articles by Andrew Rotherham (2002), an advocate, and Richard Elmore (2002), an opponent, demonstrate.

The 'threats' category of incentives is extremely complex. In part this is because the same words are used to mean very different things by different parties to the standards debate. An example of this ambiguity is found in the metaphor used by Scott Thompson, an opponent of high-stakes standardized testing, who says that the 'standards movement' has an 'evil twin' that looks just like it but is perverse (Thompson, 2000).

Tests and standards have played a central role in education throughout history. At the most basic level, every responsible teacher uses some form of evaluation to determine whether each student has learned what the teacher has taught. At the level of the individual school, tests serve to evaluate all students in a given grade and subject according to a common standard. School boards and higher-level authorities use the information from testing to guide policies, identify problems and, in some cases, to determine which schools should get awards. The movement to use tests to assure that all students at state or national levels meet the same standards is of recent origin. In the United States most observers date it from the 'Education Summit' meeting of US state governors called by the first President Bush in 1989. From that time on, the standards and accountability movement, born in a highly political context, has generated tremendous controversy and concern. The idea that there should be standards and accountability in education appears to be simple and laudable and many people continue to assume that it is. But both terms – standards and accountability – are minefields of technical, political and practical complexities that have often been overlooked.

The idea of establishing some form of standards external to the individual school and of using tests to assure that schools are doing their best to meet the standards has great appeal and has become widely accepted. It is incorporated in one way or another in the policies of virtually all US states. Some countries in both the developing and developed world have used external standards, often as a means of controlling access to secondary or higher education, for years. The controversy in the US is not over whether it is a good idea to measure achievement and impose standards and accountability. Few would argue directly against these ideas, but there is heated controversy over how to implement them without having unintended negative consequences.

Earlier chapters have mentioned the need for some form of pressure to overcome the natural human tendencies to shirk, make life easy and maximize personal welfare. Standards constitute the category of incentives most directly linked to the idea of imposing this kind of pressure. The incentives provided by standards and accountability measures are not based on market forces. They do, however, constitute an approach to monitoring the performance of agents and applying pressure to promote good performance. One can also say that standards help communicate to agents the objectives that principals want them to pursue. Standards are frequently linked with incentives based on rewards or competition in a kind of trilogy of incentive systems. For these reasons, standards, accountability and testing are considered in this book on incentives.

Is it correct to think of standards, testing and accountability for performance as a form of 'threat'? On one hand, proponents of testing argue that public funds finance public schools and there should consequently be provision for oversight, that no one should object to generating and sharing information on how well children are learning in school, and that testing (implicitly of a low-stakes variety) should not be a source of anxiety. On the other hand, when Finn, Manno and Vanourek (2000, p. 127) state that '[T]he chief aim of accountability is to find and sustain good schools while weeding out and repairing bad ones', there is no doubt that a degree of threat is intended.

I should note that the British system of school inspection, in operation for over 100 years and periodically modified and updated to reflect changing needs and realities, offers an alternative approach to maintaining quality, using on-site visits and expert judgement to identify schools with problems, and applying a form of pressure for improving performance. Such a system is much more flexible than accountability that is based on tests (although test data provide some of the information needed for supervision). It avoids problems of imposing external demands on schools that are performing well, distorting teaching behavior and narrowing the range of curricular objectives.

A full discussion of British-style supervision (and of accreditation processes used in independent schools around the world) would require almost a chapter in itself. Since the focus of this chapter is on single, centrally established standards and the use of tests to provide accountability, this subject will not be considered in depth.

The debate on standards and accountability turns on a number of questions having to do with the kinds of standards applied, the kinds of tests used, the uses to which test data are put, whether tests really lead to better performance and whether the pressure they apply has negative effects on teaching and learning processes and on equity. The following section considers the concept of accountability in education in greater depth. Section 5.2 reviews a number of the complex questions that arise in connection with educational standards and accountability. Section 5.3 examines how standards influence the institutional environments within schools, while the final section considers policy implications and conclusions.

5.1   WHAT DO WE MEAN BY 'ACCOUNTABILITY'?

In his amusing and insightful introduction to the concept of accountability, Robert Behn (2001) differentiates between two groups of people: 'Either you are an accountability *holder* or you are an accountability *holdee*. It's great to be an accountability *holder*. It's not so much fun to be an accountability *holdee*' (Behn, 2001, p. 2). Holding someone accountable, Behn says, really means punishing that person. This can take formal, legal forms such as fines, a jail term or loss of one's job, or be more informal, like some form of humiliation. While the idea that schools should be accountable for learning performance has great appeal, and has positive connotations of bravely taking responsibility for one's own work, there is a subtle underlying assumption that someone is going to be punished. Standards are the basis for holding educators accountable. It is thus not surprising that these accountability holdees will be deeply concerned about the nature of the standards. Will they be fair, take account of the true value added that a school provides, encourage the kind of authentic educational processes that produce graduates with the range of knowledge and skills needed for the modern world? Who sets the standards, with what aims in mind? Are the standards truly aligned with the tests that evaluate performance? How high should the standards be, and how do you challenge the most able students without imposing inequitable penalties on those less fortunate or less able? These are not unreasonable questions if standards will be used to determine how the accountability holdees – students, teachers and schools – are to be evaluated, rewarded or, potentially, punished.

Newmann, King and Rigdon (1997) focus on the fundamental question regarding accountability: whether it leads to improvements in school performance. They identify four components of a 'complete school accountability system': (1) information on the organization's performance (test scores); (2) standards for judging how well the school is performing (by which they mean comparison with other schools); (3) an external authority that receives the information and applies the standards; and (4) meaningful rewards or sanctions for success and improvement or failure to meet the standards (Newmann, King and Rigdon, 1997, p. 43). They conclude that such a system can have the effect of improving school performance, but only if other factors are present, specifically sound implementation of the system (including training and support for teachers), what they call 'organizational capacity', and the existence of an internal system of accountability developed by the school itself. Organizational capacity includes teachers' knowledge and skill, school leadership, adequate resources and a considerable degree of school autonomy. Later sections of this chapter will comment on these points.

The drive for greater accountability in education arises from widespread perceptions that education systems (especially in the public sector) are performing poorly. In the minds, and sometimes in the written statements, of advocates of 'strong accountability' lie assumptions about what education systems are like. Stating these in a strong, perhaps exaggerated way for clarity, some observers assume that education systems are made up of self-serving bureaucrats, lazy or incompetent teachers and indifferent students, none of whom have any incentive to do a better job. While examples of such problems can be found in virtually any education system, this is a misleading characterization of even the worst schools in the most miserable slums of some of the poorest cities I have visited. Yet this is the vision of education that some advocates of accountability and high-stakes standards seem to hold. Policies based on this vision often sound totally reasonable and desirable. Who can object to making sure that all students are making an effort and learning what they should? Or that teachers are working hard to promote learning for all students? But policies designed to whip presumed slackers into line may not be appropriate for teachers and students who are doing the best they know how and who are neither incompetents nor slackers.

It is altogether desirable for all members of school communities to do their best to accomplish learning objectives, and for there to be standards that make clear what those objectives are and tests to determine whether students and schools are accomplishing them. But interpretations of what this statement means can vary radically, as can measures for establishing and implementing the standards and tests.

Let me overstate another view for the sake of argument. It is possible to construct test instruments that determine whether a student has adequate command of core subjects such as language and mathematics, and to establish an accountability system with rewards and punishments that provide incentives for teachers and students to perform their tasks to an acceptable standard. That apparently reasonable statement begs at least five questions, as discussed in the next section. The point here is that many people do not realize or accept that many vexed questions underlie such a statement.

Standards and accountability serve the highly desirable function of focusing attention on the outcomes of education. They shift attention from inputs, which have traditionally been a top concern, to results. One of the difficult questions, as discussed in later sections, is 'What do you mean by results?' Standards and the evaluations associated with them are a source of information for various purposes. As noted in connection with school choice as an incentive, parents need information in order to make intelligent choices. They also need and deserve to know how their children are progressing in school. Education research has found that in schools whose teachers, parents and all members of school communities have high expectations that every child can learn, performance tends to be high. At best, standards can communicate high expectations, and virtually all parties to the standards debate agree that schools should have high expectations of all students. Innovations such as charter schools require that schools establish goals, including performance goals, and progress toward achieving them. Standards and tests provide the information to evaluate whether they meet these goals. All of these attributes of standards and testing are desirable, but there are important caveats and concerns associated with each.

Behn (2001) quotes the US General Accounting Office, the US agency most responsible for holding people accountable, on the definition of the term: 'Accountability is an important yet elusive concept whose meaning and characteristics differ depending upon the context' (p. 3). Behn comments that such a definition of a central concept is not very helpful. But if a highly authoritative source on accountability says that its meaning depends on context, what does that indicate regarding accountability in schools, for each of which the context varies enormously? Does it make sense to use a single set of measurement tools and a single approach to accountability to evaluate an inner-city school best described as a 'blackboard jungle', a public school in an affluent suburb, and a small charter school with a powerful vision of educational excellence to which all members of the school community adhere?

External standards and accountability are inextricably linked together. Reasonable debate and intelligent policies require that the meaning of both concepts be clear. The idea underlying both is, or should be, promoting good performance in schools. Policies need to be designed in ways that use evaluation tools without undercutting schools' efforts to accomplish learning objectives.

5.2 QUESTIONS CONCERNING STANDARDS AND TESTING

Questions about standards and tests range from very broad, 'big-think' concerns to more technical and pragmatic matters. The following sections begin with the larger issues.

Standardized or performance-based tests?

One serious controversy concerns what kind of tests should be used to determine if schools are meeting standards. The contenders are divided into two camps. One advocates tests based on multiple choice questions, the answers to which can readily be compared between individuals and groups of students. The other group favors authentic testing that evaluates student performance on tasks that require students to construct their answers, such as written composition, providing open-ended, reason-based answers to mathematical or science-related questions, or preparing portfolios in different subjects showing competence in depth and over time rather than on the results of a single test.

Looking first at performance-based tests, these are much more difficult (and costly) to prepare and grade than standardized tests. It is also much harder to make comparisons between students' performance and the validity of such comparisons is less intuitively obvious. They involve assessment (in some cases by a committee) of students' written work, oral exams or presentations, portfolios of work in various subjects, the results of group work on projects over extended periods of time and similar indicators of what students have mastered and can do. Advocates argue that they provide the only appropriate measurement of learning, and that the nature of teaching and learning that lead to good performance on such systems of student evaluation differs from (and is superior to) teaching oriented toward raising students' scores on standardized tests. They also argue that standardized, multiple choice testing diverts attention from the kind of educational processes that produce true learning. They favor tests they describe as 'worth studying for', or 'worth teaching to', and that are in fact part of the instructional process.

Various efforts to establish testing systems based on student performance were made in the US in the late 1980s and 1990s, one of the best known being the New Standards Project (NSP). NSP was jointly directed by Lauren Resnick of the Learning Research and Development Center at the University of Pittsburg and Marc Tucker of the National Center on Education and the Economy, and had the support of various donors, including the Pew Charitable Trust and the MacArthur Foundation. Numerous organizations, including societies of teachers in different disciplines and 17 US states, participated in the project, which sought to develop both well-conceived standards and methodologies and tests for measuring performance in the areas of English language skills, mathematics, science, and 'applied learning' for elementary, middle school and high school levels.

After extensive efforts to develop performance-based assessments and train teachers in their use, the New Standards Project has revised its ambitious objectives and now focuses on more limited 'reference examinations' that can be used to compare the results of assessments based on student performance. Skeptics such as Haertel (1999) concluded that, after roughly a decade of operation, the project had not achieved its original objectives. Problems included (1) difficulties in providing comparable assessments that could be used as a basis for accountability; (2) lack of sufficient training and support for teachers in both how to teach in authentic ways that would lead to high student performance and how to carry out the assessments; and (3) apparent failure to produce demonstrable improvements in student learning, and especially failure to narrow the gaps between disadvantaged and more advantaged students and the schools that serve them.

Proponents of the project and its work argued that (1) performance-based testing is based on a constructivist understanding of how students learn and is therefore more theoretically sound than multiple-choice standardized testing; (2) the effects of such testing on teaching and on the active engagement of students in authentic learning are more positive than the effects of standardized testing; and (3) the abilities that performance-based testing evaluate are those really needed by people for success in the modern world (Tucker and Codding, 1998; Darling-Hammond, Ancess and Falk, 1995; Spalding, 2000). Spalding (2000) holds that, although the New Standards Project did not lead to a 'sweeping education reform' or even have a significant impact on the powerful movement to establish accountability systems based upon standardized testing, it did have significant positive effects on the roughly 2500 teachers who participated in developing models for performance-based testing, and on thinking about authentic teaching and ways of evaluating its outcomes.

Advocates of performance-based testing would prefer to evaluate the performance of students (and their teachers) on a rich variety of skills, demonstrated in various modes and over an extended period of time rather than on the basis of a single, necessarily narrow test administered on a single day (see Newmann and Associates, 1996, Darling-Hammond, Ancess and Falk, 1995, and Darling-Hammond and Ancess, 1996). One answer is to have more than one kind of assessment system, always assuring that the two are compatible in the sense that preparing for one does not take undue time and attention away from the other. This is not easy to do technically or to sell politically. It is expensive and requires devoting a lot of precious classroom time to preparing for and administering the assessments.

Advocates of standardized testing point out that the multiple choice approach has been widely used for many years and for various purposes, including screening students for admission to selective universities or, when administered on a sample basis such as the National Assessment of Educational Progress (NAEP), for determining whether student learning is improving over time. They emphasize that standardized testing offers lower cost and greater validity and ease of making comparisons than performance-based testing. Standardized testing has been developed to a high level of sophistication by organizations such as the Educational Testing Service (ETS). Results are usually reported in a form that is readily subject to analysis for both research purposes and for applying statistical controls for socioeconomic status (SES) and other background factors when determining whether schools are doing a good job or not.

ETS and other testing organizations that specialize in standardized tests are exploring ways of introducing testing of performance, such as free-response written answers to questions, as parts of their standardized testing. This requires careful attention to design of the questions, development of criteria for evaluating responses, and training the readers to provide consistent evaluations of responses that can be compared with reliability and validity. This increases the cost of testing, and does not fully respond to the charges of critics.

Critics of standardized testing argue that it does not test student's knowledge and thinking ability in depth, focusing instead on skills developed through rote learning. They say it distorts teaching methods, discouraging teachers from using strategies such as group work or portfolio development that develop a range of valuable thinking skills. Since standardized testing is based on behaviorist rather than constructivist psychological theory, it does not use the best knowledge available about how learning happens. It misses such highly significant dimensions of learning as creativity, learning how to learn and preparing for lifelong learning, working in groups, skills of persuasive argument, sticking with a subject until it is mastered, and other abilities. Critics such as Linda Nathan (2002) say standardized testing distracts time from authentic instruction and leads teachers and students to focus on cramming for the tests. Moreover, since the tests cover only a few subjects, students, parents and teachers will insist on allocating time to subjects that will be covered in the tests.

A central issue in the argument between these two camps turns on whether the tests are used to make 'high-stakes' decisions such as whether a student will receive a diploma, whether a charter school is living up to the objectives stated in its charter, or whether a school is performing so poorly (over time) that it should be intervened or closed. This subject is discussed in depth in the following section. Suffice it to say here that the higher the stakes associated with a given examination, the greater will be the tendency to adjust teaching so that students will perform well on that examination.

High-stakes or low-stakes tests?

Testing and assessment have a number of different objectives. First, they should make it possible to determine, on a comparable basis, whether students (individually or grouped in schools) are learning what they should know. (At best the standard and the test design should reflect high expectations that all students can learn.) Second, tests should provide feedback to teachers on what students' areas of weakness are, so teachers can repair these weaknesses and adjust their teaching to overcome the problems in the future. Test scores also serve to keep parents informed of their children's progress and let school directors and higher-level administrators know how the school as a whole is performing. Testing and grades are also a source of student motivation; part of the *quid pro quo* that compensates students for the effort they put into studying. When parents have a degree of choice about where to enroll their children, tests provide information to 'consumers' of education – parents and to some degree students – about school performance so that they can make choices about what school the student should attend. Up to this point, the stakes associated with testing are fairly low. Difficulties arise when test results are used to determine whether students and schools have met standards and should be rewarded or sanctioned: denying a student a diploma, delaying or denying a teacher's promotion, revoking a school's charter, or other forms of intervention by the education authority that may include personnel changes or even closing the school. These are high stakes. They will obviously lead to changes in behavior, but the changes may not necessarily be desirable ones.

Using tests for information provides a degree of pressure, especially where opportunities for choice may mean that schools lose enrollment and resources as a result. Raising the stakes even further, for all members of school communities, unquestionably leads to changes in behavior that, while intended to encourage students and teachers to exert greater effort, may be undesirable. The most obvious outcome is the tendency to teach to the tests used to evaluate performance. If these encompass only a narrow range of abilities, those become the abilities schools emphasize in their teaching.

One of the objectives of high-stakes tests is to increase students' motivation to work hard. Even good students are likely to feel some pressure (and stress) if the tests can have serious consequences. The higher the standards and the stakes, the stronger the influence on student attitudes and behavior. High stakes will tend to reduce students' intrinsic interest in the subjects they study and increase their focus on specific content to be tested and test-taking skills. This is a motivation that lasts only as long as the tests constitute a threat. For students who are at serious risk of failing to meet the standards (and therefore not receiving their diploma), the tests can cause panic and high levels of stress and, in some cases, can lead students simply to give up hope, drop out of school, adopt disruptive behavior.

Criterion-based or norm-referenced tests

Some of the best-known tests in the US, such as the Scholastic Assessment Test (SAT), California Test of Basic Skills and others indicate how well students are performing in comparison with other students. The results of these 'norm-referenced' tests, usually presented as percentile scores, show how student performance (individual or averaged for a whole school) compares with that of others. This is fine for evaluating individual cases, as when students are selected for university admission, but has shortcomings when used as a basis for comparing schools in terms of their performance. One problem is that of comparability between scores in different years. Is the 'norm' in one year really equivalent to other years? Testing specialists are confident that they have satisfactory methods for designing tests that are comparable between years, but there are still problems in comparing percentile scores in different years, especially when trying to determine whether a school has achieved real 'value added' in terms of student learning between one testing period and the next. Another problem with norm-referenced testing is that there must always be winners and losers. By definition, half the subjects will always be below the median. A school serving disadvantaged students from low-SES communities will have great difficulty moving to the high end of the distribution (and if it moves up, some other school has to move down). And schools already performing well find it hard to show much improvement since the last testing period.

The alternative approach is to construct tests that evaluate students against a fixed 'criterion' for what students at that grade level should know. This has intuitive appeal but here, too, there are problems. First, who decides what students should know? How do you arrive at consensus about the standards that guide the design of the tests? If there are many points of view in the community (whether a local district or a state), this is a question fraught with difficulty. The end result may be standards (and tests) that attempt to satisfy all points of view, but which are very poor indicators of whether students are truly receiving a good education.

The second key problem with criterion-referenced tests is that teachers will inevitably try to prepare their students to do well on them. This means that, as a particular form of test is used repeatedly (even if specific test items are regularly changed), scores tend to increase because students have been trained in the form the questions will take and in strategies for dealing with the mechanics of test taking. Linn (2000) writes of the 'Lake Woebegone Effect', named for Garison Keilor's mythical community where 'all the children are above average'. Over time there is an upward creep in scores so that more and more students are above the criterion level. Linn illustrates a 'sawtooth effect' whereby average scores increase until a new kind of test is introduced, whereupon the scores drop sharply and begin to rise again over subsequent applications of the new test. When this occurs, benchmark tests such as the National Assessment of Educational Performance (NAEP) indicate that apparent improvements in test scores following the introduction of a new test do not reflect real changes in student learning.

In spite of problems with criterion-referenced tests, most experts on educational measurement favor criterion-referenced over norm-referenced tests as the basis for evaluating whether schools are achieving external standards. Setting aside technical issues of measurement, there is an intuitive appeal to having fixed standards for what students should know, and this tends to make standards systems comprehensible and politically acceptable to the general public.

Are the standards and the tests well designed?

Chester E. Finn, Jr and Michael J. Petrilli of the Thomas B. Fordham Foundation, strong advocates of standards and accountability, carried out a review of 'The State of State Standards' in the United States (Finn and Petrilli, 2000). The criteria they used called for standards that are specific and measurable, rigorous, and based on clearly identified subject content that students should know in each core area. They gave states 'grades' on their standards systems for English language, history, geography, mathematics and science, concluding that a hypothetical 'average state' scored only a C– for all five subject areas, while only 19 of 50 states scored 'honors' for having good English standards and only 18 states merited honors for mathematics standards (p. ix). On the other hand, they found that 'thirty states display a deadly combination of mediocre to awful (or no) standards and weak accountability' (p. 2). Worse yet, twelve states had poorly conceived standards plus high-stakes accountability.

Outside the US, countries of the British Commonwealth have long traditions of testing, often used to determine which students are allowed to progress from one level of education to the next (in other words these are high-stakes examinations). At the secondary level many Commonwealth countries use tests designed and developed through years of experience by the Cambridge Overseas Examinations Syndicate. Other countries have established their own national or regional examinations syndicates. Tests in this tradition have usually been developed for the specific purpose of screening students for advancement and are administered to virtually all students who want to proceed to higher levels (which means that many poorer-performing students do not sit the examinations). Unlike the US, these countries are not constrained by constitutional proscriptions on centrally established nationwide tests. The tests, especially those set by the Cambridge syndicate, embody high-content standards and may include some elements of performance-based evaluation (especially in open-ended writing tests).

Few countries of Latin America have testing systems covering all or virtually all students, although increasing numbers of countries have sample-based assessments that make it possible to evaluate the performance of national education systems but not individual schools or students (Laboratorio Latinoamericano de Evaluación, 2000). Chile is one of the few countries that tests all its students. Its SIMCE (system for measuring the quality of education) tests are designed to provide information on school quality (as a necessary accompaniment to its nationwide voucher system.) It is a low-stakes testing system at fourth-, eighth- and recently tenth-grade levels. In theory, providing information enables parents to choose schools on the basis of their academic performance, and the publication of rankings of schools in relation to Spanish, mathematics, history/geography and science attracts great attention in the national press. Chile is also making profound changes in the objectives and content of curricula in every subject area as part of its national Education Reform, which requires changes in the SIMCE tests so as to align them with the curriculum. These changes are of great concern to schools, which have to understand and assimilate them in a relatively short period of time. One result of the changes is that the comparability of the results between the new tests and the earlier ones is subject to question.

In every country with which I am familiar, there are concerns on the part of testing specialists, policy makers and educators over whether tests provide meaningful information about student learning, and whether they are technically well designed, challenging, and yet equitable in their impact on students. (Different interest groups have different concerns.) The situation in the United States, in which each state (and sometimes different districts within them) decides what its standards will be, leads to great diversity and, in many cases, less-than-adequate specification of what the standards should be and how they should be tested. Organizations such as the Educational Testing Service in the US and the Cambridge syndicate in the UK have made great advances in testing techniques and methods, but criticisms of the tests continue to be voiced from various quarters, usually on the basis of differences in philosophy concerning the purposes of testing. But not all testing systems are of such high quality, and many testing systems in states and countries have technical shortcomings of varying degrees of seriousness (see Meyer, 1996).

Are the standards, curriculum and tests aligned?

One of the points on which there seems to be agreement in principle but disagreement about whether in fact it is being achieved concerns the alignment between the standards that schools are supposed to achieve, the subject area curricula they are directed to teach, and the tests that will be used to measure whether schools are measuring up to the standards. The point seems obvious: you should not expect students to perform well unless the tests correspond to the materials taught in schools, nor schools to perform well according to standards that are not related to the curricula the schools are required to cover or to the tests used to measure performance.

The first area of disagreement is over the standards themselves. Are they clear, specific about the content to be covered and the level of mastery students should attain, and set forth in ways that make it possible to measure them accurately? Finn and Petrilli (2000) find that few US states have standards that meet these criteria. These authors are critical of subject matter standards established by professional organizations in the fields of English, history and mathematics, which do not meet their criteria (yet have been the basis for the standards established in some states). They also find that some states have such vague standards that they provide inadequate information to teachers or others about what students should know in each area. If the state then uses 'off the shelf' tests that are not related to the standards, there is no chance of having the necessary alignment. In such situations, teachers tend to orient their teaching to the content of the commercial tests in the absence of other clear guidance.

Curricula are sometimes influenced by educational fashion, sometimes by professional groups whose ideas and preferences differ from those of parents or the majority of teachers (readers may recall the disastrous 'New Math' fad of the 1960s), and sometimes by liberal or conservative politics. If curricula are designed to respond to the preferences of a diverse constituency, or if they are influenced by special interests such as political groups or public bureaucracies, they are likely to have shortcomings in pedagogical terms and to diverge from standards that have been shaped by other interests or at other times.

Designing tests is a demanding task, requiring high technical expertise. Assuring that the tests evaluate how well students have learned a given body of material is a crucial part of that task, but this in turn requires curricula that guide the test designers as well as teachers. If education authorities rely on tests that have been prepared without regard to the standards used for measuring performance or to the curricula students have been taught, then there can be serious problems of misalignment.

The Learning First Alliance a coalition of professional education organizations in the US that includes the two main teachers' organizations, associations of school administrators and principals, the national PTA and others – supports the movement toward standards and accountability but calls for some 'mid-course corrections' in the way these are being implemented (Learning First Alliance, 2000, pp. 1–3). The first item on its list of 'core concerns' is alignment of standards, curricula and assessments. Mid-continent Research for Education and Learning (McREL), a federally-sponsored education research laboratory, found in a study of implementation of standards and accountability that

> [w]hen the various levels are not aligned, the system shows signs of dysfunction. Teachers feel frustrated, pressured, and resentful. They may narrow the curriculum to cover only what is on the test and squander valuable learning time preparing students for a once-a-year event that is out of step with what the standards say students should learn. School, students or both receive information about students' performance that may be unrelated to what students are to learn as defined by standards. The assessments are not useful in helping teachers or students know how students are performing in relation to standards. (Mid-continent Research for Education and Learning, 2000, p. 26)

How high should you set the bar?

One of the characteristics of good schools is that teachers and other members of the community have high expectations that all students are capable of learning complex material. This is one of the basic tenets of the Accelerated Schools Project, which provides enriched and challenging education to at-risk students (Finnan, St John, Macarthy and Slovacek, 1996), and one of the characteristics identified by research on effective schools (Druian and Butler, 2001).

External standards offer one way of institutionalizing the same high expectations for all students. But how high is high? Is it possible to raise expectations and standards without overwhelming less well-prepared students? And if so, will the most able students also be challenged? This is a dilemma that affects the standards movement, and it becomes more serious and difficult as the stakes attached to the standards increase.

Some observers are concerned about the effects of standards on equity. If they are set too high, some students will be unable to meet them and are likely to become discouraged and give up hope. It is difficult to set standards that will be fair for students, including those with learning disabilities, but on the other hand there is the argument that all children deserve to be challenged to perform to the best of their ability. One solution would be to have a multi-level set of standards, with test items that include a range of ability levels and standards that screen for both 'minimum-adequate' and high-achievement levels of performance. All students would be expected to achieve the former and to score as high on the tests as possible. This, however, may lead to separating students into ability groups and differentiating the instruction offered, which would be contrary to the idea of high standards for all.

Optimally the standards and expectations established should be tailored to each student's ability and set high enough to challenge every individual but not overwhelm them. But this is not possible with common standards set at district or higher levels of authority.

What are the effects on schools' own internal evaluations?

Good schools have their own systems for evaluating student learning that serve to apply pressure, on teachers as well as students, to perform well. What effects do external standards and accountability have on schools' own evaluations? Newmann, King and Rigdon (1997) study the effects of accountability on schools that are in the process of restructuring. The picture they draw is complex. In some settings, external accountability can have positive effects on school performance, but in others it may not. They find that schools that have their own system of internal accountability as well as organizational capacity – able teachers, leadership, resources and 'shared commitment' to pursue their own goals – tend to have high performance. They find two possible implications of introducing systems of strong external accountability:

> First, to the extent that external accountability is difficult to implement [for reasons they discuss], school accountability might still be achieved through internal mechanisms. Second, to the extent that strong external accountability can be implemented, if it promulgates standards and incentives hostile to a school's internal accountability system, it may undermine school organizational capacity and thereby defeat its intended purpose (Newmann, King and Rigdon, 1997, p. 48)

Darling-Hammond, Ancess and Falk (1995) interpret research on the influence of testing as follows:

> In districts that use tests for a wide array of decisions, teachers reported themselves least able to adopt innovative curriculum materials designed to support higher order thinking and performance skills. Over 60% of the teachers interviewed described negative effects of the tests on curriculum and student learning, ranging from fragmentation and narrowing of the curriculum to lack of opportunities for in-depth study. (Darling-Hammond, Ancess and Falk, 1995, p. 9)

In schools without clear goals regarding student learning, external standards can provide orientation and stimulus that are otherwise missing. What portion of schools fits this description? In the view of advocates of external standards and strong accountability, a great many schools lack either a vision of academic excellence, motivation to achieve it, or both. For those schools that do not fall into this category, however – that is, for those that know what they want to achieve and are making sincere efforts to do so – accountability systems based on external standards may either be a diversion from the main work of the school and a waste of time, or a detrimental influence on the clarity of school goals and on performance.

What do you do for an encore?

Using tests for accountability raises questions concerning how test results will be analyzed and applied in order to cast light on the performance of schools over time. Measuring changes in school performance is a central aspect of accountability systems. The problem of the 'Lake Woebegone Effect' of upward creep of results as schools become more familiar with a particular test has been mentioned above. But there are other questions concerning how to use test results. Linn (2000) identifies several possible approaches to using test data and making adjustments and corrections to assure equitable treatment of the results: cross-sectional measurement of cohorts of students at different grades in the same year, comparisons of cross-sectional cohorts in a fixed grade from one year to the next, longitudinal comparisons of school aggregate scores without following individual students and matching their specific data, and longitudinal comparisons based on only matched student records. Some US states such as Tennessee, North Carolina and South Carolina are using highly sophisticated statistical models to analyze the results and determine which schools have met criteria for performance over time but, as Linn states: 'sophisticated statistics do not resolve questions about what data the basic model should employ'. And even though better methods of comparison through time are available, the most frequently used approach to providing data for accountability is a relatively crude comparison between schools' average scores in different years.

5.3   THE EFFECTS OF EXTERNAL STANDARDS ON INSTITUTIONS IN SCHOOLS

The main focus of this book is on the interaction between incentive systems and institutions inside schools. Like everything else having to do with standards and accountability, the impact the standards have on within-school institutions is complex.

Effects on educational goals

What about the effects of standards on the clarity of a school's goals, one of the key factors in the institutional environment in a school? On one hand, external standards, if well conceived and implemented and aligned with the curriculum taught and the tests that evaluate accomplishment, can be a powerful instrument for clarifying what a school needs to do to be successful. The McREL study of implementing standards-based education found that some teachers appreciated the orientation provided by standards (Mid-continent Research for Education and Learning, 2000, pp. 5–13). It also found that essential conditions for this to happen were for the standards to be clear and aligned with the curriculum and tests, and for the implementation process to include training to help teachers understand what the standards mean and how to apply them in their teaching. These conditions were not always met.

It can be helpful in some ways to have clearly articulated standards that provide guidance to teachers (and other actors in the education process) about the academic goals schools seek to accomplish. Clarity about goals is one characteristic of schools with good internal institutions. Goals help all parties to 'pull in the same direction'. Standards improve understanding between principals and agents about the tasks the agents are to accomplish, while tests of how well they are achieved are, if well designed, a means of measuring how well agents have performed. In order for standards to contribute to better principal–agent relations, however, the standards must be well conceived, clearly communicated, accepted as valid and achievable by all parties, and evaluated fairly and accurately. If these demanding conditions are not met, standards may do as much to harm principal–agent relations as to improve them.

The above statement assumes that external academic standards are close to those of the individual school, but what if a school chooses to pursue academic goals that go beyond or differ in some ways from those established by the standard-setting authority? What if the school's aims include preparing students to think independently, be able to analyze and construct answers to complex questions, solve problems, express themselves clearly on their feet in debate and develop other authentic academic skills? In this case, the set of goals – the objective function – becomes more complicated. Allocation of time and effort between different parts of the goal set becomes an issue, as does communicating to students about how they should focus their time and energy.

What if the school's goals include not only what can be called academics but also developing values, interpersonal skills and love of learning that will serve students well at higher education levels and in the world of work? The Matte schools described in Chapter 2 are established to serve students from poor families. Value-related goals are a central part of the written goal statements of these schools. They are communicated constantly between administrators, teachers and students, and are important reasons why parents choose to send their students to the schools. What is the effect of standards systems (that may reflect only a portion of the school's vision of the academic skills students should acquire) on attention to the value-oriented, non-academic goals? The effect need not be negative but, as discussed above, goal statements should be as simple as possible. Pursuing as many as three goals – communicating about them and persuading all actors in the community of their importance and priority – is a highly demanding task for administrators and teachers. Attempting to pursue *more* than three goals tends to dilute the meaning of them all.

The effect on goals has a great deal to do with whether standards are being applied to problem schools that are performing poorly or to 'good' schools with their own clear goals and other aspects of a sound institutional climate. Those who say that strong external standards should not cause good schools any problems ignore the effects of such systems on allocation of time and effort within schools, on the freedom of schools to develop their own internal evaluation systems, and on schools' goals and other components of the institutional environment (see Nathan, 2002). And the higher the stakes associated with the tests, the stronger the negative effects of external coercion on the functioning of schools that have their own clear goals and strong institutions.

Effects on formal and informal rules

Standards, the tests that evaluate their accomplishment, and the sanctions and rewards associated with them are externally imposed formal rules. As such they may constitute positive contributions to the internal environment. It is essential for actors to accept and 'buy into' rules if they are to be effective and if there is to be agreement between the formal and informal rules in a school community. The degree to which this happens has to do with whether members of the community – especially teachers, parents and students – feel they have ownership of the rules. Optimally this means they should have a voice in defining them, which is not possible in the case of external standards. If the standards distract from those rules that influence transactions, motivation and effort, they may damage the internal climate and, ultimately, performance. If they substitute for rules that have to do with community understanding and trust, this may also damage the institutional environment.

Congruence between formal rules and the informal rules that are pervasive in a community has a great deal to do with how well both sets of rules function. If there is a sharp divergence between the two, if the formal rules say 'work to accomplish all the school's goals' while the informal rules say 'what's important is doing well on the standardized test', this creates a tension and confusion in the minds of both teachers and students. This in turn undercuts the positive effect of rules on the institutional climate. The value of rules that are accepted and congruent is that they reduce uncertainty and provide a context in which actors can transact with confidence. If there is confusion and conflict in the set of rules, the context for transactions within the school is less favorable than when formal and informal rules converge and actors have a clear sense of what is valued and what will be rewarded.

If a school has weak or confused rules, external standards may offer a positive contribution, but if the school has different goals from those underlying the standards and accountability system, external standards introduce noise and confusion into the fabric of rules and enforcement. A more troubling outcome of external standards has to do with their effect on the relationship between the formal and the informal rules in a school. As we have seen, one of the characteristics of schools with good institutional environments that encourage all members of the school community to 'pull in the same direction' is that there is a high degree of congruence and agreement between the formal and informal rules. In such schools the subtle but real forces of school culture, peer pressure and approval and disapproval help enforce both the formal and informal rules. If the external standards are fully compatible with a school's own goals and rules, then there is no problem. Standards can reinforce good performance. This might be the case for schools that start from a situation of weak and diffuse goals and rules. (Here, however, members of the school community would not have had a voice or feeling of participation in establishing the standards/goals/rules.) It is highly improbable, however, that a set of standards established far from the school and through a political process that attempts to satisfy or trade off differing interests and preferences would be congruent with a set of strong, clear, internally generated goals and rules already existing in a good school.

Mechanisms of enforcement

A set of external standards, tests to evaluate their accomplishment and an accountability system that confers rewards and punishments based on how well the standards are achieved constitutes a powerful complex of enforcement mechanisms. In theory this should contribute to an institutional climate favorable to good performance. If the standards make sense and are understood and accepted, if the curriculum is well conceived and teachers are trained in applying it, and if the curriculum and tests are aligned with the standards, then the enforcement mechanism can indeed be a valuable part of the fabric of institutions. All these 'ifs' mean that a school, indeed all schools in the jurisdiction, must adhere to the same complex of standards, curriculum, tests and rewards or punishments. This is desirable in the case of schools that do not have their own ideas about goals, standards, curricula, tests and the reward and punishment system for enforcement. But if the school has its own ideas, as many do, an externally imposed enforcement mechanism will not serve to strengthen the institutional climate.

If the impact of enforcement is fairly slight, if information about the school indicates that it is performing poorly but this creates no serious consequences for members of the community, if no one loses their job or fails to get a diploma, then the level of anxiety can be low and the effect of the standards system may be to exert some pressure in the direction of improving perform- ance. Firestone and Mayrowetz (2000) found that in Maine, where the only sanction was negative publicity, the influence of the tests was slight. In Maryland, where the stakes were higher, the impact was greater (p. 728). If the stakes are higher, the work and study environment can become so uncom- fortable that some teachers decide to leave the profession and some students give up and drop out of school because they are convinced they cannot meet the standards. Here some may say that one of the objectives of standards is to drive poor teachers out of the profession. It may, however, be the idealistic and self-motivated teachers (with abilities and drive to succeed in other fields) who decide to leave rather than the poor teachers. Similarly, teachers whose specialties are in demand elsewhere (such as science and mathematics teachers) will tend to be among those who leave.

The effects of high stakes and the enforcement mechanisms associated with them differ between schools. In relatively good schools that pursue academic goals that are in line with external standards, students and teachers tend to take the tests and the threat of sanctions lightly. If there is dissonance between the goals that the school seeks to accomplish and the external standards, teachers and other members of the community may feel discom- fort. The most serious problems arise in schools that are struggling, in which students are on the borderline of failure and teachers feel overwhelmed by the challenges they face. In schools such as these, high standards and severe sanctions may lead students to give up, assume they will fail, and perhaps drop out of school. The equity questions raised by standards and high-stakes tests, while perhaps not as disturbing as in the case of choice, are of serious concern. When schools have difficult problems, it is hard to create a positive environment in which all members of the community do their best, but efforts to 'turn around' a school experiencing problems may be more difficult if external standards cause students and teachers to lose hope and motivation. In short, the impact of high stakes and strong enforcement threats is not uniform across all schools. They may have the desired effect of forcing actors who have been shirking to make greater efforts, but schools that are doing well will be little affected while in those where students are doing very poorly, the effects may be negative.

Effects on cooperation and trust

The effects of standards and accountability have an impact on trust and cooperation at two levels. First, standards influence trust between the school and its governing authority or board (which imposes the standards itself or acts as the agent of still higher authorities in implementing them) and between the internal school community and the external environment (as described in the model in Chapter 1). If the standards are perceived as reasonable, if they are aligned with the curriculum and tests, and if the standards system is implemented in an intelligent way with sufficient resources and support for teachers and administrators, then there can be trust between the school and higher authorities. Research and commentary on the standards movement does not indicate that many standards and accountability systems meet all these conditions.

The second level involves trust between actors inside the school community itself. How do standards influence the relationships and trust between students and teachers? The answer depends heavily on how high the stakes are. If students are feeling stress about passing the tests and obtaining their diploma, they will insist that teachers devote maximum time and effort to preparing for the tests. Trust and cooperation will depend on how closely in agreement teachers and students are on this point. If students feel daunted by testing and the stakes associated with it, their focus is likely to turn inward on their own needs and fears and away from bonds with peers and teachers. Moreover, heavy emphasis on preparing for external tests can only distract attention from other activities that tend to build social capital and trust.

Parents are likely to be interested in their students' performance and to put pressure on teachers to make sure they pass the exams. Again, the higher the stakes, the stronger the pressure and the more likely it is to damage feelings of solidarity and trust between parents and teachers. School directors, while not as directly affected as teachers, students and parents, are also influenced in ways not conducive to trust, especially if they are perceived as closely associated with the administrative hierarchy that is imposing the standards.

5.4   CONCLUSIONS ON STANDARDS AND ACCOUNTABILITY

Evaluation is a central part of education. It is essential for teachers to know how well students are learning and to have feedback on their teaching. Parents have a right to know how their children are performing in school. Equity demands that schools have high expectations for every child, and that students be evaluated according to common standards. There is a need for external evaluation to make sure that schools with low performance and serious problems are not allowed to languish, and that they receive the attention and support (even interventions) they need in order to provide a decent education for their students. Accountability is necessary and desirable and, in a world populated by humans with tendencies to minimize effort and make life as comfortable as possible for themselves, there is a need for some degree of pressure.

The questions this chapter has raised have to do with how to accomplish the desirable effects of standards and accountability without having undesirable direct and indirect consequences. Managing that balancing act is difficult, and especially so when debate is colored by political or ideological interests that have little knowledge of or concern for the subtleties of how standards influence processes and relationships inside schools.

Some of the questions are relatively easy to answer. Others are much more difficult, or may simply not have an answer. It is obvious that a system of standards, accountability and sanctions should be technically well designed and well implemented. Unfortunately it is far from obvious how to design such a system, especially when differing political and other forces influence the design. The position of the educational community that standards, curriculum and the tests used to evaluate performance should be aligned is also clearly correct. From the 'noise' in the literature on standards, it appears that these desirable and fairly obvious outcomes are not always achieved.

Norm-referenced vs criterion-referenced tests.   On the question of the nature of the tests used, there seems to be general agreement that criterion-referenced tests constitute the correct basis for a testing-and-accountability system. This does, however, raise other technical issues. In addition to Linn's 'Lake Woebegone Effect', which is an inevitable result of using similar tests over time, there is the challenge of designing a system for evaluating test scores that takes into account: (1) differences in student backgrounds or 'starting points'; (2) the school's contribution to student's learning or 'value added'; and (3) the question of 'dynamics', or determining how to provide continuing, equitable incentives to both excellent schools and struggling schools over time and repeated applications of the testing and evaluation system.

Standardized vs performance-based tests.   The separate question whether tests should be standardized or based on how well students perform complex and open-ended tasks raises a different set of issues. For a number of reasons, including not only costs but also serious matters of true comparability between students and schools, standardized tests appear to have won the argument. But the counter-arguments in favor of authentic teaching, learning and testing are very strong. How, then, is it possible to obtain the advantages of standards based upon standardized tests without diverting large amounts of time and attention from instruction that produces the kinds of abilities, understanding and approach to learning that authentic methods offer? The answer to this question has a great deal to do with how high the stakes are, which raises a complicated question of balance if not an absolute dilemma. The linked issues of authentic learning and high-stakes tests run through the remainder of this discussion.

High-stakes vs low-stakes testing.   There appears to be a growing consensus that high-stakes testing is a mistake, first because it clearly causes undesirable distortion of teaching and learning within schools, and second because it is not possible to construct an equitable system that will challenge the best students and schools while being fair and providing constructive incentives for the less advantaged (all without creating a multiple-tier system that has the effect of lowering expectations about less able students). The proponents of 'strong accountability' argue that the whole point is that there must be significant sanctions. Opponents present two bodies of thought in opposition to this argument. The first has to do with what the costs and disadvantages of such a system are in comparison with its benefits. If high-stakes tests are designed to motivate students and teachers in low-performing schools (which represent only a portion of the total schools in most jurisdictions) but their effects on schools at both ends of the performance distribution are negative, is any potential gain worth the negative effects they cause? Are there better alternatives?

The second body of thought relates to fundamental differences about the purpose of education. Opponents of high-stakes testing object to the effects of coercive measures on the motivation and performance of students and teachers, and to the way such tests encroach upon school autonomy, freedom to innovate and opportunity to develop their own internal evaluation systems. With regard to the first of these areas of concern – about the kinds of abilities students should acquire in school – opponents of high-stakes testing hold that students should have not only command of the basic tools of mathematics and written and spoken language but also the ability to think and reason, to identify problems and solve them, to organize and compose written materials and to read critically and analytically. If these are the kinds of abilities that society (and the labor market) truly want graduates to have, they argue, then it is counterproductive to have high-stakes testing based on standardized tests that measure only a narrow subset of abilities largely oriented toward skills developed through rote learning.

Extrinsic vs intrinsic motivation   A separate set of concerns revolves around the nature of human motivation, the relationship between extrinsic and intrinsic motivation, and the nature of the learning process. The work of Bruno Frey and his associates (Frey, 1997a, 1997b, 1997c; Frey and Oberholzer-Gee, 1997) focuses on the effect of monetary rewards in 'crowding out' intrinsic motivation. A less-emphasized thread in his work points to the way external threats may also damage intrinsic motivation. In a section on the effect of regulations on intrinsic motivation, he says:

> [E]xternal interventions in the form of commands, monitoring or supervision, and threats of punishment, i.e. regulation, can be perceived as controlling by the individuals concerned and therefore tend to crowd out intrinsic motivation. Indeed, a regulatory intervention is likely to introduce a stronger Crowding-Out Effect because it is a stronger form of control than a monetary reward. Both involve cost, but in the case of a financial compensation it is in the form of forgone opportunities, only, while not following regulations is directly punished by the principal; e.g. by dismissal. (Frey, 1997b, p. 340)

Similar arguments based on 'self-determination theory' are made by Sheldon and Biddle (1998) and Ryan and Deci (2000), who argue that intrinsic motivation is both highly influential in stimulating performance of certain sorts of activities yet fragile and easily damaged by either bribe-like rewards or punitive sanctions. The work of Deci and others draws upon both experience in voluntary activities such as recycling behavior and on experimental studies. Some of the experimental work is directly related to education, indicating that efforts to force teachers and students in the direction of high performance on tests lead teachers to behave in 'controlling' ways that, in turn, produce undesirable changes in student behavior. Students in the experiments lost their intrinsic interest in learning the material and, while they may have done reasonably well on the tests, engaged in rote learning rather than conceptual learning, did not enjoy the experience, and did not retain interest in the subjects. They conclude that incentive systems linked to test scores can undercut students' intrinsic interest in subjects and the development of favorable attitudes toward learning itself.

Advocates of strong accountability and high-stakes testing are unconvinced by these arguments, even though they are supported by empirical evidence. Efforts to persuade or convince opponents are unlikely to sway the opinions of one side or the other in this argument.

What about the effects of high-stakes testing on schools' autonomy? There are strong arguments that schools should be free to develop their own approach to creating learning and to build teams of like-minded professionals who are free to innovate in their pursuit of authentic learning and who have the organizational capacity to take charge of their own efforts to improve the quality of the education they provide. The same people who advocate accountability are often in favor of freeing schools from excessive regulation and 'bureaucratic intervention', yet high-stakes testing is one of the most intrusive forms of regulation and intervention.

External and internal evaluation and accountability. Newmann, King and Rigdon (1997) give considerable importance to schools' own internal systems of evaluation and accountability. They find that 'a school accountability system alone is unlikely to advance student learning. It must be combined with a high level of organizational capacity' (p. 52). They identify several separate 'ingredients' that can contribute to organizational capacity, '[b]ut only when they are organized and coordinated to advance the organization's goals' (p. 47). Among their conclusions, they found that organizational capacity was not related to accountability, that schools in situations with 'strong external accountability' tended to have low organizational capacity, and that strong internal accountability tended to be associated with schools with high organizational capacity (p. 62). The authors found that schools needed to have a fairly high level of autonomy, which enabled them to develop their own internal accountability system and build a team of teachers with shared views about goals and standards, which in turn led to 'widespread consensus around professional norms and a focus for collaborative activity' at the school level. External accountability did not contribute to developing organizational capacity in the restructuring schools in their study, nor to establishing a strong system of internal accountability. They found that, '[e]xternal accountability alone offers no assurance that a school faculty will have adequate technical knowledge and skill, sufficient authority to deploy resources wisely, or shared commitment to a clear purpose for student learning' (p. 62). All these arguments constitute a persuasive case against high-stakes testing, but this leaves open several concerns about standards and accountability that will be discussed below.

Possible solutions to dilemmas of standards and accountability

Given the problems and dilemmas discussed in the preceding sections, as well as the value of evaluation and accountability, what should one conclude about standards, testing and accountability? What about the legitimate needs for information, for accountability, for some form of pressure to deal with the natural human tendency to shirk? The answer would seem to be that simplistic, top-down measures are not appropriate for all schools; that cheap-and-easy does not work. There is a need for much more diversified, sensitive and flexible approaches to providing information, accountability and a degree of pressure where needed. In considering standards and accountability, one must ask, 'for what?' Is the objective to punish someone, or is it to improve student learning?

This chapter addresses the category of incentives I call 'threats', but one of its most significant conclusions is that standards should not be so threatening that they interfere with the healthy functioning of schools' own internal processes, including internal evaluation. Measuring how well schools are succeeding in producing student learning (or at least the part that is amenable to testing) is useful. If well designed, tests produce information that is useful for teachers and administrators to have. Where some degree of school choice is available, including choice within the public education sector, information helps parents decide which schools are right for their children. Having standards, measuring how well schools are achieving them and publishing the results can provide a modest degree of pressure for good performance, but it need not be so threatening that it leads to teaching to the test, anxiety and stress, or denying students diplomas.

Advocates of centralized systems of standards and accountability take the position that this represents a shift from concern with inputs and compliance with regulations to concern with results. This is, without doubt, a desirable change in focus. But opponents counter that it is also essential to shift from a concern for controlling to a concern for learning. Accountability advocates say that, if standards and tests evaluate skills that all students should have, what is wrong with 'teaching to the test'? But the 'if' in that proposition is a large one, and if teaching methods and student behaviors are adversely affected (which is especially likely if stakes are high), the nature of the learning produced is, at least for a majority of students in decent to excellent schools, inferior to that produced through less coercive means. Proponents of performance-based testing advocate 'tests worth teaching to', that are integrated with instruction, and that lead to positive attitudes toward learning on the part of students. The debate rages on with little prospect for resolution. Motivation theorist Kennon Sheldon suggests

> it seems a compromise is required. Local schools and boards should be open to influence from higher-level agencies, but they should not have to fear pernicious and insensitive control (as is too often the case) ... Thus, ideally, coherent national standards can be promoted in a way that supports the autonomy of local bodies in deciding how to use those standards. (Sheldon, 2001)

Avoiding 'pernicious and insensitive control' would defuse a great deal of the argument over standards and accountability.

An approach that has much to recommend it is for schools to make more information available to the public, not only on the results of single tests but also on a variety of indicators of school performance that could include rates of completion (especially for secondary level), grade repetition where this is a factor, whether schools have experienced disciplinary problems, student and teacher attendance, rates of teacher turnover and other data.

Schools usually have (or could have) such data available as a matter of course but do not usually make them public. Chester Finn, Jr and his colleagues, advocates of strong state standards and accountability, devote a chapter in their study of charter schools to 'The Accountability Puzzle' (Finn, Manno and Vanourek, 2000, pp. 127–47). They recommend a system that is not based solely on standards and high-stakes tests (because charter schools, which they favor, are created to provide flexibility to experiment with alternative pedagogies and assessment strategies). Rather, they favor an open and abundant flow of information that can inform multiple audiences about a variety of dimensions of school performance, leading to what they call 'accountability-via-transparency'. Indicators of levels of satisfaction of students, teachers, parents and other school community members would also be useful, and can be generated using questionnaires (Tucker and Codding, 1998, pp. 226–7). Robert Behn advocates 'three hundred and sixty degree accountability' in all public management situations, a concept based on evaluation of individual performance not only by superiors but also by subordinates, peers, fellow team members, and clients. The idea of such accountability is to provide feedback for improving performance, not just a basis for punishment (Behn, 2001, pp. 196–217).

Any school authority will need to develop its own detailed answers about how to provide abundant information, make it public in order to generate a degree of pressure without resulting in simplistic 'league tables', and use it as feedback for improving performance rather than as a basis for imposing punishment. As always, the devil is in the details. The core of the matter is the main concept – the underlying mindset – of information-based accountability for the purpose of feedback and improvement rather than punishment. And this differs substantially from the mindset underlying many systems of standards, evaluation and accountability.

Another approach to providing standards and accountability is through periodic peer evaluations of schools, similar to accreditation systems used in private schools and higher education. Such an approach encourages schools to develop clear goals and their own internal evaluation systems, offers a more flexible way to evaluate schools on the basis of their own objectives and plans, and would tend to be acceptable to teachers and other community members and to be taken seriously rather than considered a nuisance or unwarranted intrusion. Such evaluations would consider school performance on standardized testing, but only as one element in a rich array of indicators of school quality. They would become a focus for teamwork in solving problems rather than a source of stress or of distortions to 'teach to the test'. Their influence on intra-organizational institutions would tend to be positive. In the event of an unsatisfactory evaluation, the result would be not shame and punishment but advice and support in overcoming problems and improving performance. Peer evaluation would not be incompatible with authentic teaching and testing. Indeed it would tend to favor such approaches.

These approaches – voluntary provision of abundant information, or periodic, peer-based evaluation of schools similar to accreditation studies – could be used in conjunction with low-stakes, information-oriented systems of standards and testing. Indeed standardized test findings would form a part of the 'abundant information' approach. Either or both of them (and the two are not incompatible) would have several advantages. They would not distort teaching or damage intrinsic motivation. They would leave ample latitude for schools to develop their own internal systems of evaluation (the quality of which would be one of the things evaluated during the accreditation process), and would permit schools to use any approach to authentic learning and testing they choose. The information provided would go well beyond what standardized tests provide, without generating the resistance and antagonism sometimes associated with standardized testing. If they indicated that schools have shortcomings, this would not lead to punishing sanctions (for schools, teachers or students) but rather to constructive interventions designed to help overcome the problems. Information and accreditation-like evaluation provide positive pressure for high effort and good performance, without the damaging effects of high-stakes testing. Perhaps the most significant point is that either system would not only allow but even encourage higher degrees of school autonomy while maintaining a degree of oversight in order to identify poor-performing schools and guide efforts to rectify their problems.

Such systems would avoid the serious problem of policies based on the assumption that 'one size fits all', which is clearly incorrect. They would probably be more expensive than centralized standards and standardized testing (especially systems similar to accreditation) and they would produce findings less frequently than annual tests, but the cost of evaluation has to be measured not only in terms of the direct expense of testing but, much more importantly, on the basis of how it affects schools' internal functioning and the long-run accomplishment of student learning and other legitimate educational goals.

6. Conclusions

6.1 WHAT HAVE WE LEARNED?

The importance of incentives

The subject of incentives to improve education could hardly be more relevant than it is today. In the US the 'No Child Left Behind' legislation of 2001 conditions Federal funds for education on state actions to establish account-ability systems based on a single standardized test and encourages states to implement other approaches to providing incentives. Elsewhere in the developed and developing world, countries are experimenting with or debating various initiatives to reward or sanction schools on the basis of their perform-ance.

A great number of research studies have explored the merits of programs to provide rewards, competition or threats. Some incentive programs appear to have positive effects, or at least to be benign; yet others have failed to produce the clear improvements in student learning their advocates expected, and some simply do not work. Almost independent of the research, debate in the political realm continues to be polemical and based more on ideology than information.

This book provides a different perspective from which to consider educational incentives. It develops a theoretical framework that draws on concepts from New Institutional Economics that have not been applied to education in this way before. It is my hope that these new ideas can add to understanding the complex factors that underlie the debate on incentives.

About the theory

The theoretical framework presented in Chapter 1 and applied in later chapters helps to explain a number of things that have puzzled economists, educators and other social science researchers working in the education field. It departs from some of the assumptions underlying much economic work on schools, perhaps most importantly the assumption that schools are operating as efficiently as possible with the resources they have at their disposal (that they are at or very near their 'production possibility frontier', in economic terms).

This in turn makes it clear that school performance can vary greatly, even if inputs and the population served are very similar. Differences in schools' institutional climates help answer, at least in part, two questions: (1) Why are schools less than perfectly efficient? (2) Why does school performance differ quite substantially even when inputs are essentially the same?

The answer to the first question derives from the idea that people do not always work as hard as they can. They have a discretionary margin within which they can vary their effort and thus their contribution – as teachers, students, parents and others – to the co-production process. The institutional climate in schools influences actors' willingness to use their discretionary margin – to expend some of their property rights in labor – in ways that contribute to accomplishing the organization's objectives. And that makes it clear why, if studies do not consider institutions within schools, they will find substantial variability in performance even when they control for other variables. This also casts light on the other side of the performance question: why is it that some schools with inputs no better than others have notable success in improving student learning, even among populations at risk?

If differences in institutional climates inside schools lead to substantial differences in outcomes, this would help explain why research has found it difficult to pin down the effects of variations in inputs. With regard to incentives, the theory presented here helps us understand at least in part why competition has not produced the powerful effects on schools that market forces have in other areas. It also helps explain why intuitively appealing ideas like providing rewards to individual teachers do not work.

About empirical information on the role of institutions

A theory of institutional factors inside schools makes it possible to identify factors associated with school success that earlier studies have hitherto ignored, and to understand a variety of issues that other approaches to research have not taken into account. The empirical study reported in Chapter 2 illustrates one way of conceptualizing the nature of institutions inside school organizations and indicates that it is feasible to measure schools' institutional climate. The methodology uses qualitative assessment of documentary and interview evidence to construct a quantitative index of institutional factors and uses this to help understand differences between schools. It would of course be possible to extend and elaborate the components in the index, although greater complexity would not necessarily be a benefit. It would also be possible to alter the weights assigned to the components used here, although no single component appears to dominate the association between the index and the dependent variables (scores on two applications of the SIMCE tests plus promotion rates).

The small sample of schools studied means one must interpret the results with great caution. Still, in my opinion the associations reported in Chapter 2 are sufficiently strong that a fair-minded reader would agree that the institutional index measures something meaningful that appears to be related to school performance. At the least, the findings suggest that it would be worthwhile to replicate the study on a larger scale and to extend it to other education levels and a greater variety of schools.

A qualification about the empirical study is in order. The dependent variables studied have to do mainly with performance on standardized tests of mathematics and language (although the promotion rate is also examined). Thus this study joins many others in focusing on only a small portion of the whole spectrum of things schools seek to accomplish. One of the things we found in our study is that the values dimension is of great importance both to educators and to parents, and is a central feature in the mission statements and other indications of the objectives of the schools we studied. Moreover, in addition to being an important output, values such as self-esteem, respect for others and a cooperative and positive attitude are also intertwined with the creation of the institutional climate itself. This is a highly complex area to understand and analyze but one that merits further attention in later work.

Intersections with other theories

There are several well-known bodies of thought that point in the same direction as the theory of institutions in schools. Most of these recognize that good schools need to have a clear mission or set of objectives and that an orderly environment inside the school is a necessary condition for teachers and students to carry out their respective tasks successfully. In the area of school culture, Firestone and Louis (1999) synthesize research on how school leadership shapes the culture of a school. Deal and Peterson (1999) find that a strong school culture fosters many of the same qualities identified as part of a good institutional environment. They include these statements about culture:

- [t]eachers can succeed in a culture focused on productivity ... performance (hard work, dedication, perseverance), and improvement;
- [c]ulture improves collegial and collaborative activities;
- [s]chools that embrace norms of performance ... reinforce a learning-focused vision for the school;
- [c]ulture amplifies the energy, motivation and vitality of a school staff, students, and community;
- [culture] increases the focus of daily behavior and attention on what is important and valued;
- [culture] helps teachers overcome the uncertainty of their work;

- [a]lthough rules, job descriptions and policies can shape what a person does, the unwritten rules, the informal expectations and rites and rituals of daily life may be even more meaningful ... (Deal and Peterson, 1999, pp. 7–9)

These phrases and the characteristics they describe resonate strongly with the concept of an institutional environment favorable to good performance. The authors emphasize the role of informal rules and the importance of rites, rituals, ceremonies and traditions (pp. 32–45) and an explicitly spiritual process of promoting 'the magic and myth of education' (p. 29). Their framework draws heavily on anthropology in this sense.

Catholic schools produce good results, often for students from disadvantaged backgrounds, with inputs and costs that do not differ greatly from other schools. Research has sought to understand how this happens. Bryk, Lee and Holland (1993), associate some specific characteristics of Catholic schools with high performance. For these authors the sense of 'community' found in Catholic schools contributes greatly to their success. It encourages teachers and students to do their best and involves families in helping and urging their children to work hard (pp. 272–94). The authors constructed a 23-item index to provide a 'quantitative indicator of communal organization', including 'six indicators of shared values about school purpose, adult beliefs about student capabilities and beliefs about appropriate teacher and student behavior; six indicators of shared activities in both the academic and the extracurricular realms; six indicators of faculty collegiality; and five indicators of diffuse teacher roles' (Bryk, Lee and Holland, 1993, pp. 277–81). ('Diffuse teacher roles' means that teachers are involved in more activities than simply teaching a single subject, thus giving them broader contact with each other and with students.) The characteristics measured by their community index – a far more sophisticated and carefully developed and tested instrument than our institutional index – are fully consonant with what our study found concerning a good institutional climate in schools.

Studies of leadership in schools emphasize the role of leaders in creating positive environments within schools. One of the most important roles of a leader is to establish clarity about the school's mission or set of objectives, optimally through participatory processes that lead to internalization of the objectives and strong consensus about their 'rightness'. Good leaders also establish formal rules that are firm, fair and consistently enforced. They help create school cultures that strengthen student motivation and provide informal support to the formal rules. Giving leaders more authority by strengthening site-based management and providing greater autonomy makes it possible for them to build strong communities, cultures or institutional environments.

The Effective Schools movement, which began in the 1970s and received considerable attention in the 1980s, has identified a number of characteristics of schools that achieve high levels of performance. A statement of the 'Correlates of Effective Schools' (Association for Effective Schools, Inc., 1996) includes:

- [c]lear school mission;
- [h]igh expectations for success;
- [i]nstructional leadership (on the part of the school director);
- [f]requent monitoring of student progress;
- [o]pportunity to learn and student time on task;
- [s]afe and orderly environment ... conducive to teaching and learning; and
- [h]ome–school relations in which parents understand and support the school's mission.

Again, there are very strong parallels between what authorities on effective schools list as characteristic of such schools and what constitutes a good institutional climate. The list above includes pedagogical factors such as instructional leadership and time on task but these are fully consistent with the institutional model.

Dr Joyce Epstein has led and encouraged research on the role of families and community in improving school performance since the early 1980s (Epstein, 2001). The institutional model, with its emphasis on co-production, supports the argument that families have important roles in providing motivation to learn and assuring that conditions in the home – including rest, nutrition, avoidance of risky behaviors and allocation of time – enable the student to give full attention and energy to studying. Epstein identifies six types of parental involvement: (1) parenting, (2) communicating, (3) volunteering, (4) learning at home, (5) decision making, and (6) collaborating with the community. Some are more directly related to the co-production of learning than others but all contribute to the sense that the home and school are partners in the process of promoting children's learning.

Each of these bodies of thought has a well-developed set of concepts concerning how the characteristics they identify with good schools influence student learning. They provide insights into what constitutes a good school and how to promote an environment favorable to student learning. Taking institutional factors into account helps understand these theories better. The theoretical framework presented here constitutes an explanatory model, consistent with other research but adding to understanding of how and why various attributes of good schools work together to improve the way schools produce learning, values and other desired outcomes.

6.2   THE INTERACTION OF INSTITUTIONS AND INCENTIVE SYSTEMS

Incentives based on rewards

Merit pay to individuals and merit awards to whole schools.   Institutional factors help explain why two approaches to providing monetary incentives – merit pay for individuals and merit awards to whole schools – differ markedly in their impact and their success. Merit pay schemes encounter serious problems of high transaction costs or the simple infeasibility of obtaining the information necessary to guide and justify paying bonuses to individual teachers. Their effect on the interaction between teachers, and between teaching staff and school directors, is to undercut the role of trust and cooperation in pursuit of common goals that provide powerful means of supporting and enforcing the relational transactions between these professionals. Providing rewards to a minority of teachers creates damaging 'noise' in the system of informal rules that is part of a healthy institutional climate. In addition, monetary rewards have the potential to bring about opportunistic behavior – whether teaching to the test or some form of 'grandstanding' to improve one's image – that is prejudicial to schools' main mission.

Merit awards to whole schools, on the other hand, encourage teamwork in pursuit of academic objectives. They do not place teachers in competition with each other or put the school director in the distant position of judge and dispenser of rewards instead of team leader and coach. They strengthen community feeling within schools. There have been few studies of merit award systems and it is not entirely clear how powerful their effects on teaching and school performance are. It is clear that they involve lower transaction costs than merit awards to individuals. Such awards do not seem to generate the resistance (on the part of unions, for example) that merit pay systems do; they tend to provide some positive pressure to improve performance and not to cause damage to institutional environments. They have potential to do good and at least do not seem to do any harm.

Compensation based on knowledge and skill.   In a majority of cases teachers' pay is based on academic degrees obtained (almost regardless of their relevance to the task of teaching) and on years of service. The lack of a link between pay and performance is the source of much criticism and of calls for performance-based pay. Changes in compensation systems to emphasize knowledge, skill and closely observed performance break away from the 'lock-step' regimentation of pay based solely on academic degrees and years of service. To be successful they must be accompanied by an evaluation system that is perceived to be objective, fair, constructive in intent and based on valid indicators of performance. Optimally teachers themselves will participate in identifying the indicators by which they will be evaluated. Such evaluation requires that schools have a considerable degree of autonomy to implement the system and then to reward those who perform well (and not reward those who don't). This is readily achieved in independent schools but would be more difficult in public systems. Direct observation of teaching performance in the classroom calls for high inputs of time, especially if both administrators and peers perform much of the evaluation. The investment of time in a constructive evaluation system with the characteristics just listed can be worthwhile if the process of evaluation is a learning experience for evaluators as well as those evaluated. In this case evaluation can contribute to a rewarding environment for professional growth.

Incentives based on competition

Vouchers.   As a general observation, most voucher programs have not led to true competition based on the quality of competing schools. This is certainly the case in Chile, which has one of the oldest and largest voucher programs in the world. In most cases, providing some students with vouchers to leave the public system has not caused serious competitive pressure on the public schools, even those that lost students. There is always a limit on the number of additional places that can be created in existing private schools. The performance of private schools (where these have been created to receive the voucher-paid students, as in Chile) has not been notably better than the average for public schools. Private operators tend to create competing schools only in areas where demand is high, which leaves public schools as the only (nearby) alternative for families in poor neighborhoods and sparsely populated areas. And competition between schools in Chile and New Zealand (another country with a large-scale voucher system) has tended to be based on status and non-academic factors (an impressive-sounding name; attractive school uniforms) rather than academic performance.

Even in relatively small-scale, targeted programs such as Milwaukee, implementation is complicated (even once a program is established). There are complex issues concerning which students are eligible for vouchers, how many voucher-paid places there should be, which schools they should be allocated to, what programs they should cover, and how much the voucher payments should amount to (Witte, 2000, pp. 43–6). Larger-scale programs have their own complications (for example, a good school that has more applicants than places must necessarily select students, which introduces equity problems even in schools designed to serve the poor). Experts such as McEwan (2000a) conclude that research has not provided enough information about large-scale voucher programs to form the basis for policy decisions.

Programs that allow private schools to operate and compete for students have the potential to permit a high degree of autonomy, which in turn makes it possible for schools to develop their own educational vision or set of goals, establish a culture and institutional environment favorable to good performance, develop their own evaluation and compensation systems that reward good teacher performance, and similar desirable features. Being private does not, however, guarantee that schools will take full advantage of the autonomy, or that they will develop most or all the features that characterize excellent schools. Nor is it necessarily the case that public schools cannot have the characteristics of excellent schools (especially if choice within public systems allows true autonomy).

Charter schools.   The reasons many charter schools come into being, and the influences that shape them in many cases, tend to encourage the development of a good institutional environment. Under favorable circumstances – most importantly in jurisdictions where the legislation permitting charter schools provides a high degree of autonomy – charter schools are free to implement their own educational vision. In typical cases the school's mission and goals are the reason it exists and all those involved in its creation are, almost by definition, fully aware of and committed to its fabric of goals. In such a situation, the leadership cares deeply about the goals and makes sure that all members of the community understand and share them, that teachers have been recruited with the understanding that they agree with the mission and goals, and that families that elect to send their children to the school also understand its purposes and accept the main aspects of its rules, requirements and procedures.

Such strong consensus at the outset of a charter school's life leads to ready acceptance of rules by all parties, congruence between formal and informal rules, and a strong sense of community and that everyone is 'pulling in the same direction'. Moreover, the concepts, spirit and charisma of the founders of the school tend to pervade the school's culture and be passed on to new staff and successive generations of students and their families. For these reasons the influence of charter status on institutions within schools is stronger than the influence of simply being private. As in the case of privatization, being autonomous does not guarantee that leaders and staff will take full advantage of the opportunities charter status offers. But the chance to do so – to truly create an academic community with shared goals, innovative programs and commitment to excellence – exists for charter schools.

The main reservations concerning charter schools have to do with the legislation and the accountability system under which they operate. Strong charter legislation encourages rather than constrains the creation of charter schools and, once they are created, gives them ample freedom and autonomy to put their ideas into action. Clearly such legislation would also require accountability, but the accountability system should provide positive pressure for good performance without choking off the school's freedom to pursue its own mission, build its own team and community, and implement the innovations its founders proposed. Unfortunately, not all jurisdictions have legislation and accountability systems that meet these criteria.

Choice within public systems. The alternative of providing parents opportunities to choose among a fairly wide array of kinds of public schools has a number of advantages that neither voucher programs nor charter schools enjoy. Providing within-district choice meets most of Levin's criteria for evaluating voucher programs discussed in Chapter 4 – freedom of choice, productive efficiency, equity and social cohesion – to at least some degree. Parents are free to choose among the educational models available within the district, but for such choice to be meaningful there must be a variety of models, plus flexibility for students to transfer to the preferred school (including arrangements for transportation when necessary). In theory (and if there is flexibility for students to leave some schools and go to others) the existence of alternative educational approaches should create both a degree of competition and a yardstick effect, which together would encourage productive efficiency. For the theory to work properly, however, there would need to be agreement between the district authorities, teachers' unions and the whole of the external community (including political leadership) to provide the necessary flexibility. Within-district choice can contribute to productive efficiency just as other forms of choice, but the conditions for this to happen have to be right, and that is far from an assured outcome.

Choice among public alternatives is perhaps weakest in the area of equity. While students in poor-performing schools should have as much freedom to choose to go to an alternative school, there are likely to be limits on how many are allowed to enter some of the best schools, and the limits on information, motivation and transportation are likely to be greatest for poor or minority families. Families that value education most greatly are likely to be those that benefit most from within-district choice. As for social cohesion, this approach tends to encourage diversity to some degree. The history of magnet schools is not highly encouraging in this respect, but at least the pressures are in the right direction.

Within-district choice generates less political resistance than voucher programs or other forms of competition that are viewed as 'privatization'. It lends itself more to gradual development and mid-course corrections than a large-scale voucher program would do. Public alternative schools do not have the burdens of fund raising, advertising and management costs that voucher-paid or charter schools do. The reservations about this form of choice boil down to this: for choice within public systems to produce real benefits, the district authority must be willing to provide the flexibility and autonomy necessary for success. Districts must truly be willing to 'let loose the reins' and allow alternative schools to develop with virtually the same freedom that charter schools have under strong charter legislation. It is not at all clear to what degree this is likely to happen.

Incentives based on threats: standards and accountability

It is the nature of human beings to want to make life as easy and pleasant for themselves as they can. This includes even highly motivated people. If left completely free of oversight and control, there is an overwhelming tendency for individuals to give less effort (or to take advantage of the situation in some way) than if subject to some form of supervision or accountability. Economists call this shirking, opportunism or moral hazard.

Critics of traditional education systems argue that this general human characteristic has led education systems to protect their monopolistic position, retain information rather than make it public, and generally resist all forms of pressure to maintain or improve the quality of schooling. For this reason they favor incentive systems designed to impose standards, generate information on performance, establish accountability (and punish those who the accountability system shows to be performing poorly).

Some degree of system-wide accountability is not only good but essential to assure that public schools function close to their productive potential. This is especially true when schools are given a great deal of freedom and flexibility to innovate and follow their chosen educational model. Questions arise, however, about how much accountability there should be, on the basis of what indicators, and to what purpose.

Advocates of standards and accountability see testing as the answer to problems of what they perceive as poor quality in education (and tend not to differentiate between schools that are doing an adequate or excellent job and those that are failing to provide adequate quality). They are convinced that standardized tests can measure the most important aspects of student learning, that they will not cause distortion in the form of teaching to the test (or that any distortion will be in a desirable direction), that good students in high-quality schools should be able to pass standard tests without difficulty, and that the effects of testing will be to promote equity. They are also enamored of testing because it is relatively easy and cheap to implement from the top down. The spread of the testing movement proves that it is easy to make political arguments in support of these views.

Most educators accept the idea of some form of accountability, although they disagree with many of the advocates' views listed above. The serious problem arises when high stakes are attached to the tests. The more extreme advocates feel that the higher the stakes the better. Yet the arguments against high-stakes testing are extremely strong. The evidence and the opinions of testing specialists seem to support the arguments that high-stakes tests cause distortion in teaching, narrowing of the focus of what schools do, inequitable punishment of students in poor schools and damage to good schools that are doing their best to provide a strong and broadly based educational program.

Even low-stakes testing has a tendency to evolve into the basis for increasingly important decisions, and there appears to be a permanent and unavoidable tension between having some form of standards on one hand and allowing good schools to pursue their own vision without having to allocate often substantial portions of their scarce time and resources to preparing for standardized tests on the other. Any system that imposes a single standard on all schools is inevitably wrong for some schools.

If it were possible to combine low-stakes tests designed to provide basic information and assure that all students are achieving minimum standards of competency with other measures of school quality and student achievement, this would offer an escape from the dilemmas associated with testing and standards. This would require, however, that authorities (and politicians) be willing to undertake the more complex and challenging tasks of determining – on the basis of an array of indicators – which schools are performing badly and structuring interventions that would overcome problem situations without forcing schools that are doing an acceptable or superior job to sacrifice much of the educational quality they can provide.

The high-transparency approach suggested in Chapter 5, whereby schools provide a rich flow of information on multiple aspects of performance, would offer at least a portion of what accountability advocates seek without having deleterious effects on good schools. This would entail some costs for schools in the form of measuring and reporting, but much of the information – such as promotion and repetition rates, disciplinary actions, parental complaints and various indicators of school success – is or should already be available. Transparency would provide incentives in the form of a 'shame factor', yardstick effects, some degree of competition as a result of children being allowed to transfer out of schools with poor performance, and the possibility that very poor indicators would lead to interventions ranging from help in improving performance to severe sanctions on schools that refused to improve. It would not provide the low-cost, one-size-fits-all ease of standardized testing, and would require courage and effort on the part of administrators to identify and address problems. But it would do no harm.

6.3   CONCLUDING THOUGHTS

Social psychologist Kurt Lewin is credited with the phrase, 'There's nothing as practical as a good theory'. The theoretical framework presented here, and that forms the basis for examining various incentive systems, is an innovative approach that has many practical implications. It brings New Institutional Economics to bear, at an extreme micro level, on important questions of educational policy, and produces insights that can contribute to the often polemical debate about how to improve education and alternative approaches to providing incentives. What are the main points that one would want readers to take from this book?

Take institutions into account

If the book succeeds in drawing attention to the role of intra-organizational institutions in schools – clear objectives, sound formal rules and informal rules and enforcement mechanisms, and social capital – it will have accomplished one of its main purposes. Applications of economics to education have made valuable contributions to understanding what does (and does not) contribute to better school performance, but most studies have treated schools as black boxes and failed to examine their inner workings. There have been very few applications of institutional thinking to education and, to my knowledge, none to factors internal to school organizations.

In a conversation with education economist George Psacharopoulos some years ago, I argued that the economics of education should devote attention to school management as a determinant of educational performance. 'But Bob,' George asked, quite reasonably, 'what are the variables?' The institutional model represents a step toward identifying variables relating to management, and the exploratory empirical study makes a first attempt to show that they are measurable.

In management literature and in applications of New Institutional Economics to higher-level questions concerning the organization of economic activity and the determinants of economic performance, the role of institutions – the rules of the game – is clearly understood. It is worthwhile to apply these concepts at a micro level to understand what determines school performance.

Do no harm

One is never working with a clean slate when formulating educational policy. Existing education systems are living entities, pursuing long-established purposes, and they cannot be changed without affecting the lives and work of teachers, students, parents and others. Many interventions fail to take this into account. The makers of education policies should be required to take some equivalent of the physician's Hippocratic oath: 'First, do no harm'. Whatever the shortcomings of existing systems, beware of doing things that will make matters worse.

Incentive systems are powerful devices. They have an unmistakable impact on human behavior. But it is essential to understand what that impact is, who is affected by the incentive, and, most importantly, whether an incentive system will have undesirable side effects that can lead to displacement of the true objectives of education and damage the processes of teaching and learning.

Incentives, such as high-stakes testing, are extremely potent tools. They undoubtedly influence behavior, as has been amply demonstrated, but it is far from clear what their effects are on different kinds of schools or whether the risk of damage is justified. In a plea to keep the Massachusetts Competence Assessment System (MCAS) from damaging her school, Linda Nathan argues for a more broadly based alternative and asks, 'Why is it that the politicians who created the MCAS for public schools mostly send their own children to private schools, which rarely if ever use standardized tests to make important decisions about students?' (Nathan, 2002, p. 600). High-stakes testing is a policy with great potential for harm, yet it is being imposed upon states in spite of serious concerns about its eventual impact.

One size does not fit all

Many writers have commented on the futility of searching for a 'magic bullet' that will quickly, easily and inexpensively bring about great change for the better in education systems. Yet advocates of one policy or another continue to propose changes – especially in the area of educational incentives – that seek to apply a single intervention to the whole array of schools in national, state or local school systems. Many of these have intuitive attractiveness; they tend to appeal to one end or another of the ideological spectrum. And despite considerable research-based evidence that they have been tried extensively and simply do not work (or that we do not know enough about such interventions to implement them on a large scale), certain policy ideas continue to crop up and to become the basis for hot political controversy.

One of the characteristics of 'magic bullet' proposals is that they are relatively easy and cheap to impose from above. And in the misguided pursuit of equity, they can be imposed like Procrustes' bed on all schools regardless of whether they are needed or what their effects will be.

The British form of school inspection, mentioned in Chapter 5 but not discussed at length, offers an alternative approach to providing accountability and applying pressure to avoid shirking. The great merit of such a system is that it takes the needs and situation of individual schools into account rather than imposing a one-size-fits-all standard on all. Such an approach has its own complexities and countries of the Commonwealth that have attempted to emulate the British model have found that it is not easy to do so. A good system of inspection – or of school accreditation – has considerable costs, but these may be modest in comparison with the spillover costs of undesirable distortion of behavior caused by high-stakes testing. It would be worthwhile for those concerned with improving quality and providing accountability to consider such alternatives.

Extend the study of institutions inside school organizations

New ideas are very often resisted and almost always take a while to catch on. It would be surprising if a theory of institutions inside school organizations – incorporating unfamiliar concepts of co-production, micro-level relational contracting, and an institutional climate that reduces uncertainty and encourages actors to commit their energy and effort to accomplish school goals – experienced a different fate. A final wish of the author is that scholars explore the theory further. In particular, I hope that empirical work using the theory can be refined, strengthened and replicated, and extended to different levels of education and different educational policy issues.

Refine and replicate.   The theory deserves far more thorough empirical testing than I have been able to do to date. Obvious improvements would be larger sample size, incorporation of a greater variety of schools and refinement of the information-gathering techniques. Development of instruments that would be less expensive to administer and more readily subject to scientific analysis than the interview and focus-group methodologies used in the empirical study in Chapter 2 would be highly desirable. More sophisticated statistical methodology, which would be possible with a larger sample, would also obviously be needed.

Study other education levels and governance at the district or board level.
Applying the theory in primary schools constitutes a start but it is probable that studies of secondary schools would yield even clearer findings. This would be especially true with regard to contracting between different parties. At the secondary level it would be feasible to gather information from students and from parents that would cast greater light on the influence of various elements of the institutional climate on motivation and behavior. Applying institutional concepts would be considerably more difficult at the university level, in part because of the difficulty of identifying clear outcome variables but also because of the great diversity of sub-organizations (facul-

ties) with different institutional characteristics. It might be feasible to focus on a single set of reasonably comparable organizations (law school faculties, for example) but even here the challenges would be great.

An important extension of research on institutions would be to study governance mechanisms at the local level: school districts. Chubb and Moe (1990) conclude that 'the democratic institutions of capitalism' operating at the school district level are the source of many ills of public education. They find that institutions 'bear substantial responsibility for the bureaucratization of schools and the debilitation of their organization (p. 167). There are, however, more enlightening ways of looking at the relationship between institutions and schools. The research of Woessmann (2001), in which he used TIMSS data to analyze the effects of institutions on the performance of national-level education systems, shows that countries with certain institutional characteristics performed better on the TIMSS tests of math and science. But that research was limited by the data on institutions that were available from the TIMSS study itself, which do not permit a fine-grained characterization of institutions or a full understanding of how they work to influence performance.

Explore different issues of educational policy and management. Institutional thinking could be applied to policy issues such as site-based management to good effect. Moving to a somewhat higher level of analysis, the subject of decentralizing education has received a great deal of attention in international circles but studies have not examined what impact different approaches to decentralization have on what happens inside schools. The institutional model would provide a clear set of hypotheses with which to explore this issue.

Study of the role of networks of schools (and why some networks have greater impact than others) would be greatly illuminated by using institutional concepts to understand more fully the impact that networks such as Accelerated Schools or Fe y Alegría have on the learning environment in schools. Appendix B sketches briefly some of the ways networks influence within-school institutions, but far more work deserves to be done.

Explore how to create sound institutions. If good institutional environments are important for educational performance, and this book's main argument is that they are, then how do you create good institutions? That is a daunting question. Institutions grow out of human interaction, depend on very subtle influences in order to function, require trust between members of sometimes diverse communities, and are far easier to destroy than to build. At the level of organizations, they may depend on the charisma of one or a few individuals (which is a situation highly vulnerable to change if a key person leaves).

The literature on school culture offers some insights into how institutions may be developed and strengthened. Deal and Peterson (1999) stress that events – rites, rituals and ceremonies – can serve to strengthen bonds between members of schools communities and to create or deepen traditions. These authors also describe the role of skilled external consultants in overcoming 'toxic cultures' and providing a basis for developing positive climates within schools.

In their discussion of the implications of Catholic schooling for education generally, Bryk, Lee and Holland (1993) mention a number of factors that bear upon the creation of institutions. They, too, mention school activities that provide an opportunity for face-to-face interactions and shared experiences between members of the school community. Teachers perform many 'diffuse' functions and thus come to know their peers and the whole student body well. Catholic schools are highly decentralized, which provides the freedom to develop their own identities and institutions, but their inspirational ideology provides a lodestone that contributes powerfully to building the communities, cultures or institutions that in turn favor high performance. The sense of community, to which the authors give great emphasis, arises out of shared goals and expectations, a sense of commitment on the part of different groups, a collegial relationship between teachers (which requires building a strong sense of participation in a team), and what the authors call 'Christian personalism and subsidiarity' (p. 301). Personalism means a generally humane orientation in the relations between community members, a positive outlook that is difficult to define and impossible to mandate but that has a strong influence on the motivation of all actors. Subsidiarity means that the dictates of higher-level authorities are subsidiary to site-level concerns, in which human feelings, and dignity, mutual respect, and collegial solidarity take precedence over issues of efficiency or bureaucratic priorities. (While evanescent, such factors have a great deal to do with motivation and commitment of members of a group.) It may be hard to imagine these characteristics existing in large, public education systems but it is worthwhile to think of ways to approximate them.

Francis Fukuyama (1997, pp. 91–124) provides an insightful review of an array of mechanisms by which 'order' and social capital come into being or are strengthened. He mentions game theory and its findings about the evolution of cooperation but views this as only one of the ways norms come to be generated. The full array includes norms imposed from above by the state or some hierarchical structure, spontaneously generated norms such as the evolution of cooperation, exogenously generated norms provided by religion or ideology, and natural sources of norms such as kinship, race or ethnicity. The first two can be either rational or irrational in source. Social capital is in a sense a public good. The state may play a positive role in its creation but can also deplete it, and civil society and voluntary organizations must play extensive roles in fostering social bonds, positive mutual interactions and trust. While Fukuyama warns of a number of ways governments and other influences can damage social capital (and the positive institutions that accompany it), his reading of history leads him to a generally optimistic outlook about the possibility of generating social capital, order and sound institutions.

All these bodies of thought suggest that it would be worthwhile to gather knowledge about the role of institutions in education – from the level of the school to national policies – and ways in which to create sound institutional climates.

Appendix A: Contracting in schools

WHY DO CONTRACTS IN SCHOOLS MATTER?

One of the central arguments in the text is that members of school communities engage in transactions about who is going to do what; more specifically about how actors such as teachers and students will use their 'intangible property' – their 'property rights in labor' – to carry out their respective tasks of teaching and learning. The nature of the transactions between actors in schools varies from quite formal ones, like the employment contracts of teachers and other staff, to semi-formal ones, like written statements whereby parents agree to various rules and obligations established by the school, to the most informal bargains and 'deals' having to do with highly subtle arrangements between people. These last can be as amorphous as a teacher talking with a student about making more of an effort, or speaking up more in class (the *quid pro quo* being the implication that the teacher will give approval and perhaps a better grade). Or it could be a parent agreeing to let a student have more television rights if homework is completed beforehand. Such transactions have a powerful influence on how actors perform tasks leading to the co-production of learning.

What do we mean by contracts?   Economist John R. Commons considered that the transaction is the most basic unit for analyzing the economics of organizations (Commons, 1934). Commons' view of transactions 'began with conflict of interests, then took into account the evident idea of dependence of conflicting interests on each other; then reached a decision ... endeavoring to bring order out of the conflict of interests, known by the Court as "due process of law"' (Commons, 1934, p. 4). Even the most informal contracts between actors in schools are transactions that embody these elements.

Contracting in the education sector goes on at a number of different levels. Examples of three of these levels will help clarify what the term means in this book.

1. *High-level contracting*   This includes educational performance contracting, which was the subject of experimentation and analysis in the 1970s

(Hanushek et al., 1994, pp. 92–3; Schmidt, 1994). Hanushek *et al.* (1994, pp. 85–124) review the history of selected experiments with performance contracts and research on different approaches to using contracts to provide incentives to improve education. The more recent innovation of charter schools represents a form of high-level contracting between school boards and charter recipients. Voucher systems to provide 'school choice' are established at this level. Hill, Pierce and Guthrie (1997) propose contracting out the management of public schools (single schools or groups of schools) as a means of improving school functioning. At this high level of contracting, negotiations with teachers' unions over standard contracts take place, and state legislators make laws on charter schools and standards.

2. *Intermediate-level contracting*   This level includes formal employment contracts between school boards and individual teachers and school directors. In some jurisdictions the local board also has the power to grant charters. Also, many private schools require parents to sign formal 'contracts' indicating their agreement to pay school fees and abide by specific rules concerning their child's participation in the school.

3. *Micro-level contracting*   This includes semi-formal or informal contracting between parents and schools intended to make clear that parents support the school's objectives, agree to cooperate with the school, will assure that students have the time and other resources necessary to study effectively, and will encourage them to make diligent efforts to perform homework and other school-related tasks. Henry Levin's Accelerated Schools program requires such statements of commitment (Hopfenberg *et al.*, 1993; Hanushek *et al.*, 1994, pp. 102–3). This level of contracting is where teachers and students (and sometimes parents) establish semi-formal, informal or relational 'learning contracts'. In their most basic form, these are agreements or 'deals' governing what each party is expected to do. Tucker and Codding (1998, pp. 129–30, 136–7) recommend making explicit contracts with parents and with students that cover, among other things, completing assignments and television watching. There is a literature on 'learning contracts' established between teachers or schools and learners and establishing exactly what the learner is expected to do (for example, Boak, 1998; Knowles, 1986). This kind of contracting is used most often in distance education or with mature students (at university or technical school level) who can be expected to work without supervision and whose work can be evaluated objectively. There are, however, schools that use this kind of explicit contracting between teachers and students at the basic education level.

Complete vs incomplete contracts.   Only the simplest kinds of contracts – for example, the purchase of a standard commodity on a spot market – can be complete (Hart and Moore, 1999). The transaction costs involved in gathering information, writing more complex contracts that would cover all possible contingencies, negotiating the contract and monitoring the agent's performance would be prohibitively high. It is a commonplace to say that teachers' contracts are incomplete, but the relational contracts between teachers and students – the agreements that the student will make an effort to learn a particular body of knowledge – are even less complete. In these contracts, the degree of effort a student makes is a function of the student's choice and the monitoring and enforcement the teacher carries out. Testing and grades are the most obvious examples of monitoring and enforcement mechanisms. But a significant portion of monitoring and enforcement is performed by third parties, especially parents and peers. This has to do with whether the parties are performing in accordance with the informal rules of the game. It is based on very close observation of actors – by the people with whom they interact – and has relatively low cost. Monitoring and the informal sanctions that can be imposed by school directors, teachers, parents and peers constitute a powerful influence on the way actors use their property rights, and ultimately on school performance.

Formal vs informal contracts.   Formal contracts are usually written and enforceable by a court. There is a continuum running from highly formal contracts – for example, for the purchase of expensive and high-cost machinery that must perform according to exacting technical specifications – and the relatively informal contract whereby the person who cuts my grass agrees (usually without a written document) to do so for a cost of X dollars per cutting. In the school context there are formal contracts (the teacher's employment contract, for example), somewhat formal contracts (some schools require written agreements between parents and the school concerning the responsibilities of each party regarding the education of the child), and a large category of highly informal contracts. Many of the contract-like arrangements established between teachers and students, parents and students or any dyad of actors in the school community are unwritten agreements, pertaining to activities that are difficult or impossible to measure, and that could never be enforced in a court. Yet this kind of informal contracting is pervasive in schools and has a profound impact on how well the various actors carry out their work – the exercise of their labor – that ultimately determines how much students learn.

Standard, implicit and relational contracts.   Much traditional economic and legal theory of contracts starts from the assumption that contracts are relatively complete, made between rational actors on the basis of unlimited (and cost-free) information and enforceable by courts. Analyses may immediately begin to vary these assumptions, but that is the starting point. Increasingly since the 1970s, specialists have recognized that transactions are costly, human knowledge and rationality are limited, and truly complete contracting is effectively impossible. Thus, in the real world, most contracting does not satisfy the standard assumptions.

Standard theory also assumes that contracts are made between strangers and that factors such as reputation, expectation of benefits from future transactions, or a sense of loyalty or responsibility toward the other party are insignificant. There is a great difference between contracts in which the parties will continue to be closely involved with each other and more traditional contracts, which theoretically take place between strangers. In what are called relational contracts, the reputation of contracting parties and the informal assurances given provide incentives to honor the contracts. Key characteristics of relational contracts are that the parties are engaged in ongoing relationships and that maintaining the relationship is in the interest of all participants in the contract. Marriages and families embody one kind of relational contract. Long-term employment relationships within hierarchical organizations are another. Other examples are partnerships, condominiums, franchise agreements, retirement communities, joint ventures between firms, hand-in-glove arrangements between suppliers and producers, and a wealth of organizational arrangements in which the parties will find it beneficial to keep dealing with each other over the medium to long run. Contracts in such situations have a tendency to be self-enforcing. Some aspects of relational contracts may be clearly specified and ultimately enforced by courts. Many other aspects must depend on factors such as commitment, trust and the self-enforcing nature of agreements between parties who will have to continue to deal with each other over time. In school settings, essentially all formal and informal contracts are relational.

The concept of implicit contracts is used in labor economics to explain phenomena associated with wage rigidity in the face of involuntary unemployment, where implicit contracts offer risk-averse employees a form of insurance against job loss (Rosen, 1985; Grossman and Hart, 1981). Some writers have used the implicit contract concept as something close to a synonym for self-enforcing contracts (Klein, 1985; Pearce and Stacchetti, 1998). In most treatments of the implicit contract concept, reputation is a factor in repeated contracts between an employer and his or her employee. This certainly characterizes relationships in schools. Marvin Rozen (1990) expanded the idea to refer to contracts in which

> the behaviors and contingencies covered cannot be fully specifiable a priori since they can be neither easily described nor verified. They are subjectively perceived

by all parties, and this quality leads to a self-enforcing mechanism in which each party adheres to the understanding as long as expectations concerning that other party's behavior are broadly realized ... [E]ach party must believe that honoring implicit agreements is the best way to further its own interests. (Rozen, 1990, p. 96)

This interpretation resonates with the idea of informal contracting in schools that is the subject of this Appendix, but has not been further elaborated by others.

Baker, Gibbons and Murphy (2002) utilize the concept of 'relational contracts' in their analysis of how firms are organized. Relational contracts arise where contracting parties are involved in a long-term relationship and the continuation of that relationship is of value to all parties. Examples include 'informal *quid pro quos* between co-workers, as well as unwritten understandings between bosses and subordinates about task assignment, promotion and termination decisions ... long-run, hand-in-glove supplier relationships ... networks of firms ... strategic alliances, joint ventures and business groups' (Baker, Gibbons and Murphy, 2002, p. 39). The authors find that relational contracts can help circumvent problems in formal contracting, establish bases for ongoing negotiation when circumstances change, and promote efficiency. They find also that their design and implementation is one of the most essential functions that managers perform in the kinds of flexible organizations that increasingly characterize the modern world. While their article focuses on the issue of vertical integration vs non-integration in the light of relational contracting, their exposition of how relational contracts influence the functioning of organizations suggests how valuable this concept is in understanding schools as organizations.

In the legal literature, Ian Macneil pioneered the concept of relational contracting (Macneil, 1978). He distinguishes between classical, neoclassical and relational contracting. The last of these includes relations between management and employees within corporations, as well as 'corporate relations with long- and short-term creditors, law firms, accounting firms, and managerial and financial consultants ... Collective bargaining, franchising, condominiums, universities, trade unions ... large shopping centers and retirement communities with common facilities ... ' (Macneil, 1978, p. 887). Neoclassical contract law gives greatest weight to 'the original agreement', while in 'a truly relational approach the reference point is the entire relation as it had developed to the time of the change in question (and in many instances as it has developed since the change)' (Macneil, 1978, p. 890).

Both formal and informal contracts in the education sector are overwhelmingly relational. Schools are tightly bound to neighborhoods and communities by geography. Characteristics of education – ranging from the need to maintain continuity throughout the school year to union contracts and grants of tenure – tend to bind teachers (and school directors, students and parents) to schools on a medium- to long-term basis. As in the case of relationships within families, differences need to be resolved within the constraints of continuing relationships (barring catastrophic breakdowns such as divorce). In addition to influences that tend to force continuity in relationships, there are positive factors that encourage it (in functional families): friendship, respect, commitment and a sense of shared objectives.

The literature on industrial organization and management has dealt with this kind of contracting more deeply and extensively than economics (Anderson and Weitz, 1992; Heide, 1994; Rindfleisch and Heide, 1997). Among the best-known work on transactions within organizations and the organizational 'rules of the game' that govern them is that of Michael Jensen and the late William Meckling (1976, 1992, 1994). These last are fortunately now available in Jensen (1998). In that work, Jensen states (p. 113):

> Where the production, transfer, and application of knowledge are the primary goods being offered ... exchanges tend to take the form of long-term relationships, and the most common of these is employment contracts. Such contracts tend to be general in nature – the contents of the exchanges are not precisely specified – and they seldom are alienable. The transaction costs emphasized by Coase (1937) and Williamson (1975) are one reason such contracts emerge. Single proprietors who contract on a case-by-case basis for production and application of all knowledge would soon find themselves swamped by transaction costs in all but the smallest firms.

Jensen's work focuses on private sector firms. It is relevant to schools in many ways but not in all.

The view of contracting proposed in this book involves intra-organizational contracts that may include incomplete formal contracts but much more frequently are informal and relational contracts dealing with actors' property rights in labor. Note that the degree to which contracts in the latter category are self-enforcing depends on the importance of maintaining long-term relationships, on reputation, on shared objectives and on a degree of trust.

There has been little recognition in the economics of education of the role of such contracting within schools. Nor has there been wide recognition of the existence of the property rights with which the contracts are concerned, the role of principal–agent relationships between teachers, parents and students, or the way in which the institutional environment within schools can either favor contracting of the sort described above and promote high academic performance or undermine the ability of these actors in schools to make agreements and commitments to do their best to accomplish the school organization's objectives.

What is exchanged in contracts in schools?

The property rights of interest here are the rights individuals appropriate over their 'labor', meaning the attention, energy, effort, creativity and care they devote to the tasks for which they are responsible. In the incomplete contracts between educational authorities and teachers, and the subtle contracting between teachers and students, certain basic activities are explicit. Teachers will appear before their classes at the appointed times and teach; students will attend school and are expected to study and learn. Grades are a form of *quid pro quo* in the contracts between teachers and students, as well as a means of monitoring the performance of both students and teachers. Property rights arise because the contracts are incomplete. Transaction costs, particularly the information costs of monitoring actors' behavior, make it impossible for principals to know fully how well agents are performing. Much of teachers' work takes place behind closed doors. Parents know the difficulty of keeping track of how long, hard and well students study. Property rights – the discretion teachers and students have over their labor – arise because of the transaction costs that would be required for thorough monitoring.

Even slaves had property rights. Douglass C. North (1990, p. 33) defines property rights as 'the rights individuals appropriate over their own labor and the goods and services they possess. Appropriation is a function of legal rules, organizational forms, enforcement, and norms of behavior – that is, the institutional framework.' An extreme example is found in the rights of slaves. Barzel (1977) examined the economics of slavery and, in particular, the monitoring and enforcement of the implicit contract between master and slave. Even though a master had total control over his slave, including the power of life and death, it was too costly to observe how hard each slave worked at every moment in time. Moreover, even a slave had to be nourished and to have time to rest, otherwise his productivity would decline and, ultimately, he would be worked to death. It would make no sense for a master to destroy his valuable asset. Even in this extreme situation, the slave came to have a degree of control over (1) a modest amount of 'free' time to eat, rest and rebuild his strength, and (2) how hard he worked. Despite his circumstances, a slave was able to modulate his work effort. Since it was impossible for the master or his overseer to ensure that the slave was working as hard as possible all the time, the slave became the owner of the margin between his maximum effort and the effort actually expended. (The phrase 'saving his strength' captures the essence of this.) Thus there were informal contracts between master and slave that granted slaves some benefits in exchange for an implicit agreement to work hard; that is, use their property rights over their labor diligently.

North (1990, p. 32) describes the master/slave relationship as follows:

> There is in fact an implicit contract between the two; to get maximum effort from the slave, the owner must devote resources to monitoring and metering a slave's output and critically applying rewards and punishments based on performance. Because there are increasing marginal costs to measuring and policing performance, the master will stop short of perfect policing and will engage instead in policing until the marginal costs equal the additional marginal benefits from such activity. The result is that slaves acquire certain property rights in their own labor. That is, owners are able to enhance the value of their property by granting slaves some rights in exchange for services the owners value more. Hence slaves became owners too.

Most discussions of property rights focus on tangible property that can be exchanged in markets (for example, Williamson, 1985, p. 27). The rights of teachers and students over their own labor are quite far removed from tangible and tradeable rights to which a monetary value can be attached. They are, however, the exclusive rights of their owners and the labor could, conceptually at least, be put to alternative uses that have economic value.

Institutional climate, contracts and school performance

At the macro level, North and others have found that institutions – meaning formal rules, informal rules and enforcement mechanisms – influence countries' economic performance strongly. This book argues that institutions also exist at the intra-organizational level and that the institutional climate within a school influences its performance. This happens because having a 'good' institutional climate makes it possible for actors within the school community to engage in transactions – in effect, contracts – that contribute to the accomplishment of the school's goals.

Institutions provide security, whether at the level of nations or of schools. If security is weak and an atmosphere of uncertainty or anxiety prevails, people are not willing to enter into agreements and contracts, even though doing so would be beneficial in a secure environment. Good institutions reduce risk and uncertainty. They make it possible for people to enter into agreements and arrangements with a reasonable degree of assurance that their opposite number will uphold their end of the bargain. In a poor institutional climate, people don't respect the 'rules' that apply in more favorable situations, such as the rules and expectations that teachers and students will play their part in the education process. Thus a teacher may feel that no matter how hard and well he or she tries to communicate the content of a lesson, students will not take the trouble to learn. Or students may feel that nobody cares much not their parents, their peers or their teachers whether they learn, so they make little or no effort. Participants in the school community do not enter into contracts and agreements to try to perform their tasks well, with the obvious result that performance suffers.

Enforcement and accountability

Because, as Commons states, all transactions involve conflicts of interest (as well as mutuality and order), there is a need to monitor them and to have means of enforcing them. Even if both principal and agent are reasonably sure that the other party will uphold the contract and it will be worthwhile to enter into it, there is a need to make sure that all parties fulfill their commitments. Monitoring involves transaction costs, mainly information costs, while enforcement calls for either some third party that has the power to enforce or some form of private ordering. In schools, as we have seen above, many of the transactions are informal and enforcement is by private and often very subtle means.

Given human propensity to shirk, however, there is a need to 'keep people on their toes' and to make sure that parties to contracts are making at least reasonably good efforts to do their part. This, in turn, gives rise to demands for systems of accountability. Within the school community, school directors have some degree of control over how well teachers perform (even though they may not control hiring, firing or promotion). Teachers have tests and grades as a system for ensuring student accountability. The movement toward external standards and accountability, discussed at length in Chapter 5, seeks to exert more power and control to assure that students, teachers and whole schools perform better. Here, all the problems of transaction costs, complex principal–agent relationships, low-power incentives and other difficulties of enforcing contracts arise.

The demand for accountability and for some form of pressure to ensure good performance underlies all categories of incentives – rewards, competition and threats – and raises some of the most perplexing issues this book addresses. While the fundamental concept of conflict of interest between principal and agent is inescapable, and with it the universal human tendency to shirk, there is also a body of thought that warns us that some apparently simple and obvious policies are not necessarily optimal or even workable. This includes questions about how to elicit the best performance from workers in situations where techniques are tacit (Murnane and Nelson, 1984), the relationship between intrinsic and extrinsic motivation (Frey and Jergen, 2000), and the management and enforcement of relational contracts.

These questions lead into areas little explored in the mainstream of economic thought, dealing with the nature of humankind and the content of people's preference functions, among other subtle and complex concerns. There are many people, including both mainstream economists and strong advocates of one or another form of educational incentive system, who overlook (or deny the importance of) relational contracting inside organizations and the way it influences organizational performance. Policies that have a powerful impact on the effectiveness of hundreds of millions of dollars of public expenditure as well as the formation of the human capital of future generations should take account of the role of institutions and contracting inside school organizations.

Appendix B: Networks of schools

There is a category of schools that constitutes an alternative to traditional public education, in which schools may be private but often operate within the public system. These are 'networks' of schools that offer distinctive approaches to private education. Examples in the US include the Accelerated Schools Project, initiated by Henry Levin and now a nationwide movement, Robert Slavin's Success for All model, the Coalition of Essential Schools, the Edison Project (a private education management organization or EMO) and others. In the Latin America region the Fe y Alegría schools operated by the Jesuit Order in many countries of the region offer a well-known and successful example. In Chile the schools operated by the Sociedad de Instrucción Primaria (Society for Primary Instruction; SIP) that have been the basis for the study described in Chapter 2 provide another example. Like some charter schools, there are networks that have been established with the explicit purpose of offering children who are otherwise 'at risk' an opportunity to obtain a good education, and these appear to perform better than schools serving the same student populations that are not members of the networks.

Most of these networks provide a kind of yardstick or basis for comparison with regular public schools, although their main objective goes well beyond creating competitive pressures. Although they may be publicly financed, they are to some degree outside the main educational bureaucracy in the local education districts where they operate. Although specifics vary, the schools in the networks must comply with certain minimum essential conditions (no discrimination, no indoctrination, and so on) and must have fairly wide latitude regarding curriculum, teaching methods, teacher recruitment and selection and school management.

CHARACTERISTICS OF 'NETWORKS' OF SCHOOLS

My colleagues at the Centro de Investigación y Desarrollo de la Educación (CIDE) and I became interested in networks through our study of primary schools in Chile reported in Chapter 2. The five private subsidized schools in that study are all members of a 17-school network established and operated by the Sociedad de Instrucción Primaria (SIP) and we learned a great deal about the network while studying its member schools. Also at CIDE, John Swope and Marcela Latorre conducted a major study of the Fe y Alegría schools (Swope and Latorre, 2000). Thus the study team at CIDE was alerted to and interested in the subject of networks. Why are networks of schools exceptionally successful, we asked, even when they often serve disadvantaged students and their costs are not significantly greater than those of other schools? Does being part of such a network confer advantages on participating schools and, if so, what are those advantages? And do they have anything to do with institutions in schools?

The following sections consider three examples of networks of schools – the Matte schools, Fe y Alegría schools and Accelerated schools – to explore whether there are common factors associated with network membership that help create sound institutions and contribute to good school performance. My colleagues and I visited and interviewed in five SIP schools as well as the Society's headquarters and, although the information on the other two networks is mainly from published sources, I have discussed both at length with Henry Levin, founder of Accelerated schools, and with people knowledgeable about the Fe y Alegría schools.

THE MATTE SCHOOLS OF THE SOCIEDAD DE INSTRUCCIÓN PRIMARIA OF SANTIAGO

As described in Chapter 2, the Sociedad de Instrucción Primaria (SIP) was founded in 1856, before Chile had a public school system, with the aim of providing the children of families with 'few resources' (*pocos recursos*) an education that would enable them to become successful, productive citizens. Its original slogan, at a time when 86 percent of Chile's population was illiterate, was 'War against ignorance!' The SIP has been in continuous operation for nearly a century and a half and for much of that time the Matte family has provided strong and caring leadership as well as substantial material contributions. Patricia Matte, SIP's President, serves without pay, as members of the family have done and as do all of the most senior staff at the network headquarters.

When our study was conducted, there were 15 primary schools and two secondary schools in the SIP network, all in the greater Santiago area and intentionally located in low-income neighborhoods. The SIP schools, originally supported entirely from private contributions, were among the first to take advantage of the opportunity to become private, voucher-paid schools when Chile's voucher system came into being. They have always had complete autonomy to build their own philosophy, rules, procedures, staff, and school communities and the guiding spirit of the network is very strong. They are not religious schools as such (and religion is not a criterion for admission) but since the SIP gives great emphasis to development of values and Chile is a Catholic country, the presence of Catholic influence is clearly felt.

Private subsidized schools in Chile have higher performance than municipal schools (without controlling for other factors that might influence performance) and the Matte schools as a group have higher scores on the SIMCE (Sistema de Medición de la Calidad de la Educación) than the average for private subsidized schools (Sociedad de Instrucción Primaria de Santiago, 1999, p. 16). Since a substantial portion of the private subsidized sub-sector serves upper-middle class families in higher-income neighborhoods (who also self-select to attend private schools), the SIP schools perform better although the families they serve have lower socioeconomic status than families in other private subsidized schools. The following sections consider some of the factors that characterize this network of schools and contribute to their success.

Private status.   Being private clearly conveys benefits on this group of schools, the leaders of which have a clear idea of what they want to achieve. The schools in the network have freedom to establish their own '*proyectos educativos*' or goal statements (guided by the goals of the network itself, which are clearly articulated and widely disseminated to the schools). The SIP chooses its own school directors (many of whom have 'come up through the ranks' as teachers and leaders in the network) and the directors have autonomy to select and develop their own teams of teachers. These and other characteristics that private status makes possible undoubtedly contribute to the success of schools in this network. Not all private subsidized schools take advantage of their private status as well as the SIP schools do (nor do they, in most cases, belong to networks like the SIP).

The leadership role of the SIP.   'The Society', as teachers and directors refer to it, is the top authority to which the schools report. It occupies the position of 'board' in the model in Chapter 1. It provides an overall mission or goal statement for all the schools that is very powerful and pervasive. Schools within the network establish their own mission statements on a participatory basis, yet these all reflect the presiding spirit of the Society. This means that the principal–agent relationships between the governance authority and the schools are very close and agency problems of communication or diverging aims are minimal. Another advantage the SIP provides is continuity of governance, something the municipal sector lacks.

Further advantage of membership in the SIP network is strong instructional leadership. From 1884, when Claudio Matte edited a manual for teaching reading and writing that became widely used throughout Chile, the inputs from the Society in terms of how to improve the instructional process have been extensive and continuous. Matte became President of the SIP in 1892 at the age of 34 and continued to play a leadership role for the rest of his long life. The reading and writing method he developed, known as the Matte Method, is still used in the SIP schools. The tradition of instructional leadership is thus long and important in the organization. This professional orientation is transmitted through specific training courses for school directors and staff and is continually updated and strengthened.

Management support is provided by the network headquarters, which relieves member schools of performing some managerial functions. (The SIP plays a role in financial management and budgeting, for example.) It also provides guidance and knowledge about management functions, interacts with the national Ministry of Education on policy matters and with the association of private schools, brings in up-to-date information on management techniques from outside the network, and provides a buffer between school-level managers and some elements of the external community that might otherwise absorb time and effort.

Team building. The directors of member schools in the SIP network are chosen by the SIP, almost always from able educators who have made their way up from classroom teacher to middle-level leadership roles to directorship. The directors have a high degree of autonomy in choosing their own staff (although a new director arriving at a school inherits a staff that has been carefully chosen and trained by predecessors and the SIP system). Directors put their own personal stamp on their schools, as was evident from our interviews with five of them. They dedicate substantial amounts of time to in-class observation and play active roles of professional advisor, constructive critic and strong supporter of their staff.

Staff self-select to become teachers in the SIP network. Many among members of focus groups of teachers with whom we met had been students at Matte schools or were the children of former students, or both. Clearly there is a powerful sense of mission, tradition and commitment among this staff and there is a strong feeling of belonging to a team, of both the SIP network and of the individual school.

A substantial portion of parents who send their children to the school are former Matte school students or children of former students, or both. The Matte schools are not selective as a matter of principle but when applications exceed available places, they give preference to siblings of present students or children of former students, but this in itself provides a filter that results in a community of families that understand and support the ideas and traditions of the SIP. The proportion of 'legacies' varies from school to school. In some cases the communities where schools were originally sited, selected to be low-income communities, have changed with time and shifting demographics. Some families have also moved to other communities and yet still transport their children back to the older (and sometimes poorer) community in order for their children to attend the school.

Parental involvement in this situation is more than ordinarily strong and parents understand and feel commitment to the schools' goals and traditions. To further strengthen the links between family and school, the SIP contracts with an independent training firm to provide 'Schools for Parents' (*Escuelas para Padres*) that present courses on parenting skills and how to support the school by encouraging children to do their best.

Taking all these factors into account, the community feeling in schools in the SIP network is extremely strong. It probably corresponds to what Bryk, Lee and Holland (1993) observed in Catholic schools.

Guidance regarding rules.   The SIP has its own set of rules or *reglamento interno*, set forth in a 48-page document covering working conditions of all staff, professional advancement for teachers, directors and other senior staff, rules regarding security and risks of personnel and students, provisions for sanctions in the event of violation of the rules and related matters (Sociedad de Instrucción Primaria de Santiago, 1998). All are expressly in accordance with Chilean labor law. These general rules are binding on schools within the network, but each individual school has its own *reglamento* that deals in greater detail with rules regarding academic matters, relations between parents and the school, and responsibilities of each category of members in the school community. Members of each school community are given copies of the relevant *reglamento* and parents are required to sign written statements each year agreeing to abide by the rules and uphold their responsibilities.

The Society also plays a role, through written documents such as the mission statement as well as through other communication channels such as training and periodic inspections, in establishing and reinforcing the informal rules that apply throughout the network. The member schools also place heavy emphasis on establishing the norms of academic and personal behavior that teachers, students and all members of the community are expected to respect. In the informal sphere, the presence of these rules is felt as much through positive recognition of good performance ('best friend', 'most improvement this month', 'teacher of the month') as through negative sanctions. And in addition to explicit recognition in ceremonies of various sorts, teachers and directors emphasized the role of 'conversation' in providing guidance, encouragement and correction of behavior and performance where necessary. The Society – including its member schools – is a shaper of people.

Social capital and a climate of trust.   Repeatedly we heard teachers in focus groups and school directors mention that being part of the SIP network provides a sense of security and of being part of a 'family'. The Society's long history and traditions contribute strongly to this, as does its emphasis on values and teamwork. Teachers inside the system may have specific disagreements with each other, the director or some aspect of the Society's system, and directors may need to correct some aspect of a teacher's performance, but we were told that these things are worked out through 'conversation', in an amicable manner, within a system of rules and procedures that all parties trust. When asked about how the system deals with teachers who are not performing well, teachers replied, 'They know if they don't fit in. After a while they go away.'

One of the themes among the values the SIP schools seek to teach is teamwork and cooperative behavior. And one of the explicitly recognized means of teaching values is through modeling, in which school directors and teachers engage actively. One dimension of the formal and informal rules serves to establish an environment where all members feel secure. While there is a strong sense of discipline, this is maintained through moral pressure and carefully managed so that individuals are not shamed or hurt.

Because the directors and teachers tend to rise in their careers within the system (and often are former students), they are strongly socialized into the SIP system of values. There is agreement and consistency in the educational communities. The aims, rules and procedures have hardly varied for over a century. Having the Society as an umbrella organization shelters the school from shifting influences from external sources.

Evaluation and reward system.   Teachers in the SIP system are evaluated annually by subject and department heads and the school director. The director spends substantial amounts of time observing classes. Toward the end of the evaluation period, the director synthesizes the views of staff in supervisory positions about the teacher's performance. The teacher meets with the school director to review the evaluation report that will be sent to SIP headquarters. In most cases, criticisms are expressed in constructive and positive form, with emphasis on what needs to be done to improve. If the teacher disagrees with a finding, there is an opportunity to add a comment or explanation. The report goes to the Society's academic director, who makes decisions about rewards or, if necessary, sanctions. Rewards include both promotion through a range of positions of responsibility for outstanding teachers and monetary bonuses for excellent performance. The system provides a degree of pressure for good performance. If staff members do not live up to expectations regarding their professional performance or levels of effort, this is reflected in their records and sanctioned both through deferred promotions and by various informal means.

School directors and senior staff are also subject to evaluation by peers and supervisors from the SIP. Staff members from headquarters visit the schools regularly, attend and participate in ceremonies, observe classes and talk with the director and teachers. The system applies pressure to assure that teachers work diligently but the level of commitment – to the system and to the students – is high and not a great deal of pressure is needed. Teachers work long hours – often far more than required in their contracts – and report being happy to do so. The culture of the schools and of the SIP system to which they belong provides strong informal pressure for its members to adhere to its standards and norms and give their best toward accomplishing the schools' objectives.

Material benefits. The SIP provides network management and leadership functions that relieve its schools of some administrative burden. There are also services, especially teacher training and evaluation and activities such as 'Schools for Parents', that are provided centrally. Its staff are well informed about the findings of educational research and best practice throughout Latin America and the world, and make this information available to the individual schools, which would otherwise not have access to it. It is a source of guidance and wise advice for its member schools.

By far the largest share of income comes from the government via various categories of transfer payments, the largest being the subventions or vouchers. The second largest source of income is payments by parents through the system of shared financing or '*financiamiento compartido*' that operates in 11 of the 17 schools. Contributions from the Society itself (members of the

Table B1   Operating income of the Society for Primary Instruction by source, 2000

Expense category	Percentage
Subventions (vouchers)	73.9
Other government transfers	5.7
Maintenance allowance	1.1
SNED awards for good performance	3.2
Shared financing (parents)	15.4
Matriculation fees	0.1
Other operational income (not government)	0.6
Total	100.0

Source: Calculated from data in 'Treasurer's Report' in *Memoria, 2000*, Sociedad de Instrucción Primaria de Santiago, p. 71.

board and senior staff are required to make contributions) and donations from third parties help fill the gap between income and expenses, but in 1999 and 2000 the SIP had an overall deficit. Table B1 shows the shares of income from different sources.

The Society is the owner of the physical infrastructure and is responsible for its maintenance, but receives transfers from the government that cover a portion of maintenance costs. In addition to salaries, it provides teaching materials and supplies to the schools, which have no significant income of their own.

The Society's role is to manage the funds and allocate them between schools in the network. It has also been instrumental in arranging for shared financing in those schools where parents have agreed to this measure. It also raises funds from private donors, mainly for special projects such as providing technology for one or more schools.

THE FE Y ALEGRÍA SCHOOLS OF LATIN AMERICA

The Fe y Alegría (FYA) network was founded by Jesuit Father José María Vélaz in Venezuela in 1955. It now operates in fourteen countries of Latin America plus Spain.[1] The system was created to provide education to under-privileged children. Most of the FYA schools are located in rural areas or sometimes in or near urban slums. In each country a National Office coordinates the schools in its network and the federations enjoy a high degree of autonomy. Overall coordination is provided by a headquarters in Venezuela. The statement of guiding principles to which all schools in the system adhere is the International Mission Statement of FYA. Each National Office develops its own mission statement, and each school within a federation has its own, locally developed mission statement. This, then, is a network of networks.

The schools' main aim is to reduce the high levels of repetition and dropouts that prevail in most Latin American countries. They strive to provide a good education and to assure that students complete it. Student retention in school is the main indicator of performance, since most countries of the region lack standardized tests that would make it possible to evaluate schools on the basis of test scores. In this the FYA network is notably successful. A CIDE study of FYA in nine countries showed that, in a majority of countries, FYA schools achieved better results than the national averages for public schools in terms of 'opportune progress' (meaning completing the primary cycle within the expected number of years), lower repetition rates, lower definitive dropout rates and higher overall student retention rates (Swope and Latorre, 2000, pp. 102–14). Retention rates for girls were better than for boys in FYA schools.

FYA focuses on providing primary or 'basic' (equivalent to lower and middle school) education but, in the interest of serving the community and keeping students in school, it also provides non-formal education for adults, technical education for adolescents, and pre-school education (which increases the readiness of students – often non-Spanish speaking minorities – for the first years of primary schooling and tends to reduce repetition and dropouts). The schools are called 'learning centers' because they offer a variety of services for a range of age groups. This further strengthens the bond between school and community.

FYA schools are both public and private (with the balance varying from country to country and public schools in the majority). In most countries, the schools enjoy a high degree of autonomy, even though they may operate with public funding and under public control. This is not always fully respected but when it is, it enables the National Offices to choose their own school directors and teams of teachers, without interference from the state or teachers' unions, and to keep teachers from being transferred out of the schools unless they choose to go (Codina, 1994, p. 333). The CIDE study found that the FYA schools do not differ substantially from public schools and that they are 'a more efficient type of public school' (Swope and Latorre, 2000, p. 159).

The main source of funding for FYA schools is government transfers to cover teacher salaries, which is by far the largest expenditure item for basic education. But in order to provide a better education, the FYA schools make additional expenditures for textbooks and teaching materials, teacher training and (whenever possible) for educational innovations. This requires raising funds from other sources. The schools do this through development of school-improvement projects, which become focal points for community involvement as well as channels for communication between the individual schools (or education centers) and higher levels in the FYA organization. The international and national offices of FYA help schools prepare projects and present them to donors for financing. Projects are thus both a source of additional financing and a means of forging stronger links between the school, its community and the network.

What are the reasons FYA schools achieve better student retention than their essentially similar public counterparts? The affiliation with the Catholic Church and the mystique and charisma that this provides is undoubtedly a factor, as is the high degree of autonomy mentioned above. Pedagogical inputs are also important (although the network encourages schools to develop their own models and philosophies of education in consultation with parents and the community). There are indications, however, that the network provides an overall vision or set of objectives as well as management practices that promote the development of a desirable institutional climate in its member schools.

Mission and objectives. The international mission of FYA plays a powerful role in shaping the schools in the network. It also helps explain the network's aims and persuade communities to invite FYA to establish a school in their neighborhood. As Swope and Latorre (2000) emphasize, the language of the mission statement is 'value laden' and 'aimed at spreading an almost missionary message' (p. 26). Examples of this language include:

- popular education movement;
- commitment;
- construction of a more fraternal and fair society;
- educational action and social advancement;
- option for the poor;
- reach the poorest sectors of our cities;
- quest for a more equitable world;
- a child without a school is everyone's problem;
- Fe y Alegría starts where the pavement ends.

Such evocative language, plus a single clear focus on keeping children in school, articulates the network's objectives and helps principals and agents understand each other, communicate effectively and elicit the full potential of all members of the network and its individual school communities.

Creation of a school community. Communities must invite FYA to establish a school in their neighborhood, which provides the starting point for close relationships with parents and community leadership. FYA chooses its school directors, who then have the latitude to choose their own cadre of teachers. FYA helps provide teacher-training in its aims, techniques and methods. It is also successful in reducing teacher turnover, which is a chronic problem in schools in Latin America, especially schools in rural and poor areas. Teacher retention further contributes to a sense of community. (It is noteworthy that FYA does not attempt to provide economic incentives for teachers, yet teachers' commitment is very high.) All these things create feelings of community and teamwork.

The leadership of the school directors is of great importance. School directors facilitate teachers' professional development and often participate in training activities with the teachers; they evaluate teacher performance and provide feedback; and they participate in the selection of new teachers and in the choice of textbooks and materials. Swope and Latorre (2000, p. 209) report that, when school directors participate in teacher selection, 'teachers tend to be chosen according to personal criteria rather than technical/professional ones' and that directors in FYA schools, 'hold their teachers in high regard and seek to develop a strong school community'.

Involvement of parents and the external community.   From the time a community elects to invite FYA to establish a school, there is close involvement with the school. One of the key 'student-retention strategies' FYA uses is programs involving the community and families. These include 'workshops ... for parents as a way of having them gain a better understanding of the problems that their children face', 'increasing awareness of the importance of education', 'strategies to get parents to support school work in the home', 'programmed home visits', and 'community involvement strategies, especially those designed to involve parents in the education of their children' (Swope and Latorre, 2000, pp. 120–1).

Formal and informal rules.   Because there are obvious differences between the situations of FYA schools in different countries, as well as great diversity among schools in any one country, the FYA network does not present guidelines for formal rules in school. In general these schools, affiliated with a Catholic organization, tend to be orderly and to emphasize values and cooperation. The most important role of FYA is in the area of informal rules and enforcement mechanisms, especially in the relationships between school directors and teachers, and between teachers as peers.

Environment of cooperation and trust.   Schools in the FYA network are managed privately, although they receive public subsidy, and this facilitates the establishing of school communities in which teachers remain for extended periods, professional relationships between directors and teachers are close and positive, and parents are brought into contact with the school, encouraged to support it and to motivate their children to study well and remain in school. FYA's strong sense of mission contributes to feelings of solidarity and participation in a worthy undertaking. Writing of the 'key elements that determine the quality and efficiency of FYA', Codina says '[t]he most important, without question, is the sense of "mission", the charisma of FYA itself and its choice and spirit of service to the poor. This provides a "value added" that is a particular characteristic of FYA in all of Latin America' (Codina, 1994, p. 344).

THE ACCELERATED SCHOOLS PROJECT

One of the best-known and most successful networks of schools in the US is the Accelerated Schools Project (ASP), initiated by Henry M. Levin and colleagues at Stanford University in two pilot schools and now encompassing over 1000 schools in 41 US states. Schools in the ASP serve student populations that were 'at risk' and were performing poorly before being incorporated into the network. Sixth-grade students in the schools were reading below grade level when the schools opted to become Accelerated Schools. The basic concept is that, in such situations, children need schooling that is more intensive (accelerated) than other schools rather than 'dumbed down' because the students are below grade level in reading and mathematics. The essential aim is that students should complete primary or middle school reading, generally performing as well as (if not better than) the average for the district. The ASP applies techniques borrowed from schools for gifted and talented students, with the idea of providing for students at risk an education that anyone would want for their own children.

In most cases, schools in this network are regular public schools and not special or charter schools. The ASP obtains permission and support from the local public education authority to put its philosophy and techniques into practice (and for this to happen, the local authority must support the idea). The schools are allowed to build their own teams of personnel and to practice their approaches to pedagogy with minimum intervention from above.

Building on the experience in the 'pioneer schools' that were the first members of the network, the ASP has developed a philosophy based on three principles, a set of nine values and instructional methods called 'powerful learning' that integrates curriculum, instructional techniques and organization (Finnan, St John, McCarthy and Slovacek, 1996, pp. 15–19, 297–301). The principles are '(a) unity of purpose, (b) empowerment with responsibility, and (c) building on strengths' (p. 15). The values include 'the school as a center of expertise, equity, community, risk taking, experimentation, reflection, participation, trust, and communication' (pp. 17–18). A powerful learning situation 'is one that incorporates changes in school organization, climate, curriculum, and instructional strategies to build on the strengths of students, staff and community to create optimal learning results' (p. 18). This brief description cannot do justice to the richness of the principles, values and learning approach that have evolved since the project began in 1989. It is, however, intended to suggest the vision and guidance that the Accelerated Schools network provides to its members. Detailed information on how these overarching ideas are put into effect is found in Hopfenberg *et al.* (1993).

Becoming an Accelerated School. One of the outstanding features of the ASP is the heavy investment – especially of time, expertise of ASP staff and coaches, and the work of people at the level of the school that wants to join the network – that precedes full membership in the project and implementation of its principles, values and methods. Before schools can join the network there is what Finnan *et al.* (1996, pp. 82–103) call a 'courtship phase', involving extensive introspection and the development of strong commitment of all members of the school community – including the local board, school leadership and staff, and parents – to the philosophy. This is one means by which the ASP achieves a high degree of agreement between principals and agents.

Once the decision is made to join the project, a period of training and preparation begins. In the course of its evolution, the project has come to understand the challenges of implementing change in schools and has developed methods based on teacher inquiry to help tailor the program to each individual school and help overcome resistance to change. Much of what the ASP brings to its member schools is in the area of pedagogy but, interestingly, teaching methods that change the organization of classrooms (using study teams, project-based learning and peer tutoring, for example) and involve all members of the community in educational activities have a strong impact on levels of understanding and cooperation within the school.

Teachers have considerable voice and latitude to put their ideas into effect, which builds their sense of participation and their commitment to the program that emerges. The ASP stresses that schools are 'communities of inquiry' in which all members of the community are involved (Finnan *et al.*, pp. 126–36). 'Through universal participation in the early steps of the Accelerated schools process, school community members begin to build a unity of purpose and come to better understand the perspectives and concerns of members of different role groups' (p. 140).

The processes involved in implementing 'powerful learning' create an environment in the classroom that is conducive to learning. Finnan and her colleagues found that teachers in ASP schools have a feeling 'that collaborative practices that come about as a result of the Accelerated schools model have led to their individual professional growth and increased communication and sharing among colleagues. A by-product of this collaboration and sharing of philosophy has been a greater feeling of support from peers, camaraderie, and accountability among the staff to provide a better education for all of the students' (p. 283).

Evaluation of ASP schools.   Accelerated schools have achieved their aims of bringing students up to grade level in reading and mathematics and to levels of performance as good as or better than other schools in their district or area. Since their target populations are defined by being at risk, and would tend to have below-standard performance without the intervention of the ASP, comparison of test scores with other schools is not necessarily a valid way of assessing the success of the program. Nonetheless, there are indications that ASP schools produce good results in terms of test results. The National Center for the Accelerated Schools Project publishes information on the 'Accomplishment of Accelerated Schools' on its website, showing that ASP schools in Ohio produced higher reading and mathematics scores than the average for schools in the same districts where the ASP schools are located, and that studies in Tennessee and Texas showed that students' gains in ASP schools compared favorably with schools participating in other improvement or restructuring projects, and at lower costs (National Center for the Accelerated Schools Project, 2000).

Scores on standardized tests do not capture all the dimensions of the effects of ASP membership, however. These include not only gains in student achievement but also improvements in attendance rates; reductions in repetition, student suspensions and vandalism; increased parental involvement; and increased numbers of ASP students who meet the criteria for traditional gifted and talented programs. It is in areas such as these that the values pursued by the ASP demonstrate their impact.

The ASP and institutions in schools.   Levin has argued that the design of the ASP drew upon Harvey Leibenstein's concept of X-efficiency and research on what leads organizations to perform closer to their productive potential (Levin, 1997). He draws on 'the general literature on what makes an X-efficient firm' to identify five dimensions of efficient organizations (Levin, 1997, p. 304):

1.   A clear objective function with measurable outcomes.
2.   Incentives that are linked to success on the objective function.
3.   Efficient access to useful information for decisions.
4.   Adaptability to meet changing conditions.
5.   Use of the most productive technology consistent with cost constraints.

I suggest that, while these are undoubtedly desirable characteristics for productive organizations to have, they are not integrated into a model that explains how they influence the production process. The institutional model offers a better understanding of why ASP schools are as successful as they are. Levin's first point concerning a clear objective function is absolutely in accordance with the institutional model, and his second point, concerning incentives linked to the objective function, could be interpreted as consistent with establishing clear formal and informal rules and enforcement mechanisms. The other points appear to be at different levels of discourse and, while useful information, adaptability to change and use of productive technology all help members of an organization to function efficiently, they do not relate to the way members of an organization use their effort and are willing to collaborate with peers so as to enhance efficiency. I think the institutional model provides a better understanding than X-efficiency of the origins of the success of the ASP.

The first of the three principles of Accelerated schools   unity of purpose   is closely related to clarity of goals or the objective function, with all that this implies for reducing principal–agent problems. The ASP's values of equity, community, risk taking, experimentation, reflection, participation, trust, and communication resonate strongly with the characteristics of schools with positive institutional environments. Requiring strong initial commitment on the part of the local authority, school director and teachers, and parents, before a school becomes a member of the ASP is consistent with clarity of goals and also has overtones of contracting.

Clearly the emphasis on community has an effect on the institutional environment of ASP schools (reminding one of the findings of Anthony Bryk and his colleagues about community in Catholic schools). The ASP clarifies goals, builds powerful community feeling and commitment, and promotes an atmosphere of cooperation and trust. It has less explicit involvement in laying down formal rules than the Matte schools (in part, because it leaves each school to establish formal rules for itself) but the development of a sense of community necessarily contributes to formation of informal rules and enforcement mechanisms. This is a different kind of network; one that transmits a powerful ideology to its member schools and provides information, training and oversight to help them implement an effective program.

CONCLUSIONS ABOUT NETWORKS

This appendix considers the way networks influence institutions in schools and, as a result, contribute to good performance. On the basis of the three examples discussed above plus information on other networks, it is possible to identify the following ways in which networks operate to promote positive institutional climates within their member schools. Networks tend to have the following characteristics:

- *Short, clear principal–agent links or relationships* The operators (who may be private groups) maintain close relationships with the schools and provide their vision, guidance and supervision directly to the schools. There tends to be a high degree of consensus between the network's leadership (or operating authority) and the schools in the network. Clear principal–agent relationships are associated with strong, clear incentives.
- *A strong sense of mission* Networks are usually formed because some leader or group seeks to accomplish an educational mission. The three examples discussed above have all sought to improve education for children of families in or near poverty. Such a mission attracts participants – whether parents, teachers or others – who agree with the mission and are committed to working toward its accomplishment.

- *Clarity of objectives*   A general characteristic of networks of schools is a set of clear objectives, which are communicated effectively to the educational communities within the network. Clear objectives (and direct principal–agent relationships) are characteristic of schools with favorable institutional climates.
- *Social capital*   Several key examples of networks, including Accelerated schools, provide a sense of belonging to a parent organization within which there is trust, cooperation and mutual support, and this tends to be transmitted down to the individual schools as well.
- *Consensus within the community*   In the process of establishing a new school, or bringing an existing school into a network, some networks require that all parties to the school (including the public authority within which the school operates) understand and 'buy into' the objectives and procedures of the network. The Accelerated School Project follows a procedure whereby it consults with members of a school's community over a period of up to two years, during which it establishes firm commitments, before a school becomes a member.
- *Contribution to establishing rules*   Networks help establish a clear set of formal rules, and may lay down guidelines for their member schools to follow, but individual member schools usually have a high degree of autonomy. In small-scale networks such as the Matte schools, informal rules seem to be communicated within the network, especially those regarding the roles and responsibilities of teachers, parents and school directors. The Matte schools' network (and the Chilean education system) require that all schools have a '*reglamento interno*' or set of written rules, and parents in the Matte network are required to sign contracts specifying that they understand the formal rules and agree to abide by them.
- *Continuity*   Networks provide a degree of continuity regarding objectives, leadership, rules and pedagogical orientation, and constitute a buffer between the school and political authorities, or a stabilizing force in times of changing educational fashions. They assume the role of the board or governing authority, and the institutional relationship between the network/board and the school is thus consistent and positive. Principal–agent relations between external authority and school are clear, strong and consistent.
- *Guidance and supervision*   One of the benefits networks provide is sharing experience within the network and making information (such as up-to-date knowledge on relevant research findings or proven practice improvements) available to network members. In addition to the value of the content itself, such communication tends to provide professional stimulation. The network leadership constitutes a respected

supervisory authority. In terms of the conceptual model in Chapter 1, networks bring the role of the board into close and positive contact with the school community.

- *Administrative functions*   Some networks assume responsibility for certain administrative activities, including relationships with the next higher administrative authority, screening and hiring teachers into a pool, central purchasing, or negotiations with unions, if this is relevant. This relieves schools of some of the administrative burdens that free-standing charter schools face.

- *Evaluation of performance*   Networks may establish their own system of evaluating member schools and their staff according to their own criteria and standards. The Matte schools network has a carefully designed system that teachers understand and appear to trust.

- *Rewards and recognition*   Networks may establish systems of awards for good performance to individual member schools or teachers. Rewards may be monetary but many are based only on recognition.

- *Inputs of resources*   Most networks provide resources in the form of leadership and guidance. Some also offer curricular guidance, materials, training and, in some instances, economic resources in money or in kind. In most cases the financial resources available are limited, but some networks are adept at raising additional funding.

There are clearly strong parallels between these characteristics and (a) the findings of several bodies of research – Effective schools, Catholic schools – on what makes a good school, and (b) the characteristics of schools with a good institutional environment. Other authors have recognized the way networks can contribute to improving performance of their member schools.

In a section titled 'The Importance of Networks', Darling-Hammond, Ancess and Falk (1995) discuss the way network membership influences the five schools practicing authentic assessment that they describe in their book. All five are members of the Coalition of Essential Schools (CES) and four of the five are also members of the Center for Collaborative Education (CCE), the New York City affiliate of CES. The authors make the following comments about networks:

> While these networks have provided common ground for sharing practice and for exploring new possibilities, each school has interpreted and enacted the CES principles in quite different, contextually appropriate ways ... [This] underscores the importance of ensuring that practitioners invent models – rather than replicate models – that are embedded in and embody their knowledge of their local contexts ... As a network enables practitioners to consider these issues across schooling levels, each learns important strategies from the other. Elementary school work is strengthened as communities reflect on their values and purposes, articulating

their expectations for what students should be able to do and developing public criteria for their standards and expectations ... The network is a vehicle for reconsideration of practice from many vantage points, centering around a hub of common values supporting learner-centered practice. This makes connections between like-minded practitioners both possible and mutually profitable ... [I]t expands the possibilities for the kinds of conversations that practitioners need to have if teaching, assessment and school structure are to be organized for school success ... (Darling-Hammond, Ancess and Falk, 1995, pp. 266–8)

Linda Nathan and Larry Myatt find that, on the basis of their experience managing a 'pilot school' within a Massachusetts district, being part of a network of such pilot schools had value.

Networks are powerful tools for schools because they provide meaningful feedback as well as greater and better accountability than bureaucracies. Friendly, finely-tuned feedback from a number of sources is indispensable to a good school ... Networks of schools and educators provide the opportunity to grow and learn with and from others who share a clear purpose and whose work we know, trust and respect. Participation in our pilot network is loose and flexible, but with appropriate degrees of critical friendship at a negotiated pace and style. Feedback from peer schools can have a tough edge to it and is perhaps taken more to heart because it comes from those who know young people and profession firsthand ... Membership in a national network, such as the Coalition of Essential Schools, gives [our school] access not only to an invaluable template of school reorganization but also to the voice of the practitioner – with a democratic and multicultural tone. (Nathan and Myatt, 1998, pp. 283–4)

The subject of networks is attracting increasing interest. The RAND Corporation recently completed a study of the New American Schools (NAS) network that included consideration of other networks such as Accelerated Schools (Berends, Bodilly and Kirby, 2002). NAS is an information-based network that provides a menu of alternative models of restructuring, including detailed information on model design, to schools that are seeking to reform or restructure.

Once a school has decided on the model it wants to follow, NAS provides additional information and other inputs that help the school implement it. It is an 'external change agent' that helps schools learn from the experience of others, but it does not offer the same articulation of a mission or set of objectives, nor the same sense of being part of a broader community of like-minded professionals, to which Nathan and Myatt (1998) refer. It does not have the same kind of impact on institutions within the schools as networks such as the Matte schools, Fe y Alegría or Accelerated schools. Further study of networks would benefit, in my opinion, from taking account of the role of networks on institutions within schools.

NOTES

1. The countries in which FYA operates are: Argentina, Bolivia, Brazil, Colombia, Dominican Republic, Ecuador, El Salvador, Guatemala, Honduras, Nicaragua, Paraguay, Panama, Peru, Spain and Venezuela. Some country programs are quite small. Where data on the countries covered in the CIDE study are presented, they exclude El Salvador, for which detailed data were not available.

Bibliography

Alchian, Armen A. and Harold Demsetz (1972), 'Production, Information Costs and Economic Organization', *American Economic Review*, **LXII**, (December), 777–95.

Anderson, Erin and Barton Weitz (1992), 'The use of pledges to build and sustain commitment in distribution channels', *Journal of Marketing Research*, **24**, 18–34.

Association for Effective Schools, Inc. (1996), 'Correlates of Effective Schools', available at *www.mes.org/correlates.html*.

Baker, George P., Robert S. Gibbons and Kevin J. Murphy (2002), 'Relational contracts and the theory of the firm', *Quarterly Journal of Economics*, **117** (1), 39–84.

Barzel, Yoram (1977), 'An economic analysis of slavery', *Journal of Law and Economics*, **20**, 87–110.

Behn, Robert D. (2001), *Rethinking Democratic Accountability*, Washington: Brookings Institution Press.

Berends, Mark, Susan J. Bodilly and Sheila N. Kirby (2002), *Facing the New Challenges of Whole-school Reform: New American Schools After a Decade*, Washington: RAND Corporation.

Berkenheim, Douglas and Michael Whinston (1998), 'Incomplete contracts and strategic ambiguity', *American Economic Review*, **88** (4), 902–32.

Boak, George (1998), *A Complete Guide to Learning Contracts*, Aldershot, UK: Gower Publishing Co.

Bohnet, Iris, Steffen Huck and Bruno S. Frey (2000), 'More order with less law: on contract enforcement, trust and crowding', *American Political Science Review*, **95** (1), 131–44.

Booth, A. and J. Dunn (eds) (1996), *Family-school Links: How do they Affect Educational Outcomes*, Hillsdale, NJ: Earlbaum.

Bryk, Anthony S., Valerie Lee and Peter B. Holland (1993), *Catholic Schools and the Common Good*, Cambridge, MA: Harvard University Press.

Carnoy, Martin (1997), 'Is privatization through education vouchers really the answer? A comment on West', *World Bank Research Observer*, **12** (1), 105–16.

Chong, A. and C. Calderón (2000), 'Causality and feedback between institutional measures and economic growth', *Economics and Politics*, **12** (1), 69–81.

Chubb, John E. and Terry M. Moe (1990), *Politics, Markets and America's Schools*, Washington: The Brookings Institution.

Codina, Gabriel (S.J.) (1994), 'La Experiencia de Fe y Alegría', in Marcela Gajardo (ed.), *Cooperación Internacional y Desarrollo de la Educación*, Santiago: Agencia de Cooperación Internacional de Chile.

Coleman, James S. (1988), 'Social capital in the creation of human capital', *American Journal of Sociology*, **94** (Supp), S95–S120.

Comer, James P. (1980), *School Power*, New York: The Free Press.

Commons, John R. (1934), *Institutional Economics*, New Brunswick, NJ and London, UK: Transaction Publishers.

Corvalán, Javier and Mario Gaymer (2002), 'Efectos de la modalidad de financimiento compartido en la educación media subvencionada en la Región Metropolitana en Chile', Santiago: Centro de Investigación y Desarrollo de la Educación (CIDE).

Cotton, Kathleen (1996), 'School Size, School Climate and Student Performance', Northwest Region Educational Laboratory, School Improvement Research Series (SIRS), Close-up #20, available at *www.nwrel.org/scpd/sirs*.

Darling-Hammond, Linda and Jacqueline Ancess (1996), 'Authentic Assessment and School Development', in Dennis P. Wolf and Joan B. Baron (eds), *Ninety-third Yearbook of the National Society for the Study of Education*, Chicago: University of Chicago Press.

Darling-Hammond, Linda, Jacqueline Ancess and Beverly Falk (1995), *Authentic Assessment in Action*, New York: Teachers College Press.

Davis, Gina and Elinor Ostrom (1991), 'A public economy approach to education: choice and coproduction', *International Political Science Review*, **12** (40), 313–35.

Deal, Terrence E. and Kent D. Peterson (1999), *Shaping School Culture*, San Francisco: Jossey-Bass.

Delannoy, Françoise (2000), *Education Reforms in Chile: 1980–1998: A Lesson in Pragmatism*, Washington: World Bank, Education Reform and Management Series, **1** (1).

Druian, G. and J.A. Butler (2001), 'Effective School Practices and At-risk Youth: What Research Shows', North West Regional Educational Laboratory (NWREL), School Improvement Research Series (SIRS), available at *www.nwrel.org/SIRS/1*.

Edmondson, Amy (forthcoming), 'Managing the Risk of Learning: Psychological Safety in Work Teams', in M. West (ed.), *International Handbook of Organizational Teamwork*, London, UK: Blackwell.

Elmore, Richard F. (2002), 'Unwarranted intrusion', *Education Next*, 2 (Spring).

Epstein, Joyce L. (2001), *School, Family and Community Partnerships: Preparing Educators and Improving Schools*, Boulder: Westview Press.

Finn, Chester E. Jr and Michael Petrilli (eds) (2000), 'The State of State Standards', (January) Washington: Thomas B. Fordham Foundation.

Finn, Chester E. Jr, Bruno Manno and Gregg Vanourek (2000), *Charter Schools in Action*, Princeton: Princeton University Press.

Finnan, Christine, Edward P. St John, Jane McCarthy and Simeon P. Slovacek (1996), *Accelerated Schools in Action: Lessons from the Field*, Thousand Oaks, CA: Corwin Press.

Firestone, William A. and David Mayrowetz (2000), 'Rethinking high stakes: lessons from the United States and England and Wales', *Teachers College Record*, **102** (4), 724–49.

Firestone, William A. and Karen Seashore Louis (1999), 'Schools as Cultures', in Joseph Murphy and Karen Seashore Louis (1999) (eds), *Handbook of Research on Educational Administration*, San Francisco: Jossey-Bass.

Fiske, Edward B. and Helen F. Ladd (2000), *When Schools Compete: A Cautionary Tale*, Washington: Brookings Institution Press.

Frey, Bruno S. (1997a), 'A constitution for knaves crowds out civic virtue', *Economic Journal*, **107**, 1043–53.

Frey, Bruno S. (1997b), 'From the price to the crowding effect', *Swiss Journal of Economics and Statistics*, **133** (2/2), 325–50.

Frey, Bruno S. (1997c), *Not Just For The Money*, Cheltenham, UK and Brookfield, US: Edward Elgar Publishing.

Frey, Bruno S. and Felix Oberholzer-Gee (1997), 'The cost of price incentives: an empirical analysis of motivation crowding-out', *American Economic Review*, **84** (4), 746–55.

Frey, Bruno S. and Reto Jergen (2000), 'Motivation Crowding Theory: A Survey of Empirical Evidence', Working Paper No. 49, Zurich University Institute for Empirical Research in Economics, available at *www.iew.unizh.ch/grp/Frey/*.

Friedman, Milton (1955), 'The Role of Government in Education', in Robert A. Solow (ed.), *Economics and the Public Interest*, New Brunswick, NJ: Rutgers University Press.

Friedman, Milton (1962), *Capitalism and Freedom*, Chicago: University of Chicago Press.

Friedman, Milton (1997), 'Public schools: make them private'. *Education Economics*, **5** (3), 341–4.

Fukuyama, Francis (1995), *Trust*, New York: Free Press.

Fukuyama, Francis (1997), *The End of Order*, London, UK: Profile Books.

Fuller, Bruce and Prema Clarke (1994), 'Raising school effects while ignoring culture? Local conditions and the influence of classroom tools, rules and pedagogy', *Review of Educational Research*, **64** (1), 119–57.

Gauri, Varun (1998), *School Choice in Chile: Two Decades of Educational Reform*, Pittsburg: University of Pittsburg Press.

Grossman, Sanford and Oliver Hart (1981), 'Implicit contracts, moral hazard and unemployment', *American Economic Review*, **71** (2) (Papers and Proceedings), 301–7.

Haertel, Edward (1999), 'Performance Assessment and Education Reform', *Phi Delta Kappan* (May), 662–6.

Hamilton, Jennifer (1999), 'State by State Legislative Analysis of Charter School Policy', thesis submitted to the Graduate School of Education and Human Development, George Washington University, available at *papers. ssrn.com*.

Hannaway, Jane (1992), 'Higher order skills, job design, and incentives: an analysis and proposal', *American Educational Research Journal*, **29** (1), 3–21.

Hanushek, Eric A. (1986), 'The Economics of Schooling: Production and Efficiency in Public Schools', *Journal of Economic Literature*, **24** (September), 1147–77.

Hanushek, Eric A., Charles S. Benson, Richard B. Freeman, Dean T. Jamison, Henry M. Levin, Rebecca A. Maynard, Richard J. Murnane, Steven G. Rivkin, Richard H. Sabot, Lewis C. Solomon, Anita A. Summers, Finis Welch and Barbara L. Wolfe (1994), *Making Schools Work*, Washington: Brookings Institution.

Hanushek, Eric A., John F. Kain and Steven G. Rivkin (1998), 'Teachers, Schools and Academic Achievement', NBER Working Paper 6691, Cambridge, MA: National Bureau of Economic Research, available at *www. NBER.org*.

Hart, Oliver and John Moore (1999), 'Foundations of incomplete contracts', *Review of Economic Studies*, **66**, 115–38.

Heck, Ronald H. and Philip Hallinger (1999), 'Next Generation Methods for the Study of Leadership and School Improvement', in J. Murphy and K. Seashore Louis (eds), *Handbook of Research on Educational Administration*, San Francisco: Jossey-Bass, 141–58.

Heide, Jan B. (1994), 'Interorganizational governance in marketing channels, *Journal of Marketing*, **58**, 71–85.

Henig, Jeffrey R. (1994), *Rethinking School Choice*, Princeton: Princeton University Press.

Heyl, Vivian and Marcela Guzmán (1998) 'Evaluación del Desempeño, SNED', Santiago, Chile: Ministerio de Educación, Departamento de Estudios (processed).

Hill, Paul, Lawrence C. Pierce and James W. Guthrie (1997), *Reinventing Public Education*, Chicago: University of Chicago Press.

Holstrom, Bengt and Paul Milgrom (1991), 'Multitask Principal–agent Analyses: Incentive Contracts, Asset Ownership and Job Design', in Oliver E. Williamson and Scott Masten (eds) (1999), *The Economics of Transaction Costs*, Cheltenham, UK and Northampton, MA: Edward Elgar, pp. 214–42.

Hopfenberg, Wendy S., Henry M. Levin, Ilse Brunner, Christopher Chase, S. Georgia Christensen, Beth M. Keller, Melanie Moore, G. Rodríguez and Pilar Soler (1993), *The Accelerated Schools Resource Guide*, San Francisco: Jossey-Bass.

Hoxby, Caroline M. (2000), 'Would School Choice Change the Teaching Profession?' NBER Working Paper W7866, available at *papers.nber.org/papers/w7866*.

Jensen, Michael C. (1998), *Foundations of Organizational Strategy*, Cambridge, MA: Harvard University Press.

Jensen, Michael C. and William H. Meckling (1976), 'The theory of the firm: managerial behavior, agency costs and ownership structure', *Journal of Financial Economics*, **3** (4), 305–60; reprinted as Chapter 3 in Jensen (1998).

Jensen, Michael C. and William H. Meckling (1992) 'Specific and General Knowledge, and Organization Structure', in L. Werin and H. Wijkander (eds), *Contract Economics*, Oxford, UK: Basil Blackwell, pp. 251–74; reprinted as Chapter 4 in Jensen (1998).

Jensen, Michael C. and William H. Meckling (1994), 'The nature of man', *Journal of Applied Corporate Finance* (Summer); reprinted as Chapter 1 in Jensen (1998).

Johnson, Jean (2002), 'Will parents and teachers get on the bandwagon to reduce school size?', *Phi Delta Kappan*, **83** (5), 353–6.

Jorgenson, Dale W. and Eric A. Hanushek (eds) (1996), *Improving America's Schools: The Role of Incentives*, Washington: National Academy Press.

Klein, Benjamin (1985), 'Self-enforcing contracts', *Journal of Institutional and Theoretical Economics*, **41**, 594–600.

Knowles, Malcolm Shepherd (1986), *Using Learning Contracts*, San Francisco: Jossey-Bass Higher Education Series.

Laboratorio Latinoamericano de Evaluación de la Calidad de la Educación (2000), *Primer Estudio Internacional Comparativo, Segundo Informe*, Santiago: UNESCO-Santiago.

Ladd, Helen F. (1999), 'The Dallas school accountability and incentive program: an evaluation of its impacts on student outcomes', *Economics of Education Review*, **18**, 1–16.

Learning First Alliance (2000), 'Standards and Accountability: A Call by the Learning First Alliance for Mid-course Corrections', Washington: Learning First Alliance, available at *www.learningfirst.org/news/standards.html*.

Leithwood, Kenneth, Diana Tomlinson and Maxine Genge (1999), 'Transformational School Leadership', in Kenneth Leithwood, Judith Chapman, David Corson, Philip Hallinger and Ann Hart (eds) (1999), *International Handbook of Educational Leadership and Administration*, Part 2, Dordrecht/ Boston/London: Kluwer Academic Publishers, pp. 785–840.

Levin, Henry M. (1976), 'Concepts of Educational Efficiency and Educational Production', in Joseph T. Froomkin, Dean T. Jamison and R. Radner (eds), *Education as an Industry*, prepared for the National Bureau of Economic Research, Cambridge, MA: Ballinger.

Levin, Henry M. (1997), 'Raising school productivity: an X-efficiency approach', *Economics of Education Review*, **16** (3), 303–11.

Levin, Henry M. (2000a), 'The Public–Private Nexus in Education', National Center for Study of Privatization in Education, Occasional Paper No. 1, available at *www.tc.columbia.edu/NCSPE/*; originally published in *American Behavioral Scientist*, **43** (1), 124–37.

Levin, Henry M. (2000b), 'A Comprehensive Framework for Evaluating Educational Vouchers', National Center for Study of Privatization in Education, Occasional Paper No. 5, available at *www.tc.columbia.edu/NCSPE/*.

Levin, Henry M. (2001), 'Bear market', *Education Next*, Spring, 2001, available at *www.educationnext.org*.

Linn, Robert L. (2000), 'Assessments and accountability', *Educational Researcher*, **29** (2), 4–14.

Mac Iver, Martha A. and Sam Stringfield (2000), 'Privatized delivery of instructional services for urban public school students placed at risk', *Educational Evaluation and Policy Analysis*, **22** (4), 375–82.

Macneil, Ian R. (1978), 'Contracts: adjustment of long-term economic relations under classical, neoclassical and relational contracts', *Northwestern University Law Review*, **72**, 854–905.

Madaus, George and Laura M. O'Dwyer (1999), 'A short history of educational assessment: lessons learned', *Phi Delta Kappan*, May, 1999, 688–92.

Malen, Betty, Michael J. Murphy and Ann W. Hart (1987), 'Restructuring Teacher Compensation Systems: An Analysis of Three Strategies', in Alexander, Kern and David H. Monk (eds), *Attracting and Compensating America's Teachers*, Cambridge, MA: Ballinger, pp. 91–142.

McEwan, Patrick (2000a), 'The Potential Impact of Large-Scale Voucher Programs', National Center for the Study of Privatization in Education, Teachers College, Columbia University, Occasional Paper No. 2, available at *www.tc.columbia.edu/NCSPE/paperseriesTXT.htm*.

McEwan, Patrick (2000b), 'Comparing the Effectiveness of Public and Private Schools: A Review of Evidence and Interpretations', National Center for the Study of Privatization in Education, Teachers College, Columbia University, Occasional Paper No. 3, available at *www.tc.columbia.edu/ NCSPE/paperseriesTXT.htm*.

McEwan, Patrick and Martin Carnoy (2000), 'The effectiveness and efficiency of private schools in Chile's voucher system', *Education Policy Analysis Archives*, **22** (3), 213–39.

McMeekin, Robert (2000), *Implementing School-based Merit Awards: Chile's Experience*, Washington: World Bank, Education Reform and Management Series, Technical Notes, **III** (1).

Meyer, Robert H. (1996), 'Can Schools be Held Accountable for Good Performance?', in Dale W. Jorgenson and Eric A. Hanushek (eds), *Improving America's Schools: The Role of Incentives*, Washington: National Academy Press, pp. 75–109.

Mid-continent Research for Education and Learning (McREL) (2000), *Noteworthy Perspectives on Implementing Standards-based Education*, Aurora, CO: Mid-continent Research for Education and Learning, available at *www.mcrel/org*.

Ministerio de Educación de Chile, División de Planificación y Presupuesto (1997), 'Evaluación de la Implementación y Resultados del SNED, 1996–97' (Evaluation of the implementation and results of SNED, 1996–97), commissioned by the Ministry, performed by Alejandra Mizala and Pilar Romaguera, Santiago, Chile: Centro de Economía Aplicada, Facultad de Ingenería Industrial, Universidad de Chile (processed).

Ministerio de Educación, República de Chile, División de Planificación y Presupuesto (1998), *Reconocimiento al Compromiso Docente*, Santiago, Chile: Ministerio de Educación.

Ministerio de Educación, República de Chile, División de Planificación y Presupuesto (2000), *Performance Evaluation of Subsidized Schools: SNED 2000–2001*, Santiago, Chile: Ministry of Education.

Mizala, Alejandra and Pilar Romaguera (2000), 'Sistemas de Incentivos en Educación y la Experiencia del SNED en Chile', Centro de Economía Aplicada, Facultad de Ingenería Industrial, Universidad de Chile, Serie Economía No. 82.

Murnane, Richard and David Cohen (1986), 'Merit pay and the evaluation problem: why most merit pay plans fail and a few survive', *Harvard Educational Review*, **56** (1), 1–17.

Murnane, Richard and Richard Nelson (1984), 'Production and innovation when techniques are tacit', *Journal of Economic Behavior and Organization*, **5**, 353–73.

Murphy, Joseph and Karen Seashore Louis (eds) (1999), *Handbook of Research on Educational Administration*, San Francisco: Jossey-Bass.

Myatt, Larry and Linda Nathan (1996), 'One school's journey in the age of reform', *Phi Delta Kappan*, **78** (1), 24–5.

Nathan, Linda (2002), 'The human face of the high-stakes testing story', *Phi Delta Kappan*, **83** (8), 599–600.

Nathan, Linda and Larry Myatt (1998), 'A journey toward autonomy', *Phi Delta Kappan*, **80** (4), 278–86.

National Center for the Accelerated Schools Project (2000), 'Accomplishments of Accelerated Schools' (November), Storrs, CT: Accelerated Schools Project, pp. 1–2.

Newmann, Fred M. and Associates (1996), *Authentic Achievement: Restructuring Schools for Intellectual Quality*, San Francisco: Jossey-Bass.

Newmann, Fred M., M. Bruce King and Mark Rigdon (1997), 'Accountability and school performance: implications from restructuring schools', *Harvard Educational Review*, **67** (1), 41–69.

North, Douglass C. (1990), *Institutions, Institutional Change and Economic Performance*, Cambridge, UK: Cambridge University Press.

Odden, Allan and William H. Clune (1998), 'School Finance Systems: Aging Structures in Need of Renovation', *Education Evaluation and Policy Analysis*, **20** (3), 157–77.

Odden, Allan and Carolyn Kelley (1997), *Paying Teachers for What They Know and Do: New and Smarter Compensation Strategies to Improve Schools*, Thousand Oaks, CA: Corwin Press.

Ostrom, Elinor (1996), 'Crossing the great divide: coproduction, synergy and development', *World Development*, **24** (6), 1073–87.

Parry, Taryn Rounds (1997), 'Theory Meets Reality in the Education Voucher Debate: Some Evidence from Chile', Education Economics, **5** (3), 307–31.

Pearce, David G. and Ennio Stacchetti (1998), 'The interaction of implicit and explicit contracts in repeated agency', *Games and Economic Behavior*, **23**, 75–96.

Premack, Eric (1996), 'Charter schools, California's education reform "Power Tool"', *Phi Delta Kappan*, September, 1996, 60–4.

Putnam, Robert D. (1993), *Making Democracy Work*, Princeton: Princeton University Press.

Rapp, Geoffrey C. (2000), 'Agency and choice in education: does school choice enhance the work effort of teachers?', *Education Economics*, **8** (1), 37–63.

Richards, C. and Tian Ming Sheu (1992), 'The South Carolina school incentive reward program: a policy analysis', *Economics of Education Review*, **11** (1), 71–86.

Rindfleisch, A. and Jan B. Heide (1997), 'Transaction cost analysis: past, present and future applications', *Journal of Marketing*, 30–54.

Rosen, Sherwin (1985), 'Implicit contracts: a survey', *Journal of Economic Literature*, **XXIII**, 1144–75.

Rosen, Sherwin (1987), 'Some economics of teaching', *Journal of Labor Economics*, **5** (4) (Part 1), 561–75.

Rotherham, Andrew, (2002), 'A new partnership', *Education Next*, Spring, 2002.

Rowan, Brian and Cecil Miskel (1999), 'Institutional Theory in the Study of Educational Organizations', in Joseph Murphy and Karen Seashore Louis (eds), *Handbook of Research on Educational Administration*, San Francisco: Jossey-Bass, pp. 359–83.

Rozen, Marvin (1990), 'X-efficiency, Implicit Contracting and the Theory of the Firm', in M. Perlman and K. Weiermair, *Studies in Economic Rationality: Essays in Honor of Harvey Leibenstein*, Ann Arbor: University of Michigan Press, pp. 95–125.

Ryan, R.M. and E. Deci (2000), 'Self-determination theory and the facilitation of intrinsic motivation, social development and well-being', *American Psychologist*, **55**, 68–78.

Savedoff, William (ed.) (1998), *Organization Matters: Agency Problems in Health and Education in Latin America*, Washington: Inter-American Development Bank.

Schmidt, P. (1994), 'Private enterprise', *Education Week*, May 25, 27–30.

Mark Schneider, Paul Teske, Melissa Marschall, Michael Mintrom and Christine Roch (1997) 'Institutional arrangements and the creation of social capital: the effects of school choice', *American Political Science Review*, **91** (March), pp. 82–93.

Sheldon, Kennon (2001), 'Will standards save public education', *Teachers College Record*, (December, 2001), 101, available at *www.tcrecord.org*.

Sheldon, Kennon and B. Biddle (2000), 'Standards, accountability, and school reform: perils and pitfalls', *Teachers College Record*, **100**, 164–80.

Sociedad de Instrucción Primaria de Santiago (SIP) (1998), *Reglamento Interno* (*Internal Regulation* (of the Society)), Santiago: author.

Sociedad de Instrucción Primaria de Santiago (SIP) (1999), *Memoria, 1999* (annual report of the Society), Santiago: author.

Spalding, Elizabeth (2000), 'Performance assessment and the new standards project: a story of serendipitous success', *Phi Delta Kappan*, **81** (10), 758–64.

Swope, John and Marcela Latorre (2000), *Fe y Alegría Schools in Latin America: Educational Communities Where the Pavement Ends*, Santiago: Centro de Investigación y Desarrollo de la Educación (CIDE).

Teske, Paul, Mark Schneider, Jack Buckley and Sara Clark (2000), 'Does Charter School Competition Improve Traditional Public Schools?', Manhattan Institute's Civic Report (10), June 2000, available at *www.manhattaninstitute.org*.

Thompson, Scott (2000), 'The authentic standards movement and its evil twin', *Phi Delta Kappan*, **82** (5), 358 62.

Tucker, Marc S. and Judy B. Codding (1998), *Standards for Our Schools:*

How to Set Them, Measure Them and Reach Them, San Francisco: Jossey-Bass.

West, E.G. (1997), 'Education vouchers in principle and practice: a survey', *World Bank Research Observer*, **12** (1), 83–103.

Williamson, Oliver E. (1975), *Markets and Hierarchies: Analysis and Antitrust Implications*, New York: The Free Press.

Williamson, Oliver E. (1985), *The Economic Institutions of Capitalism: Firms, Markets and Relational Contracting*, New York, London, Toronto, Sydney, Singapore: The Free Press.

Williamson, Oliver E. (1989), 'Transaction Cost Economics', Chapter 3 in R. Schmalensee and R. D. Willig (eds), *Handbook of Industrial Organization*, Vol. 1, Amsterdam and New York: Elsevier Science Publishers.

Winkler, Donald and Benjamin Alvarez (1998), 'Reforming the School in Latin America and the Caribbean: An Institutional Analysis', Chapter 5 in Javed Burki and Guillermo Perry, *Beyond the Washington Consensus: Institutions Matter*. Washington: World Bank, pp. 89–108.

Witte, John F. (2000), *The Market Approach to Education: An Analysis of America's First Voucher Program*, Princeton and Oxford, UK: Princeton University Press.

Woessmann, Ludger (2001), 'Why students in some countries do better', *Education Matters*, **1** (2), 67–74, available at *www.educationnext.org*.

Index